Tragedy in Aurora

Tragedy in Aurora

The Culture of Mass Shootings in America

Tom Diaz

With Lonnie Phillips and Sandy Phillips

ROWMAN & LITTLEFIELD
Lanham • Boulder • New York • London

Published by Rowman & Littlefield
A wholly owned subsidiary of The Rowman & Littlefield Publishing Group, Inc.
4501 Forbes Boulevard, Suite 200, Lanham, Maryland 20706
www.rowman.com

Unit A, Whitacre Mews, 26-34 Stannary Street, London SE11 4AB

British Library Cataloguing in Publication Information Available

Library of Congress Cataloging-in-Publication Data

Names: Diaz, Tom, author.
Title: Tragedy in Aurora : the culture of mass shootings in America / Tom Diaz ;
    with Lonnie Phillips and Sandy Phillips.
Description: Lanham : Rowman & Littlefield Publishers, [2019] | Includes
    bibliographical references and index.
Identifiers: LCCN 2019001791 (print) | LCCN 2019015883 (ebook) | ISBN
    9781538123447 (Electronic) | ISBN 9781538123430 (cloth : alk. paper)
Subjects: LCSH: Mass shootings—United States.
Classification: LCC HM866 (ebook) | LCC HM866 .D538 2019 (print) | DDC
    364.152/340973—dc23
LC record available at https://lccn.loc.gov/2019001791

∞™ The paper used in this publication meets the minimum requirements of American National Standard for Information Sciences—Permanence of Paper for Printed Library Materials, ANSI/NISO Z39.48-1992.

DEATH: There was a merchant in Bagdad who sent his servant to market to buy provisions and in a little while the servant came back, white and trembling, and said,

"Master, just now when I was in the marketplace I was jostled by a woman in the crowd and when I turned I saw it was Death that jostled me. She looked at me and made a threatening gesture, now, lend me your horse, and I will ride away from this city and avoid my fate. I will go to Samarra and there Death will not find me."

The merchant lent him his horse, and the servant mounted it, and he dug his spurs in its flanks and as fast as the horse could gallop he went. Then the merchant went down to the marketplace and he saw me standing in the crowd and he came to me and said, "Why did you make a threatening gesture to my servant when you saw him this morning?"

"That was not a threatening gesture," I said, "it was only a start of surprise. I was astonished to see him in Bagdad, for I had an appointment with him tonight in Samarra."

From Sheppey, a play by William Somerset Maugham

CONTENTS

INTRODUCTION

Annus Horribilis

2012 was a bad year in America for gun violence. For public mass shootings it was horrible.

Public mass shootings are those thunderclap events when someone armed with a gun, usually a male, walks into a public space and kills as many innocent people as he can. They are a special subclass of mass shootings. Death itself—administered clinically on an impersonal and industrial scale—is both motive and objective. American polemicists produce acres of writing and terabytes of electronic disputation splitting angry hairs about what exactly is a "mass shooting" or a "mass murder," how many there are, and whether their number is waxing or waning. But public mass shootings are like pornography. You know one when you see it, or hear about it, or God forbid are caught up in it. The names of the venues are instantly inscribed in our lexicon, entries in a thesaurus of social and moral decay.

Parkland. Las Vegas. Orlando. San Bernardino. Aurora. Sandy Hook. Virginia Tech. Fort Hood. Sutherland Springs. The list goes on, and even more will be added tomorrow, next month, or next year.

This book is largely, but not entirely, about public mass shootings. "Not entirely" because it is impossible to separate all the strands that weave together all manner of gun violence in America and indeed the world. Popular firearms designs, global gun industry marketing, background checks, preventative mental health interventions, constitutional rights, cultural divisions, and ultimately the paralysis of polarized politics

1

are wound tightly around and knit through any discussion of any form of gun violence in America.

The arc of this book is the story of Jessica (Jessi) Ghawi, one victim of a public mass shooting, and the impact that her murder had on her parents, Sandy and Lonnie Phillips, and on widening circles of other people. Along the way it examines some elements of gun violence generally and the American debate about what to do about it.

This book is not an encyclopedia of public mass shootings. It is not a handbook of the moral and psychological defects of mass shooters. It is a cautionary tale about the terrible effects of public mass shootings. Its prime thesis is that America is in a crisis of cultural and moral self-definition. "The 'Great American Gun Debate' isn't really one debate but two," Yale professor Dan M. Kahan has argued. "The first, conducted primarily in social science journals and in legislative chambers, is empirical . . . [the] second gun debate is cultural. Carried out (often heatedly) in letters to the editor and in town square rallies, gun politics consists in a struggle to define what America stands for and who has standing in America."[1]

When we can seriously and heatedly argue with one other about just exactly how many public mass shootings are enough to trigger extraordinary measures to stop them, this book suggests, our society is in a dangerously infected moral state. We are not debating about empirical facts. We are arguing about culture. This is especially clear when one considers our Herculean efforts to prevent terrorism, the human toll of which in America is miniscule by comparison with that of gun violence. Something is very wrong in our comparative choices about life and death and public action. America's character—who we are and what we truly stand for beyond pious thoughts and formulary prayers—lies in the balance.

The author does not presume to know how or whether we can or will pass through that fevered crisis. The future is murky in this era of extraordinarily unpredictable flux. Equivocating, doing nothing effective about gun violence in general and public mass shootings in particular, is in itself a moral and cultural decision. Americans are deadlocked politically. Whether we break that deadlock will define who we are culturally and morally. Whatever we do or don't do will, in the end, confront each of us in judgment's unforgiving mirror.

A Devil's Calendar—Gun Violence in 2012

Perhaps years before or years since 2012 have been more terrible. But for the victims and survivors of gun violence in America during 2012, the blood-soaked evil of that year was so vile that they thought it surely must have changed everything. Ordinary people were so shocked, so horrified, so heartbroken by two public mass shootings in particular that it seemed certain that Americans would, that they must, come together at last, unite against senseless tragedy, and smash the political gridlock in Washington that for decades had blocked effective gun control in America.

Seven years later, recounting the more notable events of that *annus hor-ribilis* sounds in one's mind like the grimly measured strokes of a death knell.

On January 25, 2012, Congresswoman Gabrielle Giffords of Arizona resigned from the U.S. House of Representatives. Giffords had been shot in the head by a deranged gunman at a public event on January 8, 2011. She said she intended to concentrate on recovering from her grievous wound and that she planned to return to Congress.[2] Seven months later the man who shot Giffords pleaded guilty to killing six people and wounding thirteen others, including the congresswoman. He had been diagnosed as a paranoid schizophrenic after his arrest.[3]

Scarcely one month after Giffords resigned, on February 26 a white man in Sanford, Florida, shot to death an unarmed black teenager, Trayvon Martin. George Zimmerman claimed that he shot Martin in self-defense after a scuffle. He was charged with second-degree murder and manslaughter in the racially charged case. A jury later acquitted him of all charges.[4] The day after Zimmerman shot Trayvon Martin, a teenager shot to death three teens and wounded three others at a high school in Chardon, Ohio.[5]

On April 2, a forty-eight-year-old college dropout returned to Oikos University, a small nursing school in Oakland, California, armed with a .45 caliber semiautomatic pistol that he had recently bought. Allegedly angry that he had not received a tuition refund, the gunman shot to death seven students and wounded three others. Later diagnosed as a paranoid schizophrenic, he pleaded "no contest" to criminal charges and was sentenced to seven consecutive life terms in prison.[6]

On May 2, a former marine, neo-Nazi sympathizer, and notorious founder of an armed vigilante "border guard" shot to death four other persons—including a fifteen-month-old child—and committed suicide by shooting himself in the head. Law enforcement authorities said it was a case of domestic violence.[7]

In Seattle on May 29, 2012, the city council met with officials of the police department to discuss ways to respond to increasing gun violence. Council member Tom Rasmussen was not persuaded by the Seattle police department's ideas. He expressed the frustration that many other Americans were feeling about gun violence in 2012. "I have some skepticism about whether this will have any effect," Rasmussen said. "We have seen many community vigils, community mobilizations. We've heard about these strategies before. What's going to change?"[8]

The very next day a man walked into a bar in Seattle and opened fire with a .45 caliber Para-Ordnance semiautomatic pistol. He killed four people and wounded another in the bar. He later killed a fifth person in a carjacking as he tried to escape. Eventually cornered by police, the man shot himself in the head and died.[9] According to the Seattle city attorney, the shooter was issued a concealed weapons permit in August 2010. At that time he declared that he owned six handguns—three 9mm pistols and three .45 caliber pistols.[10]

As horrible as all these incidents were, the numbers of deaths and injuries they represented were no more than marginal notations in the grisly accounting of everyday, run-of-the-mill, ordinary, routine gun violence in America. The mechanisms underlying that dark ledger annually take the lives of about thirty thousand victims—more than half of them suicides—and leave roughly twice as many wounded but alive. In an average week in 2012, 645 people lost their lives to firearms and 1,565 were treated in emergency departments for a firearm injury.[11] In polarized America, experts bicker about the minutiae of this graveyard ledger. Are the numbers up, down, or sideways?[12] Do they evidence a national disgrace or are they the price of freedom?

Disturbing as these notable shootings were, scarcely halfway through the year, they were but pale prologue to what was yet to come in 2012.

On July 20, a young man armed with a Smith & Wesson M&P15 semiautomatic assault rifle, a Remington 870 Express Tactical shotgun, and a Glock 22 .40 caliber semiautomatic pistol opened fire in a crowded theater at a midnight screening of the Batman movie *The Dark Knight Rises* in Aurora, Colorado. Twelve people were murdered and fifty-eight were injured. Among those killed was Jessi Ghawi, a whip-smart, cheerful, funny, and beloved young woman from Texas, a student poised on the brink of a bright future as a sports journalist. Gut-punched by the news of Jessi's murder, her parents, Lonnie and Sandy Phillips, threw themselves into the ranks of the activism that they thought, they hoped, they prayed would spare others the incalculable, endless pain they suffer. Surely, the truth about this horrible event would be self-evident to the American people. It would wake them up, and change things for the better.

"My husband and I respect the Second Amendment," Sandy told *Mother Jones* magazine on the fifth anniversary of that public mass shooting. "We are longtime gun owners, who for 30 years made our home in Texas. We have no interest in taking away everyone's guns, as the National Rifle Association and other fear mongers like to claim. However, we believe our nation's laws can be vastly improved to save lives."[13]

And why wouldn't Lonnie and Sandy Phillips think that America's laws could be improved? It was late in the 2012 presidential campaign when their daughter was murdered. Plenty of attention was paid to the horrific shooting by the news media and politicians. President Barack Obama and his opponent, Republican Mitt Romney, suspended "negative" advertising in Colorado for a day or two. There were more official gestures. Flags were ordered to fly at half mast. Obama flew to Colorado and visited with victims and survivors on July 22 to do his duty as "healer in chief," a ceremonial role that President Bill Clinton played in 1999 after the mass shooting at Columbine High School, and President George W. Bush in 2007 after the mass shooting at Virginia Tech.[14] In the distinctive cadence of his acclaimed eloquence, President Obama explained his role to the media after the visit.

> I had a chance to visit with each family, and most of the conversation was filled with memory. It was an opportunity for families to describe how wonderful their brother, or their son, or daughter was, and the lives that they have touched, and the dreams that they held for the future. I confessed to them that words are always inadequate in these kinds of situations, but that my main task was to serve as a representative of the entire country and let them know that we are thinking about them at this moment and will continue to think about them each and every day, and that the awareness that not only all of America but much of the world is thinking about them might serve as some comfort.[15]

Words alone are indeed "inadequate" in the wake of public mass shootings. They count as nothing without action. But if the entire country really was "thinking about" the victims of gun violence "each and every day," and if the comfort of meaningful change was coming as a result, it nevertheless would be too late for the six worshippers shot to death by a white supremacist at a Sikh temple in Oak Creek, Wisconsin, on August 5. The gunman committed suicide after being shot by a responding police officer.[16] It would also be too late for the eight victims of a troubled employee who had been fired from the Accent Signage company in Minneapolis, Minnesota, on September 27. He shot five fellow employees and a UPS driver to death before he committed suicide with his Glock 19 9mm semiautomatic pistol. Two other employees were wounded.[17]

But evil incarnate was still not done with that horrible year of 2012.

On December 14—in the midst of the joyful Jewish holiday of Hanukkah and only ten days before Christmas Eve—another demented young man armed himself with a semiautomatic assault rifle and prepared to carry out "one of the most vicious and incomprehensible domestic attacks in American history."[18]

Lonnie and Sandy Phillips were traveling from their home in Texas to Colorado when they heard the terrible news. Sandy recalled that day for *Mother Jones.*

Five months after Jessi's funeral in Texas, which drew nearly 2,000 friends and supporters, Lonnie and I headed to Colorado to pick up Jessi's diploma and speak at her university. We managed to joke that of course she would get her degree without having to take any final exams. As we boarded the plane, we heard about the breaking news: A gunman had attacked Sandy Hook Elementary School in Newtown, Connecticut. By the time we landed in Colorado, people were checking their phones, talking in hushed, stunned voices about 20 dead children. Lonnie and I were sitting near the back of the plane. I lost it. "Shut up! Stop talking about it!" I screamed. Lonnie tried to console me.[19]

Early that morning, that young man in Newtown had gone into his mother's bedroom and shot her in the head four times with a .22 caliber Savage Mark II bolt-action rifle. He then drove to Sandy Hook Elementary School. He brought with him a Sig Sauer P226 9mm semiautomatic pistol, a Glock 20 10mm semiautomatic pistol, a Bushmaster Model

XM15-E2S semiautomatic assault rifle, and an Izhmash Saiga-12 12 gauge shotgun. He shot his way into the school, which he had attended as a child, and killed twenty first-grade children ages six and seven, and six school staff members. He then committed suicide by shooting himself in the head.[20]

Two days later, on December 16, a memorial service for the victims was held in Newtown, which is also the home of the National Shooting Sports Foundation (NSSF), the gun industry's principal trade association. Once again the news media, the politicians, and the nation entered into a ritualistic dance of political posturing, sensational reporting by solemn news readers, private pain within victims and survivors, and somber public thoughts and prayers from important figures identified as political leaders and public opinion makers.

"The streets outside the memorial service and the airwaves across the nation were filled with voices calling for legislative action," the *New York Times* reported. "The grieving in this small New England town, aired nonstop on national television, adding emotional energy to the pressure on a newly re-elected Democratic president who has largely avoided the issue during four years in the White House."[21]

"Largely avoided" was a nice of way of saying that the Obama administration had aggressively sought to distance itself from any form of gun control during the president's first term. The president and most of the Democratic Party had bought into the unprincipled utilitarian argument that gun control was the "third rail" of national politics. Its mere mention could only hurt the Democrats by offending "middle-of-the-road" gun owners, the people whom then-Speaker of the House Nancy Pelosi called "majority makers."[22] These unicorns were thought to be swing voters crucial to the party's electoral success. Electing Democrats was important, so that they could do things to help small children so long as it did not involve gun control. It was far better to tiptoe whistling past their graveyards. When, for example, Attorney General Eric Holder suggested reviving the expired federal ban on assault weapons in 2009, Obama's chief of staff Rahm Emanuel—later the mayor of gun-violence-wracked Chicago—was reportedly so angered that he sent word to Holder to "shut the fuck up" on guns.[23] Obama did not mention the issue during his eloquent speech to the Democratic National Convention in 2012. He emphasized his support for the Second Amendment during his re-election campaign. He did not propose any new initiatives after Jessica Ghawi and others were killed in the Aurora public mass shooting. In fact, the only gun legislation Obama had signed into law by December 2012 actually expanded gun rights. It allowed the carry of loaded guns in national parks and unloaded guns on the Amtrak railway system. The Brady organization—recognized at the time as the prime mover of America's gun control movement—labeled his first term a "failure" on the gun control front.[24]

In what the *New York Times* called a "surprisingly assertive speech," President Obama declared in Newtown that "in the coming weeks I'll use whatever power this office holds . . . aimed at preventing more tragedies like this."[25] The slaughter of twenty priceless and innocent children appeared at last to have jolted the president and some of the Democratic political establishment out of their passive wisdom about gun control. Two public mass shootings—senseless attacks with no motivation other than killing as many theatergoers and first-graders as possible—seemed to have brought the country to a tipping point.

"Because what choice do we have?" Obama added. "We can't accept events like this as routine. Are we really prepared to say that we're powerless in the face of such carnage? That the politics are too hard? Are we prepared to say that such violence visited on our children year after year after year is somehow the price of our freedom?"[26]

Donald Trump, then a wealthy New Yorker and private citizen, tweeted his support for the thoughts and prayers of the healer in chief on the same day. "President Obama," he wrote, "spoke for me and every American in his remarks in #Newtown Connecticut."[27]

Four months later, on April 8, 2013, President Obama again traveled to Connecticut. In an "impassioned" speech, he declared that "we have to act" to save more families from the "immeasurable anguish" that they suffered from public mass shootings in Aurora and Sandy Hook in the horrible year of 2012. "If our democracy's working the way it's supposed to and 90 percent of the American people agree on something, in the wake of a tragedy, you'd think this would not be a heavy lift," Obama said.[28]

And yet, it was not only a heavy, but an impossible lift. Even as President Obama spoke, Senator Mitch McConnell, the Republican minority leader, was threatening to filibuster a package of tough federal gun control laws that the Democrats, who then controlled the Senate, had reported out of committee.[29] In the end, no gun control legislation of any significance slipped out of the hermetically sealed gates of the Congress of the United States of America.

Five years after the slaughters at Aurora and Sandy Hook, Democratic senator Chris Murphy of Connecticut reflected on the stalemate in Washington. "I'm always a little embarrassed when I go back to Newtown," he said in an interview with the *Guardian* newspaper. "I still feel awful that we haven't enacted bigger national change."[30]

And seven years after those slaughters, on every single morning of every single day, victims and survivors, family members of bright young women like Jessi Ghawi, and the parents of twenty murdered first-graders from Newtown, all wake up to pain. The only thing that has changed at the national level is the escalation of the body count in public mass shootings and the election of Donald Trump as president. Trump's views have evolved, as politicians are wont to say when they backflip from their stated policy positions. If President Obama did speak for Donald Trump and "every American" at Newtown, Connecticut, in 2012, Trump and many other Americans have turned their backs on those words and the pain that they addressed.

The obvious question is why? Why has nothing happened to stop the killing in the seven years since Jessi Ghawi was murdered in Aurora? Gun violence reduction activists bristle at the suggestion that "nothing has happened." They point to incremental successes in a handful of states. They talk about a new era of movement building. Perhaps. But everyone knows beyond doubt that we—America and Americans—have simply failed to take coherent and aggressive-enough action. We are shadowed by the knowledge that at any minute of any day another public mass shooting might erupt.

Is American democracy "working the way it's supposed to"?

What if the way it's supposed to work isn't at all the way it actually works in real life? What if President Obama and his sympathizers were placing misguided faith in what some scholars call the "Folk Theory of Democracy," a naively romantic narrative that assumes citizens are informed, rational buyers in a marketplace of policy ideas proposed by competing political parties and chosen by voters on the basis of self-interest?[31] What if voters are in fact typically ill-informed about the substance of policy, are actually driven largely by emotions like fear and anger, and are so polarized that in the name of tribal loyalty they are willing to blithely toss aside their own self-interest and the safety of children? And if democracy doesn't work according to folk theory, if it isn't working the way it is "supposed to work," what does that mean for tens of thousands of people like Lonnie and Sandy Phillips and hundreds of millions of other Americans who have suffered pain from gun violence and want to change things?

If American democracy isn't working to make change, who or what is to blame? One usual suspect is the NRA, the National Rifle Association.

The Wizard of Fairfax—The National Rifle Association

People talk a lot about "closure," as if the pain of losing a loved one or the lifelong trauma one suffers after being shot with a gun can be neatly folded up and put away in a chest of emotional drawers. Many victims and survivors of firearm violence are more likely to talk about accommodation, or coming to terms, or declaring a truce with their emotional and physical pain. These realities will never go away for them. But here is another cruel reality. Like even the most urgent email imaginable, sent to "every American," their personal stories gradually slip down the queue of the nation's inbox. Their reality inexorably falls out of the public's sight. Their anguish is superseded at the top of the urgent-message rank by newer and often more ghastly events. This is particularly so in the case of public mass shootings.

On October 1, 2017, for example, a man whose motivations remain a mystery brought to the world's attention one of the American gun industry's more deadly inventions, a mechanism known as the "bump stock," a legal means for increasing the rate of fire of semiautomatic assault rifles, in effect converting them to more rapidly firing machine guns. Armed with more than a dozen AR-15–type semiautomatic assault rifles fitted with bump stocks, he opened fire from his hotel room on the thirty-second floor of the Mandalay Bay Resort and Casino in Las Vegas, Nevada. His targets were people enjoying an open-air country music festival. By the time he committed suicide, he had killed fifty-eight people, the most in a public mass shooting in America at the time of this writing. According to the final police report, 869 other persons suffered nonfatal physical injuries, of which 413 were caused by gunshot or shrapnel.[32] One year later—while the Trump administration was dragging its heels in the lengthy process of issuing a federal regulation banning bump stocks—a Texas company was still cheerfully selling them.[33]

Eight months after the Las Vegas public mass shooting, on February 14, 2018, a male teenager walked into the Marjory Stoneman Douglas High School in Parkland, Florida, armed with a Smith & Wesson M&P15 semiautomatic assault rifle—the same make and model gun that was used to murder Jessi Ghawi in the Aurora theater public mass shooting. He killed fourteen students and three staff members and wounded another seventeen victims.[34] Public reaction to the Parkland public mass shooting was immediate and widespread. There was the predictable media race for "breaking" gun violence porn and the public display of deep thoughts and pious prayers from politicians. President Donald Trump tweeted his.

My prayers and condolences to the families of the victims of the terrible Florida shooting. No child, teacher or anyone else should ever feel unsafe in an American school.
12:50 PM–14 Feb 2018

Something different happened, however. It again raised hopes that this time, everything really was changed. This time the tipping point really had been reached. The surviving students of the public mass shooting at Marjory Stoneman Douglas High School firmly rejected the role usually assigned to victims of all types of shootings, that of passive props, exploited for tearful sound bites by the news media and assembled as grieving background extras for politicians making speeches into cameras and microphones.

One of the students, senior Emma Gonzalez, threw down the gauntlet at a rally just three days later. "Every single person up here today, all these people should be home grieving," Gonzalez said. "But instead we are up here standing together because if all our government and President can do is send thoughts and prayers, then it's time for victims to be the change that we need to see."[35]

It was a powerful moment. The formless grief and anger of the Parkland survivors crystallized into the spontaneous core of a movement as the students visited, talked, cried, and shared their thoughts and reactions among themselves. They rejected what psychiatrists call "learned helplessness," the mind-set that there is "nothing I can do" about abuse or violence, often seen in victims of domestic abuse.[36] Like crystals erupting out of inchoate matter, the "Parkland kids" connected with other students and other gun violence victims and survivors. They expanded their reach beyond advocacy for gun control to the more primal forces of voter registration and movement building.

"We started," David Hogg and his sister Lauren wrote in their book *#Never Again*, "by going to war with the NRA."[37]

The National Rifle Association (NRA) would without question be an essential symbolic and tactical target of any effective gun control (or "gun violence reduction") movement.[38] The NRA is at a minimum a bloody flag. It is a useful tangible symbol for recruiting and mobilizing activists, just as the NRA itself uses grimly stylized images of Democratic leaders in Congress like Charles Schumer and Nancy Pelosi, and feverish warnings about their evil intentions, to mobilize their own activists.[39] More substantively, the NRA is universally recognized as one of the most effective lobbying organizations in America at the state, local, and federal level. It is the point of a cultural spear that repeatedly impales the efforts of those who seek stronger gun control laws.

Examples of the NRA's prowess are legion. A week after the Parkland public mass shooting, President Trump announced through his Twitter stream that he was supporting several moves to tighten federal gun laws, including raising the minimum age for buying rifles, requiring background checks for all gun sales, and ending the sale of bump stocks.

> I will be strongly pushing Comprehensive Background Checks with an emphasis on Mental Health. Raise age to 21 and end sale of Bump Stocks! Congress is in a mood to finally do something on this issue—I hope!
> 5:13 AM–22 Feb 2018

The president mocked members of Congress in a televised White House meeting, snidely telling the legislators that although the NRA has "great power over you people, they have less power over me."[40] Trump's stated support for strengthened federal gun laws prompted Senate minority leader Schumer to invite Trump to back proposals to ban semiautomatic assault weapons like the AR-15–type rifles used at Aurora, Sandy Hook, Parkland, and elsewhere. "If the president can get some Republicans to vote for the assault weapons ban," Schumer said, "we can pass it soon."[41]

Later that same day, however, Trump and Vice President Mike Pence met in the Oval Office with senior NRA officials. After that meeting, Chris Cox, the NRA's chief lobbyist, confidently tweeted that "POTUS & VPOTUS support the Second Amendment, support strong due process and don't want gun control. #NRA #MAGA."[42] And within a month the president publicly backflipped again to get in line with the NRA.

> On 18 to 21 Age Limits, watching court cases and rulings before acting. States are making this decision. Things are moving rapidly on this, but not much political support (to put it mildly).
>   6:22 AM–12 Mar 2018

What Trump did not explain in his cryptic Twitter reference to "court cases and rulings" was a telling backstory. After the Parkland shooting, the Florida legislature quickly passed and the governor signed into law the Marjory Stoneman Douglas High School Public Safety Act, which, among other things, prohibited gun sales to anyone younger than twenty-one. On March 9, 2018, the day that the governor signed the bill, the NRA filed a lawsuit challenging the new age limit, arguing that it violated the constitutional rights of young people between the ages of eighteen and twenty-one.[43] It is safe to assume that the NRA's Florida lawsuit was among the unnamed court cases that the president would allegedly be "watching."

Check. Mate. Stalemate.

Yes, the NRA is a powerful force. But a danger lies in mistaking the NRA for the simple cause rather than the complex effect of America's polarized political and social order.

There is a popular, simplistic view that the NRA is the cause of all of this gridlock, an evil wizard of violence. Operating from its headquarters in Fairfax, Virginia, lurking behind a curtain of secrecy and vile bluster, the Wizard of Fairfax pulls levers, seduces politicians with its bags of cash, and suckers millions of otherwise correct-thinking voters into a patently absurd love affair with guns, the harlot of Babylon.

There are two major problems with this view.

The first is that the NRA shares its cash only with politicians who already agree with its clearly stated policy views. They are mostly Republicans.

In any case, taken in the broader view of political finance, the NRA's individual campaign contributions ($1.1 million in 2016) are not enough to buy any politician's vote. "Compared with the towering sums of money donated to House and Senate candidates in the last cycle—$1.7 billion— the N.R.A.'s direct contributions were almost a rounding error."[44] As one analyst observed, the NRA's money is spread out over so many campaigns that it "may be enough to keep the volunteers in donuts, but it won't swing any races."[45]

The second is the marginal role that this simplistic view necessarily assigns to the millions of Americans who are members of the NRA, and to millions more that polling shows own and like guns and support at least in part the NRA's opposition to gun control. According to polling by the nonpartisan Pew Research Center, 30 percent of Americans say that they own a gun. In a population estimated to be about 330 million in 2018, that would mean that roughly 99 million Americans own a gun. Another 36 percent say that they are open to owning a gun in the future—another 118 million Americans. Taken together, therefore, there are about 217 million Americans who are not opposed to gun ownership.[46]

If the NRA were indeed the simple cause of America's gun violence problems, it would follow that these millions of Americans must either themselves be co-conspirators with the NRA, or gullible enough to be fooled by the Wizard of Fairfax's dark powers. Absent the NRA, they would beat their guns into plowshares. This dismissive view of a large part of the American electorate—the real source of the NRA's clout—may be emotionally satisfying, but it ignores political reality.

Positing the mere existence of the NRA (and the more broadly and vaguely decried "gun lobby") as the ultimate cause of the failure of gun control in America is not just poorly informed practical politics. It ignores the deeper cultural forces that have shaped polarization and gridlock in America across a spectrum of contentious policy issues. It fails to grasp that the NRA is as much a product of those deep forces as a driver of them. Those forces must be understood and addressed in an organized and informed way if the NRA is to be disempowered or matched in influence.

There are other problems with simply blaming the NRA for America's gun violence. That mantra has for decades papered over failings of gun control (or "gun violence reduction") advocates themselves. By excusing these failings, it has helped prevent the formation of a genuine and effective grassroots movement. And it has encouraged ineffective and unprincipled politicians to pose as friends full of sympathetic thoughts and prayers, but who actually do little. It permits these sunshine friends to shrug their shoulders and walk away from the third rail because the wicked NRA, that Wizard of Fairfax, simply will not let them do their job. As political science professor Kristen Goss wrote in her astringent critique *Disarmed: The Missing Movement for Gun Control in America*, "the nation has never witnessed a vigorous, nation-spanning social movement to control access to firearms" in part because the would-be leaders of such a movement "have chosen political strategies that are anathema to movement building."[47]

> Unlike other movements, such as those against tobacco, smoking, and abortion, the gun control campaign struggled to obtain patronage, to craft a resonant issue frame, and to settle on a strategy that could deliver movement-building victories. As a result . . . gun control remained remote—difficult to relate to, difficult to rally around. Somewhat counterintuitively, gun control did not inspire a true social movement, in part because its elite leaders for decades did not think one necessary.[48]

The fact is that the NRA and other conservative issue- and value-oriented groups have better understood "movement building" and have consistently better navigated the riptides of polarized America than have the top-down national gun control organizations that oppose it. The NRA's true power lies in its ability to energize real people on one side of America's political and cultural polar divide. In order to understand this point, it is useful to review the work of a number of social scientists and other perceptive authors who have explored and sought to explain three key issues:

- The causes and consequences of America's current cultural, ideological, and political polarization.

- How the NRA and the gun industry have successfully exploited this polarization.

- The weakness of the model that gun control efforts have historically used.

American Tsunami—The Causes and Consequences of Polarization

"It has become obvious to both scholarly and non-scholarly observers that partisan conflict among political elites has greatly intensified," Alan Abramowitz wrote in his book *The Great Alignment*. "What is not as widely acknowledged is that polarization is not confined to the elites. The American people—especially those who participate in politics—have also become polarized."[49]

To be sure, not every political scientist accepts the proposition that the American people themselves are polarized. Morris Fiorina, for example, argues that the "political class" is polarized, but "normal people" are not.[50] This school agrees that Americans have sorted themselves into two political parties with distinctly different ideologies, values, and positions on specific issues. But advocates of this view hold that, taken as a whole, most Americans still fall into the middle of a bell-shaped curve about most issues. In short, most of us are still centrists. We are sorted into sides, but not polarized. There is a disconnect between us and our polarized political leaders.

Abramowitz argues that data from the American National Election Studies (ANES)—scholarly surveys of voters taken before and after every presidential election, with data going back to 1948—refutes the centrist argument. "Sorting and polarization are almost indistinguishable," he states. "As the American electorate has become increasingly sorted by party, the distributions of ideological positions, policy preferences, and even candidate evaluations have become increasingly polarized, with fewer Democrats and Republicans found near the center and more near the opposing attitudinal poles."[51] There is no "disconnect," he concludes. "America is a polarized country where leaders reflect the diverging priorities and values of the constituents who elected them."[52] Current polling and recurring events like the bitterly contested 2018 confirmation of U.S. Supreme Court justice Brett Kavanaugh seem to indicate that Americans are indeed deeply polarized along ideological and cultural, and thus political, lines.[53]

How did we get here? The three phases of a typical tsunami provide an interestingly apt model for tracking how America arrived at its current polarized state.

A tsunami is a series of waves of ocean waters of such height and speed that they can swiftly destroy low-lying coastal areas. A tsunami in the Indian Ocean in 2004 had waves as high as one hundred feet. It killed nearly a quarter of a million people on coastlines from Indonesia to South Africa.[54]

There are three phases in tsunami events that are analogous to cultural and political polarization in the United States over the last half century: (1) a precipitating event that causes the waves to form; (2) a sudden flow of water away from the shore just before the tsunami strikes; and (3) the swift and destructive force of the tsunami as it sweeps over the coast.

The first of these phases, the triggering event, is an abrupt and large-scale movement on the ocean floor that displaces billions of tons of seawater.[55] The displaced water spreads outward in concentric waves. Most tsunamis are caused by earthquakes. Underlying these formative events is the constant friction between massive tectonic plates that move over and under each other beneath the earth's crust at about the same speed that fingernails grow. Occasionally, the accumulated energy in these plates is released through the sudden and massive shift of a plate—an earthquake. When an earthquake forces one of the plates upward from the seabed, those billions of tons of water are displaced.

The tsunami waves created by the displacement appear small in the open ocean. But when they reach shallow waters close to shore, the huge volume of water is forced up from the seabed, resulting in much bigger waves. As a tsunami nears a given coastline, the first noticeable event may be something that happens if the trough of the wave arrives first: a sudden outward rush of water so vast that the sea disappears off the shoreline and exposes hundreds of yards of seabed. Tragically, this classic early warning is often misinterpreted. People are drawn to explore the exposed seabed, where fish and underwater artifacts appear for the taking. Many of these people die during the third and final phase when the walls of water arrive, race across the beach, and sweep far onto the shore.

Scary, yes. But what does this have to do with American polarization politically and culturally? Obviously, nothing directly. But the analogue is compelling.

The Tectonic Shift of the 1950s

In 1977 a political scientist named Ronald Inglehart published a book titled *The Silent Revolution*.[56] Inglehart first postulated and then demonstrated that the equivalent of a vast shift in the world's cultural

17

and political tectonic plates had occurred over several decades after the end of the Second World War. He argued that high levels of economic and physical security reshaped values and worldviews to which people all over the world had been bound and believed in since the Industrial Revolution. He explained in a 2018 article that the shift was fundamentally from Materialist "survival values" that emphasize "economic and physical security above all," to Postmaterialist "self-expression values" that give "top priority to individual autonomy and self-expression." The emphasis on Postmaterialist values "led to massive social and political changes, from stronger environmental protection policies and anti-war movements, to higher levels of gender equality in government, business and academic life, greater tolerance of gays, handicapped people and foreigners and the spread of democracy."[57]

The revolution was "silent" because it was the product of a new generation, figuratively growing at the speed of fingernails. It was not inspired by a call to the cultural barricades or by impassioned speechmaking. It was organic to a new economic order. Many of the older generations under whom all this was happening felt threatened, especially by social tolerance and ethnic diversity. "People take the world into which they are born for granted. It constitutes their baseline for what seems familiar and normal."[58]

The change was not just happening in America. In his book *The Big Sort*, author Bill Bishop wrote, "Inglehart's post-materialist trend has been true for every country; the higher the level of economic development, the more widespread the values of self-expression."[59]

The Waters Roll Out—Sudden Dealignment in 1965

Among the consequences of the silent revolution was a change in the dynamics of practical American politics. People were less easily led by political parties and their bosses. Americans, Bishop wrote, "began to define themselves by their values, and that altered what it meant to be either a Democrat or a Republican."[60] And then, precisely in the summer of 1965, "post-materialist politics in the United States reached a point of no return."[61] In January and February of that year, Gallup polling showed the highest levels of party loyalty since the question was first asked in 1945. But in October 1965 the same polling showed that party loyalty had suddenly plummeted.

"There's often talk about realignment of political parties," observed Bishop. "In 1965 there was a sudden *de*alignment, a mass withdrawal of support for *both* parties."[62] The phenomenon was not limited to political parties. It was happening all across American society. People were also dropping out of religious denominations, civic and social clubs, and even recreational leagues. "Institutions that had been gaining members for hundreds of years suddenly stopped their advance and began to decline."[63]

Professor Robert Putnam explored this dynamic in his book *Bowling Alone*. In the 1960s membership in community groups "shot up year after year." Churches and synagogues were packed "as more Americans worshipped together than only a few decades earlier, perhaps more than ever in American history."[64] But that changed. Between 1973 and 1994 the number of Americans who attended just one public meeting or served as an officer or committee member of any local church or organization each fell by 40 percent.[65] "Americans have been dropping out in droves, not merely from political life, but from organized community life generally."[66]

This movement away from traditional parties and community institutions was like the rushing of coastal waters away from the shore before the arrival of a tsunami. The outward rush was accompanied by another change. People's trust in government plummeted. "In the two decades after World War II, people maintained a remarkable trust in government," Bishop wrote. "By 1966, however, American's faith in government had been replaced by doubt."[67] Thus, at the very time that ambitious government initiatives were being pursued in Washington—including what was to become the Gun Control Act of 1968—large numbers of people were dropping their belief in government solutions.

"President John Kennedy had been able to proclaim a 'New Frontier' and President Lyndon Johnson could declare a 'Great Society' because Americans trusted government," according to Bishop. "After 1965, however, Democrats were forced to become ideological contortionists. In the new political climate, they proposed solutions to public problems that were to be carried out by a government that most people—even Democrats—no longer trusted to act in society's best interests."[68] Americans rich and poor alike had begun to think that government was unfair and dishonest.

The Democrats, Abramowitz suggested, were "victims of their own success." The very people who had benefitted the most from the Democrat's New Deal of the Great Depression began to think of themselves

19

in the prosperity following World War II "less as beneficiaries of public spending than as taxpayers supporting programs that benefitted others—others who increasingly looked different from themselves and whose lifestyles many found distressing."[69]

Other tides were rolling out as well. Religion is one important example. "We know in retrospect that just as Catholics and the traditional Protestant denominations were promoting racial reform and world religious cooperation, members of most of these churches were beginning to leave," Bishop wrote. "They were headed to the independent Evangelical and fundamentalist churches that distrusted ecumenical religious organizations."[70]

The "dealignment" of voters from both political parties was a mostly white phenomenon. Black and other racial and ethnic minority voters were consolidating with the Democratic Party. The social tensions of the civil rights movement, the disorders of Vietnam War protests, and the perception that street crime was out of control in America combined with the new personal values orientation to strongly influence large numbers of white people to leave both major parties.[71] It is impossible to sugarcoat the consequences. "Perhaps the most important and potentially dangerous long-term consequence of the great alignment has been the increasing centrality of issues of race and ethnicity in American politics," according to Abramowitz. "No other development in American politics has had a greater impact on the rise of partisan polarization over the past thirty years," and attitudes toward race and ethnicity "are increasingly connected with attitudes toward other major issues in American politics."[72] The original policy differences are no longer the essential driver, observed Professor Lilliana Mason. "The parties have grown so divided by race that simple racial identity, without policy content, is enough to predict party identity," she wrote in her book *Uncivil Agreement*. "The policy division that began the process of racial sorting is no longer necessary for Democrats and Republicans to be divided by race. Their partisan identities have become firmly aligned with their racial identities, and decoupled from their racial-policy positions."[73]

Cultural changes left some white men "deprived of positive identities . . . and left them feeling besieged and confused," Douglas Kellner wrote. "This situation gave rise to a new strain of white male identity politics . . . often exploding into violence and finding solidarity in militia movements, right-wing hate and extremist groups, Christian fundamentalism, survivalist sects, and talk radio and internet subcultures."[74]

For a decade or so, the effects of dealignment seemed benign, even ideal from the point of view of practical politics. Partisanship declined. An ambivalent public split its votes. In 1960, 73 percent voted straight party tickets. That declined to 50 percent in 1966 and was down to 42 percent in 1972.[75] "Party elites in Washington were content with a politics of compromise and tempered ideology."[76] It seemed to be the golden era of cooperation that many long for today. "During the 1950s, 1960s, and 1970s, it was much easier to build bipartisan coalitions to pass legislation."[77]

It is worth emphasizing that none of this vast change was obvious, nor was it apparent to people who made a nice living as gurus and experts with their fingers on the country's pulse. "The political and journalistic elite was the last to know what was happening in the country."[78] Many politicians, cultural leaders, and media elite were content to enjoy themselves out in the newly nonpartisan seabed. Few were aware that the American people were starting to align themselves in an entirely different way.

The big wave was about to roll in.

Tsunami—The Resorting of the 1970s and Beyond

Nobody ordered it. Nobody dreamed it up. Nobody schemed to make it happen. But starting in the mid-1970s and continuing today, Americans abandoned a way of life in which most of them routinely interacted in many different ways, levels, and places with people whose views, life experiences, and values were different from their own. Historically, Democrats and Republicans came in different stripes, from liberal to conservative and all of the permutations in between and along the margins. But their diversity was fitted in along a spectrum within their respective parties. "The most important difference between the American party system during the 1950s and that of today," Abramowitz wrote," is that the parties in the fifties were less ideologically aligned: liberals and conservatives were found in considerable numbers in both parties."[79]

Americans also had "cross-cutting" community connections with each other outside of politics, in their neighborhoods, social and public-service clubs, recreational leagues, and religious institutions. They were exposed to different ideas about which they could disagree without thinking of one another as fools, monsters, or mortal enemies.

All that political and communal cross-pollination of ideas was washed away when the tide rolled back in. People slotted themselves firmly into geographical and ideological communities that were most like themselves. And when people started flowing back into the ranks of both political parties, their new focus was more on shared ideology and culture than on the details of policy proposals. They weren't buying ideas in the marketplace of Folk Democracy. Nor were they mixing their ballots based on assessing the fine print of proposals advanced by competing parties or candidates. They were self-balkanizing, choosing sides across the trenches of a growing culture war. That sorting out is reflected in America's politics today. Hundreds of studies have shown that "mixed company moderates, like-minded company polarizes," Bishop explained. "Heterogeneous communities restrain group excesses; homogeneous communities push toward the extremes."[80]

This was the tsunami. It wiped out what Bishop calls any "sense of the whole."

The change has in one dimension been geographical, a "partisanship of place," and that has had an impact on national politics. Given a choice, people wanted to live in communities where their neighbors shared their values and their politics, and there has been migration in that direction all over the country. "Congressional districts are, as a rule, growing more politically homogeneous," Bishop wrote. "When older officials leave office, they are inexorably replaced by someone further to the right or the left."[81] But there are important exceptions that have a different result, districts changing from red to blue or purple, and vice versa. Colorado and Georgia are two examples.

Colorado is a once dependably Republican state that is becoming increasingly Democratic, although not in every district. The counties with the highest inflow from other states are tending to be more Democratic while those least affected by migration are becoming more Republican, Bishop found. "The people moving to the fast-growing counties around Denver were three times more likely to have come from 'blue' counties outside Colorado than the people moving to the slower-growing (and heavily Republican) counties along the Kansas, Oklahoma, and Nebraska borders," he wrote. "The county that sent the most people to

Colorado between 1991 and 2004 was deeply Democratic Los Angeles County, California."[82]

In 2018, the *Atlanta Journal-Constitution* examined in depth a similar phenomenon in Georgia. "No county has experienced a greater jump in Democratic voter participation between the 2010 and 2018 primaries than Gwinnett, a fast-diversifying suburb teeming with neighborhoods and strip malls," the paper reported. "And no county experienced a GOP awakening as much as Brooks, a sparsely populated, rural territory laden with mossy oaks and peach groves perched atop the state border with Florida."[83]

Brooks County's population of less than sixteen thousand has not changed much since 1960. It was once solidly Democratic, its voters so-called "Yellow Dog Democrats," meaning that they would have voted for a yellow dog so long as it was a Democrat. But the tsunami hit Brooks County in 2010. "Eight years ago we still had conservatives running as Democrats," said a peanut factory owner the newspaper described as the county's unofficial historian. "It became obvious that you couldn't sit down and be a Republican but then vote in a Democratic primary."[84]

As Gwinnett County "transformed from a rural backwater to a sprawling suburb," it experienced a trend in the opposite direction. "The primary reason is a swirl of changing demographics," the paper reported. "More than 60 percent of Gwinnett's 900,000 residents are black, Latino or Asian—a tidal shift for a county that was almost exclusively white in the 1990s. Transplants from major cities in the Northeast and Midwest are also changing the county's mix."[85]

But polarizing trends are much broader and much deeper than simple migration. At the same time that waves of Americans were self-segregating into opposing value-based tribes, new organizations and institutions were being founded, and some older ones (including the NRA) were dramatically changing from within. "The new groups weren't broad based, and they weren't democratically controlled," explains Bishop. "They were run from the top and organized around policies or issues. They weren't for fraternization; these new groups had agendas."[86] From a partisan point of view, argues Mason, "The Republican Party did a better job of organizing sympathetic social groups behind it."[87]

Beginning in the mid-1970s, historically separated strands of conservatives—religious fundamentalists, free-market capitalists, libertarians, and intellectuals—coalesced under the banners of a plethora of new issue-oriented organizations and institutions. "In the late 1960s, conservatism was still a movement tightly linked to, and governed by, the interests of business, grassroots activists, and Republican elected officials," Steven Teles wrote in his book *The Rise of the Conservative Legal Movement*. "Those interests are still vital parts of modern conservatism, but they have been increasingly joined by, and in some cases rendered subordinate to, a network of conservative organizations whose members are primarily motivated by ideological principle rather than coalitional affiliations."[88] The rise of this ideological network had significant political effects. "Parties have gone where the action is in American politics, seeking to control government not just through electoral warrants from the voters but also by coordinating the behavior of actors across society and among the different branches of government," Teles wrote. And "in the transformed party system that came into being in the 1970s, these nonelectoral dimensions of party activity have become increasingly important."[89]

New phrases and names entered the American political vocabulary: the New Right, the Moral Majority, the Christian Coalition, the Heritage Foundation, the Cato Institute, the Federalist Society, and more. Some on the left saw a "vast conspiracy" behind the creation and growth of these new entities, while those on the right saw themselves as merely having caught up with a model pioneered on the left by the Rockefeller Foundation, the Ford Foundations, the Brookings Institution, and others.

None of this conservative mobilization has been more important to the question of gun control than the rise of the conservative legal movement.

In no other area of conservative mobilization, Teles states "was the process of strategic investment as prolonged, ambitious, complicated, and successful as in the law."[90] The conservative "strategic investment" materialized in the form of public-interest law firms, academic revitalization in teaching and scholarly works, judicial appointments, and, most importantly, "strategic litigation." Strategic litigation is important, Teles explained, because courts have less "agenda control" than other political institutions. Therefore, "social actors who are mobilized and skilled at organizing litigation campaigns are likely to prevail over their unmobilized and unskilled counterparts." Viewed through the lens of a recent series of gun-rights successes in the Supreme Court, it becomes clear that these wins happened because conservative lawyers were organized, coordinated, and on a strategic offensive. "Whether the Court hears a case at all depends on the ability of litigants to produce a conflict between circuits, and whether the cases produce the outcomes they want depends upon those litigants' ability to effectively shape the fact pattern presented to the courts."[91]

The consequence of all of this sorting, organizing, and enlisting for cultural war was polarization. So far as gun violence reduction at the national level is concerned, that has meant not just gridlock, but a rolling tide of success for the pro-gun side.

In Our Own Image—The Consequences of Polarization

In the halcyon world of Folk Democracy, Americans would listen carefully to the debate over what to do about gun violence generally and public mass shootings in particular. They would rationally weigh the pros and cons of specific policy details advanced by both sides, seeking the right balance among civil rights, personal interest, and public safety. Then they would vote for the party or candidate who proposed the most sensible solutions. But that's not what happens in America's polarized world. "In this political environment," Mason wrote, "a candidate who picks up the banner of 'us versus them' and 'winning versus losing' is almost guaranteed to tap into a current of resentment and anger across racial, religious, and cultural lines."[92] America's division into two sides fighting a zero-sum game has resulted in behaviors and attitudes that reject compromise as a value and make it all but impossible for partisans to hear one another's case.

News reports regularly illustrate Mason's observation that "Democrats and Republicans have grown to 'dislike, even loathe' each other," and Abramowitz's statement that each side thinks that the other's partisans have "questionable motives and pursue goals that would do grave harm to the country."[93] A Republican senator compares Democrats to the Nazi Brownshirts, whose thuggish harassment of Hitler's political opponents helped bring him to power in Germany.[94] A Georgetown University professor tweets that Republican senators "deserve miserable deaths . . . we castrate their corpses and feed them to swine."[95]

Americans are, in Mason's words, "informationally isolated." The emergence of a plethora of new media sources has made it possible for both sides to "protect themselves from any exposure at all to arguments and opinions on the other side."[96] This means that "even when we sit down to relax and watch TV, Democrats and Republicans are different kinds of people."[97] Americans are even sorted by the slant of the political books that they choose to read, preferring to read only those that reinforce their existing ideology.[98]

Even when divided partisans hear the other side's arguments, they engage in "motivated reasoning," which is "the process by which individuals rationalize their choices in a way that is consistent with what they prefer to believe, rather than what is actually true."[99] Research about how Americans listen to presidential debates has shown that "voters watch debates to reinforce what they already believe," an inclination known as "confirmation bias." When two people with opposite opinions listen to the same report, "both hear confirmation of their preexisting beliefs."[100] Moreover, the dynamic of polarized groups keeps pushing their respective partisans to the extremes by means of "a kind of self-propelled, self-reinforcing loop" in which "they all vie to stand out as the most Republican or most Democratic in the group."[101] Finally, polarized partisans are angry, and anger "leads to increased political activity based not on policy goals but on knee-jerk identity-defense responses."[102]

All of this clearly has an impact on what millions of Americans hear, want to hear, and most importantly choose to believe about guns, gun violence, and what to do about them. It infuses race and immigration deeply into the debate, especially about criminal use of guns. A brief examination of the NRA's ideological history suggests that it is several laps ahead of the gun violence reduction side on exploiting the dynamics of polarization.

The NRA's Ideological History and Polarization

There are several books examining the NRA and its ideological history. Sociology professor Scott Melzer's book *Gun Crusaders* is the best of the lot in the context of polarization and its effects.[103] Melzer interviewed NRA leaders and members and reviewed NRA documents and publications to map its ideological metamorphosis in the mid-1970s. Tracking perfectly the American tsunami of ideological sorting, an internal revolt transformed the NRA from a courtly national sporting club, often ambivalent about gun control, to a bare-knuckled, militant Second Amendment religion. Melzer quotes a former director of the NRA's lobbying arm on the hard-line NRA of today. "You would get a far better understanding if you approached us as if you were approaching one of the great religions of the world."[104] There are no shades of gray in that Spartan religion. You are either for it or against it.

The NRA was originally founded in the late nineteenth century as a means to improve the marksmanship of American military conscripts. Although it continued to promote marksmanship, the NRA gradually became a civilian association oriented largely toward hunting and sporting use of firearms.[105] By the late 1960s and early 1970s, many of the NRA's staff were "hired managers with no particular interest in guns."[106] The NRA's leaders, the "Old Guard," had effectively surrendered to what they perceived as a societal sweep against guns. These leaders "became convinced of the inevitability of the complete extinction or extreme regulation of the shooting sports."[107] They devised a grand plan to pack up and move the NRA headquarters from Washington, D.C., to Colorado. There the organization would build a giant sporting complex the very name of which—the National Outdoor Center—deliberately eschewed the words "gun" or "shooting." These were moves to "re-direct" the NRA "from the gun control area into the safe and uncontroversial area of conservation and sports."[108] They did not sit well with a core of "hard-liners," who fumed at the views of the Old Guard.

The reactionary tsunami swept right over the NRA at its annual meeting in 1977. The hard-liners, bent on engaging in a culture war, "organized and carried out the 'revolt at Cincinnati,' effectively transforming the NRA into the primary defender of the Second Amendment."[109] The NRA, writes Melzer, "gained power and influence at the same time as did many other conservative, reactionary movements . . . [and] recently its agenda has broadened beyond gun rights to conservative politics, and it has ridden the conservative wave to new heights of success."[110]

In polarized America, the NRA of today is a multi-issue Viking with a broad ax waging culture war. Edward Leddy captured its self-image in one short paragraph in his book *Magnum Force Lobby*:

If the National Rifle Association were to portray itself as a symbolic person, he would be a pioneer heading west with a rifle. He is self-reliant,

27

morally strong, and competent. He is also peaceful by preference, but ready to defend himself from attack. He believes in personal rather than collective responsibility.[111]

But there is another side to the self-reliant pioneer. "Listening to NRA leaders and speaking with members, their most palpable emotion is *fear*," Melzer found. They are afraid of big liberal government, which they see as "part of a broader culture war threatening gun rights, individual rights and freedoms, and independence, and, ultimately, white men's status and power." And just beneath the surface "lies the politics of gender and race."[112] Leddy describes the NRA's opponents as the "adversary culture," whose adherents are "concentrated in professions, academia, and the media, where their opinions are easy to spread, and where they can prevent the distribution of opposing views."[113]

Melzer's assessment is that the NRA "is winning the gun battle."[114] And it's not because of bags of cash. It's because the NRA has mobilized a grassroots base energized through "multiple tactics" and "several strategies." It involves its base of voting Americans every hour of every day. Its annual convention draws tens of thousands of the faithful every year. It sponsors local fund-raising banquets, publishes several magazines, has an extensive online, multimedia presence, puts on firearm training sessions and workshops, awards grants to friendly scholars, and hammers its opponents without quarter.[115]

The NRA's deep grass roots and its comprehensive, unified, and unwavering ideological programming stand in stark contrast to the divided, top-down, and kid-glove approach of the other side.

In Search of the Unicorn—Gun Control Groups

Until very recently, America's gun control organizations fell into two categories: foundation babies and direct mail marvels. They were comparatively small bureaucratic entities that orbited independently in the empyrean ether of Washington, New York, Chicago, and Los Angeles. There is still no equivalent of the NRA's national convention, nor is there a sophisticated, comprehensive online media presence promoting a unified "for us or against us" message. Although there are a few law centers fighting a valiant rearguard action, there is nothing comparable to the aggressive, widely interlocked litigation strategy of the conservative legal renaissance. Gun control groups have had almost no true grass roots, although some are trending in that direction now. And most of all, they have eschewed hands-on political organizing—putting aside occasional marches, prayer vigils, and random memorial services—in favor of an "expert-led, inside the Beltway strategy."[116]

The favored action of this model has been the scholarly production of exquisitely moderated "evidence-based" studies, eventually translated from their dense statistical calculations and neutral academic-speak into politely moderated English by one or another "activist" organization, or the generation of largely anecdotal studies by the organizations themselves. The strategic theory, to the extent there is one, appears to be that there is a centrist body of unengaged and undecided opinion in the public and in the Congress that can be swayed by yet another report demonstrating yet again that guns do indeed kill people, and that lots of guns, and particularly military-style guns, kill lots of people. The crux of this approach has been a sonorous call to the unicorns of the middle-of-the-road, who, if only they can be persuaded, will swing elections and stand up and be counted in congressional votes for the correct side of the gun control fight.

This is a model that worked in the era of warm feelings about and liberal dominance of government, when progressive forces were winning in courts, independent regulatory agencies, and Congress. It is still advocated with a straight face by adherents of a centrist political denomination called "The Third Way," whose catechism sanctifies as an article of faith that gun control is the dreaded "third rail" of politics. It is a strategy of doubtful utility in polarized America.

One flaw in this soberly "expert" approach is that the pursued unicorn probably does not exist. There are almost no survivors in the no-man's-land between the polarized trenches. Yes, some people do like to call themselves "independents." According to Abramowitz, "the independent label appeals to many voters: being an independent means thinking for oneself rather than voting blindly for one political party." In actual practice and when pressed, however, "most of these 'independents' make it clear that they usually lean toward one of the two major parties." While there are some "pure independents," these are people who are "much less interested in politics and much less interested in voting."[117] So it turns out that if you want friends on the issue of gun control, you must mobilize the people on your side of the trenches. Which is exactly what the experts inside the Beltway chose not to do:

> By choice and circumstance, gun control was a top-down political campaign without a bottom-up social movement. Pro-control sympathizers were marginalized, lacking the resources, collective identity, and prospectively winnable opportunities that inspire civic participation. They were left to get mad and write futile letters to their Congress members or send a contribution to a lobbying organization in Washington.[118]

Sandy and Lonnie Phillips walked grieving and naively into this asymmetrical legal and political warfare in 2012. They were determined to make change. They thought a natural force for mobilization—for building a movement and breaking the gridlock—would be America's millions of gun violence victims and survivors. But they had a hard time convincing the elite leaders of the gun control entities orbiting the empyrean of that crucial and game-changing point. Meanwhile, the Phillipses—like other victims and survivors—were subjected to unspeakable abuse by partisans from the pro-gun side. They were exploited, and then knocked to the mat twice by their own side. But they got up, dusted themselves off, and rejoined the war.

They are still fighting today. They have a message that they are determined to deliver to America. They call it "Jessi's message."

CHAPTER ONE
PRELUDE

The story of a murder can begin anywhere, any time. This one begins on a late midwinter night along a lightly traveled street in Toronto, Canada.

Canada may seem an unlikely place to start a story about a murder in Aurora, Colorado. But the fabric of gun violence is complex. It respects no boundaries and crosses national borders with ease. Gun violence erupts in many different forms, from a toddler shooting someone with a tragically found handgun[1] to the almost inexplicably intentional carnage wrought by a mass murderer shooting as many complete strangers as he can with military-grade weaponry.[2] It is often cruelly random. A person might dodge a bullet one day and be shot to death the next.

The varied causes of gun violence are not peculiar to any given country, race, ethnicity, creed, or socioeconomic status. They are universal among humanity and include fear, anger, greed, depression, jealousy, revenge, fanaticism, and some forms of mania, among others. Plentiful and easily obtained guns are a pool of gasoline waiting for any one of these very human sparks to ignite violent tragedy.

The globalized gun industry, the militarization of its civilian products, the greed of its owners and executives, and the passivity and in some cases complicity of the world's politicians have filled that volatile pool to overflowing.[3] They have poured an unceasing stream of guns throughout the world, most heavily in the United States. "With the world's factories delivering millions of newly manufactured firearms annually and with far fewer being destroyed, civilian ownership appears to be growing globally," according to the authoritative Small Arms Survey.[4]

The inescapable questions for any civilized, which is to say caring, society are what should be done—what can be done—to contain the eruption of these universal causes of gun violence? Notwithstanding the utopian view that some Americans hold of Canada—and many Canadians of themselves—it too has a long history of grappling with these frustrating questions. The forces at play in Canada's efforts to restrain gun violence illuminate its special relationship with the singular gun culture of the United States, and the difficulties of dealing with the transnational influences of a globalized and militarized civilian gun market.[5]

Except for the actual gunfire—those brief, shocking, unbelievable moments when bullets rip through flesh, shattering bones, exploding tissue, and shredding organs—the warp and woof of the daily gun violence that blankets the world is for all practical purposes invisible. In the United States, for example, millions of civilian gunshot victims—including the physically wounded and the emotionally scarred—live among us with no distinguishing badge. Over the years 2001 through 2016 alone, some 1,204,058 Americans suffered nonfatal gunshot injuries.[6] They are the walking, and in some cases wheelchair-bound or bedridden, wounded. According to a survey by the Pew Research Center, 44 percent of Americans say they know someone who has been shot by a gun.[7] An analysis of American social networks and gun violence data by scholars at Boston University produced an estimate that 99.9 percent of Americans will know at least one victim of gun violence in their lifetime.[8]

The millions of dead gunshot victims, of course, lie silently moldering in their graves. More Americans have been killed by gunshot wounds in the last fifty years than the total of all U.S. military personnel killed in all of the wars that the country has ever fought.[9] Some past and future sociopathic perpetrators of gun violence skulk among us, masking their marks of Cain. Others more "normal" and socially accomplished, however, would be horrified if they could look into a crystal ball and learn that at some irretrievably damning second in the future, their fingers too will squeeze the deadly simple lever of a firearm's trigger and kill or injure another person.[10]

Pick a single thread out of this blood-dark cloth of gun violence. Follow it far enough, and you will find that it bends, twists, and doubles forwards and backwards, a sinuous strand that crosses other strands, loops acrobatically, and wraps itself tightly around all of us—you, me, the strangers around us, and the people we know intimately and love well.

The thread of this particular story begins with Todd Irvine, a young Canadian arborist who was driving down Gerrard Street in Toronto on a chilly, overcast winter night in 2012. It has been said that Todd can expertly trim a fifty-foot tree while dangling perilously above the ground, identify more than a hundred species of trees, consult on the legal and botanical aspect of landscaping projects, and conduct engaging tree walks through leafy neighborhoods. He was once described as Toronto's "tree whisperer." He does not particularly care for the phrase. He suspects that it might be a slight mocking of his love for trees and the profession that he takes quite seriously.

The American woman Jessica ("Jessi") Redfield Ghawi was living at that moment in Denver, Colorado. She had begun her education at home in Texas but had enrolled the year before in Metropolitan State University in Denver, where several established friends were helping her break into sports journalism. She had three internships and was covering the Avalanche hockey team for a local radio station. She was a vivacious, witty, and compassionate young person, who loved and was beloved, poised just on the cusp of what had every promise of being a rich and fulfilling life as a television sports reporter. She smiled often.

Cute, beautiful, impish, intelligent would all work to describe Jessi. But her funds were tight, and she had decided to get a less expensive apartment in the nearby suburb of Aurora. She did not know that her parents, Lonnie and Sandy Phillips, were planning to surprise her in July with some much-needed financial relief.

Todd Irvine and Jessi Ghawi would never meet. But both would be brushed in Toronto by the wings of the Angel of Death. Those dark wings shuddered around the man Todd saw lying spread-eagled in the eastbound lane of the road shortly after 10:00 p.m. on the night of February 28, 2012.[11]

There were several possible explanations for a man being sprawled on his back across an entire lane of traffic, his arms and legs spread wide like Leonard da Vinci's drawing of classic human proportions. Gerrard Street runs east and west through central Toronto. At this spot and time it marked a cultural and socioeconomic border between an upscale, gentrified neighborhood of Victorian row houses to the north, inelegantly named Cabbagetown, and the elegantly named but poverty-stricken sprawl of beaten-down public housing to the south, Regent Park. Artists, writers, musicians, and the urban hip lived north of Gerrard Street in Cabbagetown. Immigrants, gangs, and the poverty-bound lived south of its border in Regent Park.[12]

"Literally, on one side of the street were two-million-dollar homes, and on the other side were blocks and blocks of planned housing, where there were no roads and people lived in this ghetto of separation," Todd recalled in an interview six years later.

The Violent Spark of Economic Inequality, Marginalization, and Hopelessness

Dating from 1948, Regent Park is Canada's oldest public housing project. Designed as a utopian "garden city" of low-income housing facing inward on green squares, Regent Park was effectively closed off from the rest of Toronto. Over time the design itself isolated the project's disadvantaged and increasingly immigrant population. Economic inequality such as that so dramatically parsed by the geography of Gerrard Street fairly breeds violence, a fact concisely summarized by Peter Squires. "Taken as a whole, the more unequal [any] given society, the more health and social problems the society will exhibit . . . including a range of crimogenic influences."[13]

The False Validation of Guns

Inequality, manifested in stunted opportunity, discriminatory exclusion, and the resulting hopelessness, is a common vector of gun violence throughout the world. Its frustrating grip invites the most marginalized to escape their wretched fate in the false validation of street crime, gang violence, ethnic and racial conflict, and terrorism. Not all, but some significant proportion of the disempowered youth who are born in, or migrate into these environments of chronic violence turn to the local outlet of the global gun market to acquire power in the form of thoroughly militarized civilian firearms.[14] As Duke University scholars Philip Cook and Kristin Goss observed about one American city, "Gun crime is a devastating problem in Chicago's high-poverty inner city neighborhoods and a relatively minor problem in its wealthier neighborhoods."[15]

Chicago's gun violence is concentrated in the city's West and South Sides, predominantly black neighborhoods where schools have been closed, social service budgets including mental health services cut, entire blocks consist of litter-strewn vacant lots or boarded-up buildings, and there are more liquor stores than food markets. The violence, a local activist told the *Guardian*, is an example of "what happens when you crowd people into a space where there is little to no resources, where there have been decades of disinvestment, where there is hyper-policing but not hyper-education or access to mental health care."[16]

In a 1997 essay examining the alleged crime-reducing utility of carrying concealed handguns, Valparaiso University Law School professor Albert W. Alschuler observed, "The most promising responses to youth violence focus less on the violence itself than on the conditions that breed it. If despair and hopelessness remain the all-but inescapable lot of millions of Americans, neither our police nor our prisons nor the firearms in our shoulder holsters are likely to save us."[17]

It's Their Own Fault

Not everyone agrees with this view of the relationship between poverty and gun violence. Many believe that "urban decline is the fault of the urban poor, they alone are responsible for the violent mess they have made for themselves."[18] One of the indicia of America's cultural and ideological polarization is the strength of the difference of opinion between the extremes on which is the cause and which is the effect of poverty and crime in low-income neighborhoods, a debate that often degenerates into argument warped with tribal opinion about race and ethnicity. Edward Leddy wrote about these different views in his chronicle of the NRA, *Magnum Force Lobby*. Leddy contrasted the NRA's cultural ethic with that of what he calls its "adversary culture."

> Largely, the adversary culture views crime as the product of oppressive class conditions. Crime is deterministically fostered in lower class individuals by socio-economic conditions. One should feel sympathy for the criminal not his victim. For others, most notably America's traditional

middle-class groups, crime is essentially the free act of a human being choosing evil over good.[19]

Similar dichotomies exist in the matters of deciding which are the "wrong hands" to keep guns out of, which guns should be kept out of most or all hands, and the role of mental illness versus free will and moral choice in assessing accountability for public mass shootings.

Tensions about race, ethnicity, and immigration lie not far below the moral dichotomy regarding crime and poverty. These tensions were crudely articulated in 1991 by the late Jeff Cooper, a former member of the NRA's board of directors and a popular gun columnist, notorious for his scarcely hidden racism. Commenting on the high murder rate in Los Angeles, Cooper wrote in his monthly column that "the consensus is that no more than five to ten people in a hundred who die by gunfire in Los Angeles are any loss to society. These people fight small wars amongst themselves. It would seem a valid social service to keep them well-supplied with ammunition."[20] It is no coincidence that in 1991, whites represented only about 41 percent of the population. The remainder were Asian (10 percent), black (11 percent), and Latino (38 percent).[21]

In a 2017 interview, Dr. Ben Carson, the Trump administration's secretary of housing and urban development, illustrated the polar divide when he opined that "poverty to a large extent is also a state of mind." He went on to contrast the deserving and the undeserving poor. "You take somebody that has the right mind-set, you can take everything from them and put them on the street, and I guarantee in a little while they'll be right back up there." But, he noted, helping the undeserving accomplishes little. "You take somebody with the wrong mind-set, you can give them everything in the world—they'll work their way right back down to the bottom."[22]

Presidential candidate Donald Trump deftly and implicitly dog-whistled this perspective on the disadvantaged among us in an August 2016 speech ostensibly aimed at soliciting African-American votes. "You're living in poverty, your schools are no good, you have no jobs, 58 percent of your youth is unemployed—what the hell do you have to lose?" he asked, veering off of his prepared script.[23] The mercurial candidate put the blame squarely on black voters themselves, specifically for their longtime support of Democratic politicians. "One thing we know for sure is that if you keep voting for the same people you will keep getting the same result."[24] The message implicit in Trump's subtle whistle went beyond voting for the wrong political party. It was patently about opposing sides in America's culture war and pointed the finger of blame for poverty and its consequences at the victims themselves, people with "the wrong mind-set."

If there were any doubt about this subtext, it was erased two years later when the Trump administration made the message explicit by unilaterally declaring the nation's so-called War on Poverty "largely over and a success."[25] What remained on this simplified view of the socioeconomic battlefield were malingerers, people with the wrong mind-set who, for their own good, need to be put to work to earn their porridge. The unilateral declaration of victory may have been at least in part a reaction to the sting of the previous month's United Nations report on poverty in America. "The United States, one of the world's richest nations and the 'land of opportunity,' is fast becoming a champion of inequality," the report stated.[26]

A Bloody Event in Toronto

In Toronto, the decline of Regent Park turned the green spaces of the "garden city" into turf to be contested and fought over by some of the young men stranded in its socioeconomic desert. By February 2012 work was underway to tear down and rebuild the entire project. The reconstruction and resulting displacement created more turmoil within the neighborhood.

Todd's fiancée, Dale Duncan, was in the passenger seat that evening as they drove by Regent Park. The couple were coming from a Home Depot store, where they had gone to order special doors for the house they had bought but not yet moved into. The transaction had taken time and care. They were probably the last to leave the store, sometime after ten o'clock. It was a happy time. As Todd drove west on Gerrard, the two chatted about their new home and its fittings.

Then Todd saw the man lying in the opposite lane of the roadway. One might easily have imagined that a man lying in the road at that particular location must have been a drunk or a drugged-out addict who had stumbled out of Regent Park and simply fallen down in a stupor on Gerrard Street.

"We were the first to come upon him, or maybe other people had just driven around him, although that would have taken quite some effort. At first I thought he had been hit by a car. But he wasn't curled up in a fetal position, he was spread out like a starfish, like he had lain down there on purpose. It could have been someone on drugs, making a scene, whatever."

As they got closer, Todd slowed the car, lowered his window and saw that the man was lying in a pool of blood.

"I can see that he's in distress, and I can see blood," Todd recalled.

As are many who come upon scenes of violent trauma—from motor vehicle crashes to public mass shootings—Todd is haunted by the memory. During a telephone interview six years after the fact, his voice broke as he recalled what he saw and did that night.

Psychological trauma is also one of the invisible strands of gun violence. It ensnares law enforcement officers, medical first responders, victims and survivors, and all of their families, a ribbon tied around unwelcome memories—the sights, sounds, and smells of blood and pain, death and loss. "You never forget your first dead body," Dr. John Nicoletti, a national expert in police and public safety psychology, observed in an interview.[27] The experience is much worse when there are dozens of bodies of the dead and the wounded.

Todd Irvine is a man of humane conviction. He was never going to drive around that scene. His chosen profession as an arborist is inspired by his love of trees. His human relationships are lifted up by empathy and care for others. Todd positioned his car in the street to block any oncoming traffic in the eastbound lane and got out.

Christopher Husbands, the young man lying in the street, was covered in his own blood, frightened, and fading into shocked unconsciousness. His wrists and legs appeared to have been bound with duct tape, as was much of his head.

"Call 911!" Todd said to Dale as he knelt beside Husbands, from whom thick blood was oozing.

"You're going to be all right," he assured the young man. "Hang on and stay awake."

But in the moment it was not clear that Husbands would be all right. The wait for the police and the EMT seemed an eternity, even though it was actually only a matter of minutes. After help arrived, Husbands was taken off in an ambulance. Todd gave his statement to the police. Then he went home and sent out a short tweet.

"Tonight I stood over man laying on street bleeding from stab wounds. I talked to him as we waited for help, hoping he would not die. The police arrived shortly after and took over. The scariest 4 mins of my life. I hope guy is okay. Be safe everyone!"

Six months later most of Toronto was very angry at Christopher Husbands. Many wanted him locked away for life. A few questioned whether Todd Irvine regretted saving the young man's life. It was a question Todd dismisses out of hand.

"What I saw was a frightened, bloody young man. I think he had lain down in the middle of the street because he knew it was his only chance to be found, to be saved. I would do the same thing if it happened again today. It was a matter of life and death, and I wanted him to live."

The Mysterious Beating

Christopher Husbands was bleeding to death because he had been beaten and stabbed in the back at least twenty-two times. The complete story of what led to Husbands's agony that night is still shrouded in the cloak of *omerta*—the universal code of the mean street and its violent crimes. Keep your mouth shut. Tell the cops nothing. Get your own justice later. "Talking to the police, the street lifestyle, it's a very dangerous thing to do," Husbands later testified about why he had never identified his attackers to police. "It could get you in more trouble than if you just shut up."[28]

Some part of the events that led up to Husbands's injuries are known from his own testimony during his criminal trial several years later on felony charges growing out of his personal exaction of violent justice—revenge. But even that tale is masked here and there. The whole truth will probably never be known to a moral certainty.

What is known is this. Christopher Husbands may have been a member of a gang, the Sic Thugs (or Sic Thugz) of Regent Park. His father thought he was a gang member. But Toronto's gangs are fluid, not as well organized and tightly disciplined as, say, America's MS-13 and other spawn of Los Angeles. Husbands may also have been involved in drug dealing.[29]

At the time of the assault in February 2012, Husbands certainly was out on bail and under house arrest on a sexual assault charge from

November 2010 (of which he was convicted in October 2012). He was also facing an even older seventeen-count indictment. Those charges resulted from his being found sleeping in a car on March 29, 2010. A stash of marijuana and a loaded Heckler & Koch .40 caliber handgun were also found in the car. That indictment specified nine weapons charges, two counts of obstructing a police officer, five counts of breaching bail conditions, and one drug possession charge. The weapons charges evaporated in a plea bargain in April 2012.[30]

Husbands's meandering criminal record included other brushes with the law. It was altogether ominous. Research has demonstrated that the risk that an individual will use a gun to shoot another person is significantly increased if the individual has access to a firearm and has ever committed a violent crime, including violent misdemeanors, a crime of domestic violence, or a crime in which drugs or alcohol are involved.[31]

It was Christopher Husbands's story that he was lured to visit an apartment in Regent Park that afternoon to enjoy a sexual liaison with an older woman who lived there. The woman was the mother of one of his friends. She had seduced young Christopher and shared her favors with him for months. Christopher did not know that sex was not at all on that evening's agenda. Nor did he know that the apartment was in fact vacant. His paramour had moved out. When he knocked at the door, several men in masks grabbed him and dragged him into the apartment. There he was blindfolded, robbed of several hundred dollars, threatened with a gun held to his head, bound up with tape, taunted, dumped into a bathtub, beaten, stabbed, and finally left alone in an empty room, bleeding and awaiting an uncertain end to his ordeal.[32]

Christopher claims still to be puzzled by why this violence happened to him.

"To this day," Husbands told the court during his criminal trial in November 2014, "my memory's not clear about what happened that night."[33]

Husbands eventually realized that most of his assailants were gone. He could hear conspiratorial whispering in another room among the two or three who remained. Seizing the moment, Christopher leaped up, crashed through a door, ran away through the winter-bound night, and fell down in the road, panting and bleeding.

There he was found and saved by Todd Irvine.

Jessi Ghawi and Christopher Husbands also would never meet. But in a few months their paths would cross in Toronto's busiest, most famous, and most popular commercial and tourist venue.

The Angel of Death would again be hovering nearby. This time it would be carrying a handgun.

The Threatening Gesture—A Shooting in Canada

Saturday, June 2, 2012, was a drizzly evening in Toronto, and Jessi Ghawi was out on a mission.

At shortly before 6:00 p.m., the rain was dwindling and the winds were calming. The temperature was in the low sixties. The coming days would be pure Canadian Spring, a week of clear skies and rising temperatures.

"I was on a mission to eat sushi that day," Jessi wrote later, "and when I'm on a mission, nothing will deter me."[34]

That was the decidedly tough side of Jessi talking, the verbal armor of a beautiful and determined young woman. Jessi was an exceptionally talented writer who loved sports—among many other things in her full life—and wanted to break into television sports reporting. She used the pen name "Jessica Redfield" in honor of her grandmother, whose aspiration to become a journalist was never realized.

"Jessi was smart, friendly, and amazing," her friend and fellow journalist Cheryl Bradley would later write. "A red head through and through, she was a ball of energy and fire, with a quick wit and an infectious personality."[35]

Among all the things Jessi loved, ice hockey was her passion.

"I Like My Hockey How I Like My Men" was the title of the first essay on her blog, *A Run On of Thoughts*, posted almost a year earlier on August 8, 2011. "Men are like the game of hockey to me," she wrote, "and NHL teams are easily compared to a collection of male archetypes that everyone can relate to." She wittily dissected and matched types of men to National Hockey League teams. Her typology ranged from "The Guy You Lost Your Virginity To" (the Phoenix Coyotes) to "The Unicorn" (Boston Bruins).[36]

Jessi was in Canada to console her boyfriend, Jay Meloff, a hockey player whose dog had recently died. She and Jay originally met about one year earlier when Jessi interviewed him over Skype for a sports story. "We spent more time talking rather than interviewing," Meloff told the *Toronto Sun*. "She was just so funny and witty, she didn't miss a beat."[37]

"We just had such a bond right from the very first time we ever spoke to each other," he told another newspaper, the *National Post*. "We were like the same person. It was perfect how we got along."[38]

Like Jessi, Jay was trying to break into the big leagues, but as a player rather than as a journalist. He was scrapping among the middling journeymen "who fight for every minute of ice time they get throughout their careers."[39] Jay strapped on his first pair of skates when he was two years old. He scored his first goal when he was three. After years of playing in a succession of college and minor leagues, Jay was moving to Denver to try out for the Denver Cutthroats, a new Central Hockey League farm team for the NHL's Denver Avalanche.

Jessi regularly confounded Jay's father with her knowledge of Canada's national sport, its players, statistics, and history. Jessi was "just an absolute hockey and sports factoid machine," Jay's mother said. "My husband's been a coach forever and ever in hockey and she could tell him things he didn't know."[40]

At least publicly, Jessi never said where Jay fit into her hierarchy of men and hockey teams. She avoided the potential appearance of conflict that some might have imagined had she mixed her private life with Jay and her professional work as a journalist on, for example, her Twitter feed.

But being a fetching and conscientious sports geek was not nearly enough. Elbows are thrown in sports journalism, just as they are in sports themselves. To make the team, one needed to be tough enough to take as well as one gave. So however vulnerable Jessi might have been on the inside at twenty-four years of age, she made it a point on the outside to show "sass, class, and a bit of crass."[41]

"She could hang with the guys," her mother, Sandy Phillips, said in an interview. "She could talk their talk, but she was all girl."[42]

Jessi's Twitter feed reads like a rolling sound track, the uncensored life and ruminations of the "fiery Texas redhead" she billed herself as—alternately witty, deeply thoughtful, occasionally bitingly sarcastic, never cruel.

A Fiery Redhead's Mission

Jessi's immediate objective that Spring evening was a place called Sushi-Q, located in the Toronto Eaton Centre's food court, the "Urban Eatery."

The Eaton Centre is not just any shopping center. It was among the first of the vaulted, glass-ceilinged atrium shopping spaces in North America. Its vast, airy design inspired the architects of the best-known galleries in the United States. Eaton Centre is a weatherproof commercial heart beating at the center of a complex of transportation links, artistic venues, hotels, and office buildings. In addition to its purely commercial attraction, it is Toronto's number one tourist attraction, drawing almost fifty million visitors a year. That number is claimed by Toronto's boosters to be more than the number of annual visitors to New York City's Central Park.[43]

Not all of the visitors are tourists. Residents of Toronto and nearby towns in the province of Ontario regularly shop at Eaton Centre or eat in its food court. And among the hundred thousand people visiting the mall that day, there were seven in particular who were also bound for the Urban Eatery. They were in three separate groups, each heading independently toward Sushi-Q.

The lives of these seven people would intersect. When they did, they would be forever changed by a sudden explosion of violence. None of them could have imagined that traumatic eruption would engulf them, on that day, at that time, in that place.[44]

Jessi Ghawi never made it to Sushi-Q. An invisible, disquieting finger touched Jessi's soul and pushed her away from her mission. She missed the fateful convergence of those seven lives by two minutes. But what happened among them had an effect on Jessi as profound as a blinding burst of celestial light.

"When I arrived at the Eaton Center mall, I walked down to the food court and spotted a sushi restaurant," Jessi wrote. "Instead of walking in, sitting down, and enjoying sushi, I changed my mind, which is very unlike me, and decided that a greasy burger and poutine would do the trick." (Poutine is Canada's national comfort food, a mélange of french fries, melted cheese, and grease.)

Jessi hurried through her burger and poutine. But a disturbing feeling set its hooks inside her. It kept tugging at her insides. "After that purchase, I said I felt funny," she wrote. "It wasn't the kind of funny you feel after spending money you know you shouldn't have spent. It was almost a panicky feeling that left my chest feeling like something was missing. A feeling that was overwhelming enough to lead me to head outside in the rain to get fresh air instead of continuing back into the food court to go shopping at Sport Chek."

Jessi and Jay walked around outside the mall for a while. And then something astounding happened. "People started funneling out of every exit."

The World We Live In

Professional baseball player Brett Lawrie, then a third baseman for the Toronto Blue Jays, was inside the Eaton Centre. "It was instant panic," Lawrie said. "It was almost like as if you stepped on an anthill and then everyone just flooded right out of the whole place."[45] Another witness described it as "a massive crowd of people screaming, running, freaking out."[46]

Jessi saw that panicked flood pouring out into the streets. Then she heard someone say, "There was a shooting in the food court. Some guy just opened fire." Sirens wailed. Police and emergency medical services personnel arrived. Jessi stayed. "I'm not sure what made me stick around at this point instead of running as far away from the mall as possible," she wrote. "Shock? Curiosity? Human nature? Who knows."

A growing mass milled around in the streets outside the mall, a whirlpool of chaos. After a short while police started pushing the crowd back, yelling for people to make room. "I saw a young shirtless boy on a stretcher, with his face and head covered by the EMS as they rushed him by us to get him into an ambulance. The moment was surprisingly calm."

The light struck Jessi as the ambulance doors slammed shut. "That's when it really hit me," she wrote. "I felt nauseous. Who would go into a mall full of thousands of innocent people and open fire? Is this really the world we live in?"

The answer to Jessi's first question would be answered within forty-eight hours. Her second question is a matter of passionate debate and the ultimate subject of this book. Is this the world we live in? And if it is, can it be changed for the better?

The man who had gone into a mall full of innocent people and opened fire turned himself in to police. He was Christopher Husbands—the bloodied young man that Todd Irvine found sprawled in the road three months before.[47] One of the innocent people that Husbands struck down was Connor Stevenson, the thirteen-year-old boy that Jessi saw being rushed out on a stretcher. Connor was not one of Husbands's targets. He was hit in the head by a random bullet. The first responders who wheeled him out thought that he was unlikely to survive his wound.

Surveillance tapes, trial testimony, and Jessi's own writings lay out the uncanny sequence of life-threatening events that her panicky feeling spared her.

The register receipt showed that Jessi bought her burger and poutine at 6:20 p.m. Had she not been diverted, had Jessi continued on her mission for sushi, she would have been at Sushi-Q at that minute. That was when and where young Connor Stevenson was standing in line with his mother, Jo-Anne Finney. Connor, his mother, and his older sister Taylor had been to a theater matinee across the street from the Eaton Centre. They decided to stop in at the food court, eat, and do a little shopping before driving back home to Port Hope, about sixty miles east of Toronto. Taylor wanted pizza. Connor and his mom wanted sushi.[48]

Grainy blue security surveillance tape—the now-familiar witness to so many shootings in the world—shows Connor and his mom waiting in line at Sushi-Q. Directly behind them in line is a young woman who is later identified as LaChelle John. Standing off to one side is John's companion—twenty-three-year-old Christopher Husbands. Connor and his mother collect their order. They then join his sister, Taylor, and seat themselves at a table only yards away, next to a structural column.

At 6:22 p.m., just after John is handed her order of sushi, Husbands suddenly pulls out a handgun and starts shooting at a passing group of five young men. Chasing the men for a few yards through the food court, Husbands fires all fourteen rounds of the .40 S&W ammunition in his Glock high-capacity semiautomatic pistol's magazine in thirteen seconds.[49]

Two of his targets fall to the floor. One of them, twenty-four-year-old Ahmed Hassan, is struck by four bullets and dies instantly. Husbands straddles the other, twenty-two-year-old Nixon Nirmalendran, who had also been hit already by four bullets. Holding the gun in a two-handed grip, Husbands empties what's left in the magazine of his Glock semiautomatic pistol execution-style into the young man's chest—four more bullets. In less time than it takes to read this paragraph aloud, the shooting was over. Husbands fled, blending into the pandemonium and out of the mall.

Outside the mall, Jessi watched a man being rushed out on a stretcher. She could see "multiple gunshot wounds in his chest, side and neck." That man was Nixon Nirmalendran. He died nine days later. According to his trial testimony, Christopher Husbands had always known that Nixon was one of the men who had dragged him into that empty apartment months before and assaulted him to within a bloody inch of his life. Ahmed Hassan, however, apparently was not among those assailants. Why he was shot and killed—other than being in the wrong place at the wrong time—was not made clear.

Young Connor Stevenson had nothing to do with any of this. He was simply a victim of random chance and a stray bullet.

O, Canada! O, America! So Near, Yet So Far Apart

The thought of gunfire ripping through a Canadian shopping mall no doubt strikes many advocates on the gun control side of America's polarized debate as a chord of jarring cultural dissonance, a vandalous slash across their Romantic gallery image of a more perfectly peaceable union north of the forty-ninth parallel. "In Michael Moore's 2002 documentary 'Bowling for Columbine,' the filmmaker presented Canada as a sort of magical place, where people didn't lock their doors and gun deaths were extremely low."[50] North of the border, gun control for many progressive Canadians has historically been, among other things, "a means of distinguishing Canada from the United States."[51]

Canada is geographically and culturally the nearest example of how some partisans on both sides of the American gun control divide find the perfect solution to the country's gun violence problems in another country's idealized laws. Libertarian author David Kopel addressed this phenomenon in his book *The Samurai, the Mountie, and the Cowboy*, and argues in effect that both sides are pounding square pegs into round holes, and specifically that Canadian gun control laws cannot be pounded into American culture.

"The pro-gun and the anti-gun sides shout at one another, each trying to justify its own policies by citing the laws of other countries," he wrote.

"The two sides never achieve any resolution, because neither side bothers with more than a superficial glance at the realities of gun ownership in the other countries." Gun control advocates cite the strict regulatory regimes of England, Scotland, Canada, Australia, and even Japan. Gun-rights advocates point to the supposedly more relaxed regimes of Switzerland and Israel. "Each side wishes America could be more like its favorite foreign country."[52]

One or another of these foreign exemplars might be useful if the United States were a great deal more culturally homogeneous than it is. But polarization has created something of a country with two different cultural personalities. Kopel's argument implicitly assumes that American culture is or ought to be static. But cultures change and America's culture has changed over the centuries. Looking more closely at Canada's experience with guns and gun control might help clarify what American culture is, what it is not, and what it might become.

Canada's culture might serve as an instructive model toward which Americans might aspire in their quest to control gun violence. Of course, the very thought of becoming anything like Canada is anathema to the gun-rights pole of divided American politics. It is an example of what the NRA's Wayne LaPierre and others like him calculatingly denounce as the "political disease" of "European-style socialism."[53]

Canada and the United States share a predominantly British founding culture and both have frontier histories. "Located on the same continent, with the majority of their populations speaking the same language (although important minorities do not), they are probably as alike as any other two peoples on earth," Seymour Martin Lipset wrote in *Continental Divide,* a study of the different values and institutions of the two countries. "Today they are both wealthy and democratic societies, but they still march to a different drummer, as did the rebels and loyalists, the Whigs and Tories, two centuries ago."[54]

Canada enjoys significantly lower absolute numbers of gun violence incidents and lower rates of gun homicide and suicide than the United States. The prime question is why? What makes Canada so different from the United States in the matter of gun violence? Another recently emerging question is whether Canada can continue to effectively suppress gun violence in the face of the twenty-first-century forces of a globalized firearms industry, a transnational gun lobby, and the chronically violent friction among criminal networks and local gangs.

Gun Violence in Canada and the United States— The Same but Different

There is no question that, by any objective measure, there is less gun violence in Canada than in the United States. A comprehensive study of violent death rates among high-income countries published in the *American Journal of Medicine* reported that in 2010 the U.S. firearm homicide rate was "7 times higher than that of the second highest country, Canada (3.6 vs. 0.50 death per 100,000 population)."[55] The Canadian rate of firearm suicide was also much lower than that of the United States (1.7 vs. 6.3 per 100,000 population).[56]

A Canadian government analysis published in 2014 documented in more detail the same disparate relationship—higher gun violence numbers and rates in the United States than in Canada in 2012 (the year in which Christopher Husbands unleashed his .40 caliber Glock pistol at the Eaton Centre):

> Violent crime in the United States tends to involve firearms more frequently than violent crime in Canada. There were 8,813 homicides involving firearms in the United States in 2012, accounting for 69% of all homicides, while in Canada, firearms [172 homicides] accounted for 33%. . . . In addition, when looking at specific offenses, the rate of firearm-related crime is higher in the United States than in Canada. In the United States, a firearm was present in 22% of all major assaults, compared to 4% in Canada. . . . The rate of firearm-related major assault in the United States was about ten times higher than in Canada in 2012 (53 per 100,000 compared to 5 per 100,000). Similarly, robbery in the United States was more likely to involve a firearm than robbery in Canada (41% of all robberies versus 12%).[57]

Canada is like the United States in one grisly aspect, however. The majority of firearm-related deaths in Canada (about four out of five) are not crime-related at all, but are rather the result of suicides (and some much smaller number of accidents and legal interventions).[58] In the United States, an average of 60.5 percent of firearms deaths were suicides in the decade ending in 2012.[59] Suicide rates in general have increased dramatically in America over the last decade, more than 30 percent in half of the states, and as high as 57.6 percent in one, North Dakota.

Guns were the means of suicide in almost half of those deaths. "American suicide is predominantly a firearm issue," psychologist Michael Anestis told National Public Radio in June 2018.[60] Anestis is a professor in the Department of Psychology at the University of Southern Mississippi. He is the author of *Guns and Suicide: An American Epidemic*.[61] Given the cultural stigma and social embarrassment widely associated with suicide, these deaths frequently go unreported in the news media and are often overlooked in public discussion of gun violence and ways to reduce it.

Even though firearms violence accounts for a "relatively small proportion of violent crime in Canada," the Canadian federal government nevertheless officially recognizes that gun violence "can have considerable physical, emotional, and psychological effects on those who are victimized, on families, and on communities." In Canada gun crime thus remains "a significant social concern" for the national government, and across a spectrum that is broader and uses more sophisticated means than the traditional mechanisms of law and order—police, courts, and jails.[62]

These differences between the extent and rates of gun violence in Canada and in the United States did not just happen. They reflect differences in how the citizens of these two highly developed frontier nations with a shared British heritage have defined their political and social cultures generally. The Canadian cultural personality is often perceived as the key to its comparatively more peaceable dominion. Filmmaker Moore, for example, suggested that Canadians have less violence than the United States because theirs is a more collaborative culture. The evidence suggests that he was right. Cook and Goss point out that such cultural differences are "difficult to prove empirically," and that at a more practical level "Canada has much stricter gun laws than does the United States and much lower handgun ownership rates."[63] But Lipset and Kopel describe specific historical and cultural influences that brought Canada to these stricter gun laws and gun ownership rates. The differences between Canada and the United States are the concrete result of both cultural and political factors that, like river and river bed, are inseparable and influence one another. "Canada has been and is a more class-aware, elitist, law-abiding, statist, collectivity-oriented, and particularistic (group-oriented) society than the United States."[64]

The first difference is cultural, manifest in the gross difference in the prevalence of firearms in the two countries. According to a 2018 Small

Arms Survey report, the United States has the highest rate of civilian fire-arm holding in the world, at 120.5 guns for every one hundred residents. Yemen is second at 52.8, and Canada fifth at 34.7.[65] Put another way by the *Washington Post*, there are enough guns in the United States "for every man, woman, and child to own one and still have 67 million guns left over."[66] Those "left over" guns would be slightly more than five times the total of 12.7 million civilian guns held by Canadian residents.[67]

This mountain of guns is higher in some regions of the United States than in others. "Geographically, gun ownership is less concentrated in the Northeast than in other regions in the country, and there is a vast urban-rural divide across regions. Among adults who live in rural areas, 46% say they own a gun. By comparison, 28% of adults who live in the suburbs and even fewer—19%—in urban areas own a gun."[68] The huge number of guns in America is the result of a culture that is—according to Dr. Robert J. Spitzer, an authority on the American politics of gun con-trol—generally recognized as a "key component of the American mythic tradition." Spitzer, a professor of political science at the State University of New York, described in one of his books what is meant by the term "American gun culture."

> The phrase usefully summarizes the long-term sentimental attachment of many Americans to the gun, founded on the presence and proliferation of guns since the earliest days of the country; the connection between personal weapons ownership and the country's early struggle for survival and independence followed by the country's frontier experience; and the cultural mythology that has grown up about the gun in both frontier and modern life, as reflected in books, movies, folklore, and other forms of popular expression.[69]

The second difference is political, evident in the history of Canadian efforts to control gun violence through control of access to guns, and to protect the country from what Canadians have seen as dangerous trends within the American gun culture and undesirable influences emanating from its gun industry.

It would be a mistake, however, to suggest that Canada does not share with the United States some problems of gun violence chronic in the twenty-first century. For example, even though its rate of firearms-related homicide is far less than that of the United States, Canada has in recent decades suffered a number of public mass shootings and ongoing gang violence.[70] Solutions have proven difficult and the debate about these problems has been contentious, if not as raw or culturally divisive as that in the United States. The Canadian federal government's imposition in 1998 of a costly system of central licensing and registration of long guns (rifles and shotguns) invigorated the Canadian gun-rights movement and set off a bitter struggle that ended with repeal of the law under a Conservative administration in 2011.[71]

Nevertheless, key attitudes and actions taken relatively early on in Canada's history laid the foundations for a public policy that has been more effective at suppressing gun crime and violence than that of the United States. And as David Kopel wrote, "Canadian gun control cannot be understood outside the context of that country's history."[72] Before examining the specific differences in Canadian and American gun control laws, it is valuable therefore to set the stage by looking briefly at how history shaped the two societies' different organizing principles, their divergent views on government and its role. The starting point is 1776 and the American Revolution.

History's Stage—1776 and All That

"Americans do not know but Canadians cannot forget that two nations, not one, came out of the American Revolution," Lipset wrote. "The United States is the country of the revolution, Canada of the counter-revolution."[73] A good part of Canada was settled in the eighteenth century by Tories—British loyalists—fleeing the American Revolution. "In the south, the colonists' emphases on individualism and achievement orientation were important motivating forces in the launching of the American Revolution," observed Lipset. In the north, however, "both English- and French-speaking Canadians sought to preserve their values and culture by reacting against liberal revolution."[74] Canadian intellectuals and politicians in succeeding decades "emphasized the crudity of American 'mobocracy.' They were not impressed by the advantages gained from democracy as distinct from liberty. . . . They believed, in short, that 'freedom wears a crown.'"[75]

This disdain for America's "'mob' democracy," Kopel wrote, "would powerfully influence Canada. In contrast to the American revolutionaries, the Loyalists were not afraid of what the government would do to them; they were afraid of what would happen if the government collapsed."[76] And Lipset asserts that Canada "remains more respectful of authority, more willing to use the state, and more supportive of a group basis of rights than its neighbor."[77]

There is another important difference in the two countries' historic molds. "From the start," Kopel explains, "the Canadian advance on the frontier was much less violent than America's . . . while America had sixty-nine Indian wars, Canada had none."[78] One of the practical differences was that, unlike in the American West, law enforcement was on the scene to keep order and discourage gunplay even before settlers arrived. These were the "Mounties," the North West Mounted Police (later renamed the Royal Canadian Mounted Police). There was no such national police force in America, and law and order devolved into the hands of random individuals on the frontier. Lipset describes the cultural effect.

> These rugged individualists—the cowboy, the frontiersman, and even the vigilante—not the uniformed, disciplined Mountie, are the heroes of American western settlement. The frontiersman, on the other hand, has never been a figure for special glorification in Canadian literature as he has been in American. Conversely, the Mountie has been treated in laudatory fashion by historians, journalists, and novelists.[79]

The stage thus set, we can examine the large differences between guns and gun control in the United States and Canada, and what they might mean for the ambitions of American activists.

CHAPTER TWO
THE MAPLE LEAF AND THE EAGLE

Jessi Ghawi slowly emerged from the horror she felt immediately after the shooting at the Toronto Eaton Centre. "Feeling sick to my stomach trying to wrap my mind around everything I saw."[1] Many of her Twitter followers offered their support. "Thanks for the well wishes," she responded. "Hoping the victims are ok. You never know when and where it's your time. Really freaked out by this."

She was filled with scorn for something else she saw in the turmoil. "A man dressed as Batman is charging tourists to take pictures outside the Eaton Center yelling "MY PARENTS ARE DEAD!" she wrote. "Very tacky & heartless."

The man in the Batman costume was more than tacky and heartless. He was in retrospect a chilling portent, a threatening gesture, a flutter of the Angel of Death's wings. Yet no one on this planet could have read such a meaning into that fleeting, surreal moment until many weeks later.

A Mother's Comfort

Jessi naturally turned for comfort to her mother, Sandy Phillips, with whom she was extremely close. "We talked a number of times every day," Sandy said in an interview. "And if we weren't actually speaking to one another we were texting to one another. We were in constant contact."[2]

"She always ran things past me before she published," Sandy added. "Like her blog about the hockey teams. She rewrote that several times, and each time it got better and better and better. She ran it by us every single time because she wanted it to be just right. In fact, afterwards she said, 'I don't think I'll write anything that good again.'"

"Our conversations were always very honest," Sandy said. One of Jessi's tweets left a witty trail to one such frank conversation.

"My mom and I are having a conversation about my butt, maple leaf tattoos, strippers, and money," Jessi tweeted in July 2012. "Just don't ask."

"It was so typical," Sandy said with a laugh when she was asked about that particular conversation. Her answer opened windows into Jessi's soul and her irrepressible personality.

Her butt, for starters.

"She had this whole body dysmorphic thing," Sandy said. Jessi had an eating disorder in her mid-teens, and it had serious consequences. "She had been a dancer in her youth, and she was trying to stay tiny and little-girlish so that she could continue to dance. And by starving her body, she was starving her heart as well."

Jessi developed a heart condition known as SVT, which stands for "supraventricular tachycardia."[3] In lay terms, people with SVT experience episodes when their hearts suddenly race at abnormally high rates. There are various treatments, depending on the nature and extent of the specific condition. Some people do nothing. Others take pills. But in Jessi's case, surgery was necessary, a procedure known as "SVT catheter ablation." Long, thin, flexible wires are inserted through the inner thigh and guided to the heart. Once in place, they destroy the tissue causing the abnormal heart rhythms. "We went through the first procedure just fine," Sandy said. "She changed her life and got therapy on her own."

But about a year later, Jessi's symptoms returned and she had to undergo a second operation to destroy some of the tissue missed the first time. "She was fine after that." By the time of that tweet in 2012 Jessi had worked through her disorder and was now "much more comfortable with her body." But Sandy still paid close attention whenever the subject came up. "She was always either fat, or she didn't have a good shape. In this case, she was trying on a bathing suit and she was worried about her butt."

The maple leaf tattoo was a lighthearted riff.

"She liked Canadians and Canadian hockey, so she was talking about getting a maple leaf tattoo," Sandy said. "But it was all a joke. She wasn't going to do it."

Jessi already had a tattoo. The story of what it was, why, and how she got it illuminates the deep bonds she shared with her mother.

"She got that tattoo when she was old enough to get a tattoo and she tricked me into getting it," Sandy recalled. "She said, 'I want to get a tattoo.' And I said, 'Jessi, you know how I feel about tattoos,' and she said, 'Hear me out.' She said, 'You know how mam-maw's [Jessi's grandmother] writing means so much to you and you treasure anything that has her writing on it?' And I said, 'Yes,' and she said, 'I want to have "mizpah" in your handwriting tattooed on my foot so it doesn't show but I'll always have it.' And I thought, boy, you really roped me in on that, so I can't say, no, you can't have my handwriting on your body so that when I'm dead you can look at it."

The English word "mizpah" is derived from several passages in the Hebrew Bible that refer to a pillar or stone erected as a symbolic watchtower, signifying specifically that the Lord will keep an eye on the parties to a covenant, even when they are apart, to make sure that neither cheats on their agreement. In popular usage—tattoos and jewelry, for example—it refers to a phrase from the Bible, specifically Genesis 31:49, "May the Lord watch between you and me, when we are out of sight of each other."[4]

The biblical passage refers specifically to the Lord's oversight of an agreement between Joseph and his father-in-law, Laban, dividing territory between them and memorializing their respective promises not to harass each other. Popular culture morphed the phrase "watch between you and me" from its original meaning of legal monitoring by the Lord into something entirely different. In popular usage it asks that the higher power keep watch over emotionally bonded people when they are apart. The passage has evolved into a sort of common prayer and good-luck charm. During the Victorian era the phrase was popular on jewelry, often a coin-shaped pendant cut in two.[5] Today, tattoos like the one Jessi had on her foot may have only the single word "mizpah," which is meant to incorporate by reference the entire biblical phrase.

So, what Jessi wanted and got was not an arty tattoo, but a physical reminder of the deep connection between her and her mother, and the hope that it would be safely preserved.

The allusion to "strippers and money" left Sandy puzzled for a moment. Then it came back to her.

"Strippers? Oh, right," she said. Jessi's last year in college was coming up. "Jessi was really, really tight on money and we had tapped out of the money we had saved for her school. So, she said, 'I am going to have to get a job as a stripper.' I said, 'Yeah, like that's going to happen,' and she said she had a friend who was in media who actually worked at a strip joint as a cocktail waitress and made money without stripping. She said, 'Maybe that's what I should do' and I said, 'No, not you, you know better. That's the kind of world you do not want to be a part of.'"

"Jessi had a really good moral compass," Sandy added on reflection. "When she first moved to Colorado, she was looking for a job as a waitress, even cocktailing. She went over to Coyote Ugly, a cowboy bar franchise, the girls wear very little clothing, not her kind of thing. Anyway, she went over for an interview and she saw how the girls were behaving and what they did to make their tips and she said, no, I can't do that. I know that's who she truly was. Every time she started getting off course, she would right herself and say, no, that's not who I am, and that's not who I want to be."

Sandy remembered that she was gardening in the back yard of her home in Texas when Jessi called from Canada to tell her about the terrible events at the Toronto Eaton Centre. Sandy missed the call. She had left the phone in a charger inside. When she came in from the garden, she called Jessi back immediately.

"I listened to what she was telling me and I could tell that she was very, very upset," Sandy recalled. "She said, 'I don't know if these people are going to make it. There was blood everywhere.' It was very traumatic for her, and I said, 'Well, you have seen the worst of humanity today, and you'll never see that again.'"

Sandy paused.

"And that wasn't true."

Sandy knows now that humanity had something even worse in store. And yet she did what any loving parent would do. And, according to some experts, it was exactly what a parent should do. She reassured her daughter.

"Parents . . . can help children feel safe by establishing a sense of normalcy and security," the National Association of School Psychologists advises in its points for talking to children about violence. "Reassure children that they are safe. . . . Although there is no absolute guarantee that something bad will never happen, it is important to understand the difference between the possibility of something happening and the probability that it will affect you."[6]

And, after all, as unlikely an event as a random shooting in Canada—barely noticed in the American news media—seemed even more unlikely to repeat itself in any person's life, including Jessi's. An examination of the differences between Canadian and American gun control might illuminate an invisible thread that may have changed the odds.

Regulation of Handguns Compared, Part One—The American Love Affair

The most significant difference between Canada and the United States on gun control is how the two nations have culturally related to and politically regulated handguns. A great deal of attention is paid to the use of semiautomatic assault rifles like the AR-15 and its many variants in public mass shootings. But high-capacity semiautomatic pistols—many of which can be charged with fourteen or more rounds of ammunition in a single loading—have played at least as deadly a role in many mass shootings.

In the United States, handguns and their perceived utility for self-defense are powerful symbols and an emotional touchstone of the gun-rights movement. In his opinion for the majority in the landmark Supreme Court case of *District of Columbia v. Heller*, Justice Antonin Scalia wrote "the American people have considered the handgun to be the quintessential self-defense weapon. . . . Whatever the reason, handguns are the most popular weapon chosen by Americans for self-defense in the home." The decisions in *Heller* and the case of *McDonald v. City of Chicago* were results of strategic litigation mounted by the conservative legal revival that began in the 1970s. Based on a "new theory of the Second Amendment" that Professor Robert J. Spitzer has criticized as "stunningly and fatally defective,"[7] these decisions nevertheless firmly established the individual adult American citizen's right to acquire and possess handguns free of almost any state impediment.[8] According to one recent academic study, Americans own handguns not only for protection from crime, as suggested by Justice Scalia, but also because of a generalized belief that "the world is an unpredictable and dangerous place and that society is at the brink of collapse."[9] These same layers of fear contribute to handgun owners' support for the broad Second Amendment right articulated in *Heller*, and to their belief that they have the right to shoot and kill in self-defense.

Concealed Carry of Handguns

Keying off of these fearful layers, gun-rights advocates, conservative legal strategists, and the gun industry—working in tandem over the last several decades—have succeeded in dramatically relaxing individual state laws governing the issuance of permits to carry concealed handguns. In the mid-1970s, prior to this wave of change, all but five states either forbid the carrying of concealed handguns or required those who wished to do so to obtain a special license.[10] Most states that allowed permits controlled their issue under a discretionary "may issue" system, which meant the state may or may not issue such a license. The burden was on the person desiring the permit to show a good reason why it should be issued. The gun-rights coalition succeeded in dramatically loosening state laws against concealed carry and reversing the burden of proof in those states that require licenses. Most states now operate under a "shall issue" system, meaning that the burden is now on the issuing authority to show why any applicant should not be granted a permit. If the state cannot meet that burden within a set period of time, it must issue the permit. By 2014, these presumptive "right-to-carry" laws were in effect in all but eight states and the District of Columbia.[11] In 2017, a federal appeals court ordered the District of Columbia to loosen its strict system, and by early 2018 the nation's capital also was issuing hundreds of permits under its new shall issue system.[12]

Federal legislation that would compel every state to recognize every other state's concealed carry permit, no matter what its own law, has been passed by the House of Representatives but has never cleared the Senate. The gun lobby has made passage of mandatory reciprocity a central item on its national agenda.[13]

Stand Your Ground Laws

Gun-rights advocates have also succeeded in changing the law in many states to protect gun owners who use their concealed weapon to shoot and kill or injure another person in what they claim to be an act of self-defense. So-called "stand your ground" laws have reversed fundamental premises of the ancient common law of self-defense. The long-standing duty to avoid violence by retreating from a public confrontation where possible has been erased. The burden of showing proof regarding whether one actually was in reasonable fear of mortal danger to justify use of lethal force has also been switched. The burden has been shifted from the defendant to the state, which must now prove the negative proposition that the shooter was not in reasonable fear.

Forces behind the American Handgun Wave

A number of factors lifted this wave of pro-handgun change over the commonsense objection that "increase in the prevalence of gun carriers would likely tend to increase the potential for deadly violence in any tense confrontation, such as barroom and other angry arguments, highway collisions and disputes, and police stops of pedestrians and drivers."[14]

One influence was the tectonic shift going on in American society, most specifically in this case the decline in Americans' trust in their own government. Commenting on right-to-carry laws in 1997, scholar Albert Alschuler wrote:

> These laws reflect America's distrust of government and a self-help siege mentality. Difficult though it is to believe, as late as 1964 76% of Americans thought that they could trust the government to do what is right most of the time. The figure is 19% today. Right-to-carry laws indicate how our faith in the social contract has faded: they take us a step backward toward Thomas Hobbes' state of nature.[15]

Another powerful force behind the change was the gun industry, motivated by profits from the opening of a new market in smaller handguns suitable for concealed carry. "The gun industry should send me a basket of fruit—our efforts have created a new market," Tanya Metaksa, the NRA's chief lobbyist, said in 1996.[16] The NRA and other gun-rights advocates lobbied heavily at the state level. They were helped by the hidden hand of conservative strategic litigation, and by legislative lobbying by conservative organizations not ordinarily involved with the gun industry or pro-gun activism. This included ALEC, the conservative American Legislative Exchange Council, which promoted "model legislation" favoring expanded gun rights.[17]

But the indispensable source of intellectual cover, the putatively empirical basis, for changes that many thought defied common sense was a man named John Lott, author of the influential book *More Guns, Less Crime*.[18] Although his work has been repeatedly savaged by independent experts and by scholars of the academic community over and over again, Lott was and is the prime voice among a small band of pro-gun analysts who argue that "feared or actual presence of armed citizens may deter violent crime."[19] In simple terms, Lott's argument is that more guns equals less crime. It is the basis for the slogan that NRA executive vice president Wayne LaPierre first emitted one week after the public mass shooting at Sandy Hook Elementary School. "The only way to stop a bad guy with a gun is with a good guy with a gun."[20]

John Lott—The Ever-Ready Academic

Until Lott popped up, most studies by public health researchers and academic analysts were hammering the pro-gun side of the debate. The argument that more guns equals more gun violence from suicide to domestic murders was winning intellectually, if not politically. In the polarized era of informationally isolated partisans—driven by motivated reasoning and dismissing contrary arguments through confirmation bias and self-reinforcing loops—the conservative side needed a "scientific" authority to refute the accumulating empirical evidence, to rebut the cultural force of the gun control side, and to fuel the reflexive loops of its pro-gun base.

John Lott fit the bill.

"The entire ideology of the modern gun movement has been basically built around this guy," historian Saul Cornell told *Mother Jones* magazine.[21]

Lott entered the fray about 1997, with a research paper followed by his book, which was based largely on the paper. Since then "John Lott has been the leading go-to guy for 'scientific' evidence to support the political advocacy of gun-rights associations like the NRA and Gun Owners of America," which not only frequently reference his work but promote his book and enlist him for speaking engagements.[22] He has been useful not only for his "scientific" attacks on gun control proposals and his strategic advocacy for looser gun laws. He also serves up a menu of friendly reports supporting a variety of conservative causes wholly aside from guns.

What Lott brings to all of his advocacy, his many critics charge, is a black box of statistical machinations. This box of "econometrics" emits "scientific" conclusions remarkably uniform in their conformity with the interests of pro-gun and other conservative advocacy. The internal mechanics of Lott's magic box are impenetrable to lay persons, indeed to anyone not fluent in the statistical sciences, but that is hardly the point. The messages that the black box spits out are what matters to polarized pro-gun advocates. The mechanics of Lott's black box have been opened up and intellectually destroyed time and again by critical scholars, even including some friendly to the pro-gun side. The consensus of Lott's critics is that he tinkers inside his black box with a mathematical gear here and a statistical ratchet there, fine-tuning its machinations to come up with conclusions friendly to his policy proclivities. "In other words," wrote two scholars unrelentingly critical of his work, "Lott simply cherry-picked the evidence that supported his conclusion and disregarded the rest."[23]

Rutgers University professor Ted Goertzel wrote a scathing article in 2002 in which he surgically destroyed four examples of what he called "junk science" that used "mathematical models with no demonstrated predictive capability to draw policy conclusions." These models purport to produce numerical "'facts' that can be used as debaters' points in policy arguments," but are actually no more than "will o' the wisps" that evaporate with slightly different settings of the gears. Goertzel included Lott's "econometric model"—his black box—that supposedly demonstrated that more guns results in less crime.

> Lott's work is an example of statistical one-upmanship. . . . He demands that anyone who wants to challenge his arguments become immersed in a very complex statistical debate, based on computations so difficult that they cannot be done with ordinary desktop computers. He challenges anyone who disagrees with him to download his data set and redo his calculations, but most social scientists do not think it worth their while to replicate studies using methods that have repeatedly failed.[24]

If most social scientists did not think at first that Lott's dubious work merited serious enough notice to bother going down his statistical rabbit hole, some began to pay attention when pro-gun organizations and conservative media like Fox News started to promote his "scientific" conclusions. Lott's books became the well-thumbed reference bible of pro-gun political preachers. Lott said it. They believed it. That settled it.

Individual researchers closely examined and tried to replicate Lott's work. Some of these independent researchers found, for example, that with the thumb off of the scale, the evidence showed the opposite of Lott's assertions, that in fact "more guns were linked to more crime, with right-to-carry states showing an eight percent increase in aggravated assault." Florida State University criminology professor Gary Kleck—who originally wrote a glowing review of Lott's first book—told *Mother Jones* magazine that when he reexamined Lott's work, "It was garbage in and garbage out. Do I know anybody who specifically believes with more guns there are less crimes and they're a credible criminologist? No."[25]

In 2005, the private, nonprofit, nonpartisan National Research Council of the National Academy of Sciences delivered to Lott's "more guns, less crime" thesis what would have been the knockout punch in a world other than one rendered paralyzed by the stubborn anti-intellectualism of the polarized right. A panel of distinguished experts included Lott's pro-gun canon in its critical study aimed at improving research information and data on firearms and crime. The experts dived down Lott's rabbit hole. When they came back out, their report stated (in polite scientific language) that the facts that Lott's black box produced "have proven to be very sensitive to the precise specifications used and time period examined." Lott's model, "when extended to new data, does not show evidence that passage of right-to-carry laws reduces crime." The tinkering with these gears ended up "casting serious doubt on the proposition that the trend models estimated in the literature reflect effects of the law change" to greater freedom in concealed carry of firearms. "Thus the committee concludes that with the current evidence it is not possible to determine that there is a causal link between the passage of right-to-carry laws and crime rates."[26]

As a result of these and many other negative critiques, Lott's "professional reputation was in tatters, his bold claims undermined by accusations of shoddy research and questionable ethics."[27] Be that as it may, John Lott still regularly pops up, an indefatigable Whack-a-Mole, thick-skinned and obstinate, with a contrived answer in his pocket for even the most devastating critique. It is not surprising that outlets like Fox News often feature Lott and his work. What is curious is why so-called "mainstream media" do the same. Journalist Julia Lurie discovered that editors and producers are "unconcerned by his baggage." His appeal, one media person told her, is simple. "He's got a controversial position and he's smart. What more could you want?" And criminologist Kleck explained,

"All that discrediting is based on technical issues that people don't understand or care about."[28]

Lott has many unfriendly critics, but Professor Louis Klarevas presented as fair and balanced an assessment as might be expected in his book *Rampage Nation: Securing America from Mass Shootings.* Klarevas used the brilliant metaphor of a hypothetical dilemma facing a newly diagnosed cancer patient trying to assess a recommended oncologist with decidedly mixed qualifications. On the one hand, a first internet search reveals that the doctor "attended the best schools, completed his residency at a major research hospital, and published articles in top-tier medical journals." But the patient keeps digging and discovers that the doctor's "research methodologies and findings have been called into question by the leading experts in the field; that he has been accused of fabricating some of his research results; and that, after being criticized on online rating websites, he created a fake sock-puppet account to enter fake reviews and artificially inflate his scores in an effort to salvage his reputation." Lott, Klarevas observes, is "a prominent example of a researcher who has been plagued by such controversy."[29] The metaphor is especially powerful when one considers that gun violence is indeed like a cancer on America's cultural and political health.

Lott's sock-puppet was supposedly a former student of his named Mary Rosh. Mary wrote pages of gushing online support for Lott when he was under attack by his academic peers. She vigorously defended his methodology and his character. When a skeptical writer for the libertarian magazine *Reason*—a reliable opponent of gun control—compared the Internet Protocol (IP) addresses of John Lott and Mary Rosh, he discovered that they were one and the same. Lott confessed to his moral and intellectual duplicity, but with a makeshift excuse. "I shouldn't have used it, but I didn't want to get directly involved with my real name because I could not commit large blocks of time to discussion."[30] The editor-in-chief of *Science* magazine observed that "in most circles this goes down as fraud."[31]

In light of all this, Klarevas pointed out that not only Lott's work, but also the policy recommendations that flow from it have been called into question, the latter like the fruit of a poisoned tree. On the merits, more credible and recent analyses support the view that more concealed gun carriers increases the potential for deadly violence.[32] For example, one significant corollary of the supposed deterrent effect of concealed carry of handguns would be a decline in crime with long guns. Those who might want to commit their crime with a long gun should be just as deterred as those who carry handguns by the thought that someone might have a concealed handgun with which to protect themselves. But a peer-reviewed study published in 2017 found that not to be the case. "Shall-issue states had handgun homicide rates that were 19.8% higher . . . but rates of long-gun homicide were not significantly different in states with shall-issue compared with may-issue laws."[33]

A Curious Artifact—The Crime Prevention Research Center

After John Lott's academic career and his series of brief stints at a few credible think tanks cratered in the wake of exposures of his flawed work and his Mary Rosh sock-puppet scheme to rehabilitate that work and his reputation, Lott finally landed on a home-office perch of his own creation, the Crime Prevention Research Center (CPRC). The center's federal tax return reports that it was incorporated in 2013. It describes the center as "a research and education organization dedicated to conducting academic quality research on the relationship between laws regulating the ownership of or use of guns, crime, and public safety, educating the public on the results of such research, and supporting other organizations, projects, and initiatives that are organized and operated for similar purposes."[34]

On the subject of "academic quality research," two points are worth noting. "Lott is not affiliated with any university, and hasn't been for years," journalist Peter Moskowitz found when he looked into Lott's record. "Little of his gun research has been published in peer-reviewed journals."[35]

Peer review has been an essential part of scholarly communication since the first scientific journals appeared in the seventeenth century. It is the quality-control process by which academic articles are reviewed before publication by other scholars working in the same field as the author (the peers). Peer reviewers evaluate the quality of a proposed paper by assessing the validity of the research methodology and the procedures that the researchers followed. If peer reviewers detect problems in either of these, they may suggest revisions in the paper, or in some cases reject it entirely. Peer review is a scholarly safety valve. It protects against bias and shoddy work.[36] "Lott's recent research hasn't gotten the same scrutiny most scientific researchers do," experts told Moskowitz, because if it did, "it would be torn apart."[37]

Curiously, Lott's center promotes hot-button causes of the political right that seem to wander beyond the scope of its stated focus on "laws regulating the ownership of or use of guns, crime, and public safety."

For example, Lott claimed in one of his center's recent emissions that undocumented immigrants in Arizona are at least 146 percent more likely to be convicted of a crime than other Arizonans. A blogger at the libertarian Cato Institute soon pointed out that Lott had apparently misunderstood his own data set, mixing legal and undocumented aliens together, making his analysis useless. No matter, the damage had already been done. Conservative outlets like Fox News and the *Washington Times* newspaper trumpeted Lott's faulty conclusions. Attorney General Jeff Sessions cited them in a speech.[38]

Lott also testified as an expert for President Trump's since-shuttered and discredited federal voting fraud commission.[39] Addressing a meeting of the commission in September 2017, Lott suggested that election officials should require all would-be voters to be vetted through the federal gun purchase background check system. Given Lott's disdain for that system, a number of observers concluded that he was simply "trolling" the gun violence reduction movement, for which a robust and comprehensive gun-buyer background check is an article of faith.[40] Law professor and author Adam Winkler dismissed Lott's proposal as "patently absurd." He told the *Washington Post*, "Given the previous criticism of the background check system by John Lott, and the fact that the structure of voting regulation is actually different than the regulation of guns, it's hard to believe that this is a serious proposal."[41]

Judged by the Company He Keeps—CPRC's Board of Directors

A much clearer understanding of CPRC's mission is gained by looking beyond its antiseptic "statement of purpose" to the membership of its board of directors. That board includes two of the most toxic of the NRA's public voices—rock guitar player Ted Nugent and former Milwaukee County sheriff David Clarke. It is not likely a coincidence that both of these men have served simultaneously on the CPRC's and the

NRA's boards of directors.[42] Both have a history of stoking the anger of the right pole of divided America.

Nugent recently crowned his long record of racist,[43] anti-Semitic,[44] and threatening language[45] with a round of attacks on the teen-aged student leaders who survived the public mass shooting at the Marjory Stoneman Douglas High School in Parkland, Florida. "The lies from these poor, mushy-brained children who have been fed lies and parrot lies," Nugent said during a March 2018 radio interview, according to the *Washington Post*. "It's not only ignorant, dangerous and stupid—it's soul-less."[46] Nugent continued his attack in April 2018, focusing on student leader and survivor David Hogg. "This guy is a lost cause. He is consumed with hate," Nugent said, according to the *New York Daily News*. "He is part of the problem, not the solution."[47]

Ted Nugent's False Flag

Like many of his peers in the gun-rights movement, Nugent wraps the American flag around himself. "Nugent says his blood runs red, white, Reagan and Bush, and if they had a war—a real war—he would fight his way to the front line." He said he was "proud that the Michigan legislature this year [1990] proclaimed him a 'wholesome, traditional' man of 'honor, integrity, loyalty, and patriotism.'"[48] But Nugent's "patriotism" did not extend to serving his country in military uniform. The Michigan guitar player is an admitted draft-dodger. Because he has cleaned up his story over several decades of interviews, the only open question is exactly how Nugent evaded military service during the Vietnam War.

In two different interviews in 1977 and 1990, Nugent claimed to have so physically fouled himself before his draft board physical examination that "those guys in uniform couldn't believe the smell."[49] In the first inter-view, he asked rhetorically, "Do you think I was gonna lay down my guitar and go play army?" Nugent claimed that in order to arrive at this putrid state, he "stopped all forms of personal hygiene . . . and a week before his physical, he stopped using bathrooms altogether, virtually living inside pants caked with his own excrement, stained by his urine."[50] As a result of this foul condition, Nugent then claimed, "I got this big juicy 4-F."[51]

Later on, after he had become a conservative idol, Nugent changed his story. He claimed that he was spoofing the media in his earlier interviews—in other words, lying—and had actually evaded the draft with a student deferment. "I did not want to get my ass blown off in Vietnam."[52] However, after its own independent investigation, Snopes.com found that Nugent's draft evasion record was still cloudy. The entire episode raises the classic lawyer's question in cross-examination of a witness with inconsistent stories. Was he lying then, or is he lying now?

> An analysis of Ted Nugent's Selective Service classification record doesn't prove or disprove either version of the story. He did indeed receive a high school student deferment (1-S) in 1967 and then (as he stated) a college student deferment (2-S) in 1968. However, he was reclassified as "available for military service" (1-A) in 1969 and then subsequently rejected as a result of a physical examination and given a 1-Y classification. (The 1-Y classification denoted persons "qualified for service only in time of war or national emergency" and was generally assigned to registrants who had exhibited medical conditions that were limiting but not disabling.) After the 1-Y classification was eliminated by the Selective Service at the end of 1971, Nugent was reclassified as 4-F ("registrant not qualified for any military service").[53]

Whatever the truth about Nugent's draft-dodging, neither it nor his apparent racism and anti-Semitism prevented his being invited to dinner at the Trump White House and being given a private tour of the premises by the president himself in April 2017.[54]

The Sheriff of Fox News

Former Milwaukee County sheriff David Clarke shares Nugent's penchant for venomous, unsubstantiated attacks. He has also had extraordinarily abrupt and oddly explained turns in his career. (Clarke is no longer on the NRA's board of directors at this writing.)

Like his fellow CPRC board member, Clarke attacked the Parkland student leaders. He also packed his February 20, 2018, tweet with dark reference to the far-right's paranoid conspiracy theme, simultaneously working in a dog-whistle call to anti-Semites by accusing the hate-mongers' default target, Jewish billionaire George Soros, of orchestrating a Parkland conspiracy.

> The well ORGANIZED effort by Florida school students demanding gun control has GEORGE SOROS' FINGERPRINTS all over it. It is

similar to how he hijacked and exploited black people's emotion regarding police use of force incidents into the COP HATING Black Lives Matter movement.[55]

Clarke and Donald Trump were a case of love at far right. "Clarke became the Make America Great Again movement's tactical response to Black Lives Matter."[56] The sheriff—who affected a large white cowboy hat in public appearances that reportedly earned him hundreds of thousands of dollars—spoke at the Republican National Convention in 2016. Lurking beneath an operatic score of a brave black cop willing to take on the snowflakes of the left and minority-identity politics were jarring counterpoints. There were, for one thing, allegations of gross mistreatment of inmates at the jail he supervised, "where an inmate died of 'profound dehydration'—ruled a homicide by the courts—and where three inmates and a newborn baby have died in his custody and under questionable circumstances."[57] There were also rumors of extra-marital affairs.[58]

Clarke was also entangled with the NRA in the machinations of alleged Russian undercover agent Maria Butina. He was a member of an NRA delegation that visited Moscow in 2015. That group was hosted by Butina and two senior-level officials close to Russian president Vladimir Putin, Alexander Torshin and Dmitry Rogozin, both of whom are under sanction by the United States.[59] According to a Fox News outlet in Wisconsin, Butina's group paid $6,000 of Clarke's expenses and the NRA picked up another $40,000.[60]

> Clarke has served as a virtual Bering Land Bridge between the NRA and its counterpart in Russia, The Right to Bear Arms, taking a trip to the country . . . with a who's who of NRA brass. Present on this bizarre excursion were ex-NRA President David Keene, NRA First Vice President Pete Brownell—who also just happens to run an enormous firearm accessory empire—and NRA Women's Leadership Forum executive committee member Hilary Goldschlager.[61]

Goldschlager's father, Arnold, a major NRA contributor who was also on the 2015 Moscow trip, told the McClatchy news agency that the NRA junket was a "people-to-people mission," and that he was impressed by Torshin. "They were killing us with vodka and the best Russian food," Goldschlager said. "The trip exceeded my expectations by logarithmic levels."[62] Vodka and logarithms aside, the FBI has been reported to be investigating whether any Russian money was funneled through the NRA to Donald Trump's presidential campaign.[63] The gun-rights organization reportedly broke its own record in spending thirty million dollars to support Trump. The FBI is said to likely have obtained the organization's tax returns in order to look at secret donors who would not be listed in other public documents and through whom Russian money could have been laundered.[64]

The Case of the Vanishing Senior-Level Job

Any or all of these factors could have contributed to Clarke's suddenly and mysteriously being cut out of a high-ranking job at the U.S. Department of Homeland Security only weeks after he had announced that he had accepted it. At least one observer has noticed that Clarke also seems to have been cast into the equivalent of the right wing's outer darkness. He has "stopped appearing on Fox. His once-ubiquitous cowboy hat has all but disappeared from Hannity."[65]

The final act has yet to be played, but the saga of Clarke's evaporating DHS job becomes more and more intriguing as more becomes publicly known about Special Counsel Robert Mueller's investigation into Butina's alleged Russian influence operation. In May 2017, Clarke announced on a Wisconsin radio broadcast that he would be leaving his sheriff post in June to take up an offer from the Trump administration to become an assistant secretary in DHS's Office of Partnership and Engagement.[66] That announcement "set off alarms in Wisconsin and in Washington."[67] Then, for reasons that still remain opaque, Clarke abruptly announced in June that he had "rescinded his acceptance of the agency's offer." Clarke was reported to have decided that "his skills could be better utilized to promote the president's agenda in a more aggressive role."[68] A few months later, the sheriff unexpectedly quit his day job,[69] signed on with a pro-Trump "super PAC" called America First Action, and set up his own consulting business with one of the women with whom he is alleged to have had an extramarital affair.[70]

Overlooked in the shuffle was a sentence buried deep in the *Washington Post* story about Clarke's "rescinding" his acceptance of the DHS job offer. The newspaper's staff had seen the offer letter and reported that it stated that the offer was contingent upon "final approval by the Office of Personnel Management."[71] That bland reference was to the role of the National Background Investigation Bureau (NBIB), which is "the primary executive branch service provider for background investigations for eligibility for access to classified information [and] eligibility to hold a sensitive position."[72] What the NBIB may have concluded about Clarke's "eligibility" for high office remains an interesting secret. But a thumbs-down on a clearance from that agency ordinarily would torpedo the prospects of a candidate for a sensitive government post.

Lott and his center are obviously free to keep any company they wish. But they should be judged by that company as well, especially its board of directors, whose fiduciary duty requires it to be directly involved in the center's policies. "Management is responsible for running the organization on a day-to-day basis while the collective board is responsible for the strategic direction of the organization in order for it to run effectively and efficiently."[73]

Dishonesty Condemned

In February 2018, the conservative commentator Kevin D. Williamson summed up the moral and intellectual rot within the dishonest advocacy of ideologues, specifically calling out Ted Nugent and David Clarke. In a blistering essay in *National Review*—titled "An Epidemic of Dishonesty on the Right"—Williamson scathed Clarke, whom he derided as "the sheriff of Fox News," and asked "is there any act of depravity to which the less respectable right-wing media cannot imagine a connection for George Soros?"[74] He decried both the moral and political consequences of untruthful rhetoric. "When people get used to hearing prominent conservatives lying about their opponents," he warned, "it makes it easier for honest and fair-minded people to dismiss conservative arguments and conservative claims out of hand." The conservative movement, Williamson lamented, "has become infected with Trump's dishonesty." A final thunderbolt summed matters up.

> David Clarke should be ashamed of himself, and not just for his ridiculous hat. And conservatives should be ashamed of them, too, and for bending the knee to . . . Ted Nugent, and every other third-rate celebrity

who has something nice to say about a Republican from time to time. And we should be ashamed of ourselves if we come to accept this kind of dishonesty in the service of political expediency. If conservative ideas cannot prevail in the marketplace of ideas without lies, they do not deserve to prevail at all.[75]

There is plenty of shame to go around. Producers and editors in the so-called "mainstream media" often see Lott, Nugent, Clarke, and others like them as boons to their programming—controversial and contrarian, they are click bait and ratings drivers. By uncritically broadcasting conceptually flawed and often dishonest statements, the media spreads the infection of dishonesty for a cheap one-news-cycle stand. Consumers of these media should demand from all media more vigorous and rigorous screening of whom they promote as "experts" and of the quality of their work. As political reporter Alex Seitz-Wald wrote in 2012 after the Sandy Hook shooting:

> News programs should be free to bring on whomever they want to interview—there's no value to viewers in censoring certain guests by keeping them off the air. But, if you choose to bring on someone like Lott, who has been so thoroughly questioned by his peers, broadcast journalists owe it to their audience to give all the pertinent information, or at the very least, challenge the arguments the guests are making, so they may better make up their own minds.[76]

Consequences in America

The changes in the laws of concealed carry of weapons and self-defense have made a difference in the likelihood that a handgun owner in the United States will carry a concealed and loaded weapon. A study published in the *American Journal of Public Health* in 2017 found that "consistent with the increasing number of permit holders . . . nearly 1 in 4 of the approximately 38 million adult handgun owners in the United States carried a loaded handgun on their person in the past 30 days." The study also found that "proportionately fewer . . . carried a concealed loaded handgun in the past 30 days if they lived in states with laws that allowed issuing authorities to exercise substantial discretion in granting concealed carry permits."[77]

While politicians who rely on John Lott's work continue to dispute the bad effects of relaxed concealed carry laws, there is no credible argument against the proposition that handguns have a disproportionate role in gun violence in the United States. Even the conservative source the Daily Caller News Foundation reported that "handguns are used in about nine times as many murders and eight times as many nonfatal violent crimes than rifles, shotguns and other firearms combined."[78] Significantly from an ideological perspective, however, the point of the foundation's "fact check" was not to lament the undesirable consequences of relaxed regulation and handgun proliferation. It was rather that proposed restrictions on civilian possession of semiautomatic assault weapons miss the mark, because gun crime in the United States is overwhelmingly handgun crime. That spin notwithstanding, the Daily Caller's fact-check closely tracked the findings of a 2013 U.S. Department of Justice survey of firearm violence between 1993 and 2011. "Handguns accounted for the majority of both homicide and nonfatal firearm violence. A handgun was used in about 83% of all firearm homicides in 1994, compared to 73% in 2011. Other types of firearms, such as shotguns and rifles, accounted for the remainder of firearm homicides. For nonfatal firearm violence, about 9 in 10 were committed with a handgun, and this remained stable from 1994 to 2011."[79]

Regulation of Handguns Compared, Part Two— The Canadian Cold Shoulder

The Canadian approach to gun control in general and handgun regulation in particular has been remarkably different from that of the United States.[80] According to David Kopel, "a majority of Canadians believe that they have a right to own a gun. The important point is that they do not believe that the right extends to handguns, and they do not seem to believe that the current system of controls violates their right to a gun."[81]

From the creation of the Canadian Confederation on July 1, 1867, until the late middle of the twentieth century, the Canadian government generally declined to regulate long guns (rifles and shotguns) except in times of war. On the contrary, concern about potential aggression from the United States led the Canadian government to encourage the civilian use of rifles as a means of bolstering the nation's defensive forces.[82] "Many

Canadians wondered how long they would survive the American boast that 'manifest destiny' would allow them to rule the entire continent."[83] The American purchase from Russia of the two countries' common neighbor Alaska in 1867 was a troubling example, as were probes by American commercial representatives into the Canadian Red River Valley, the expansion of American armed forces during the Civil War, and incursions into Canada after that war by Fenians, militant Irish liberationists.[84]

In response to these concerns, the new national government armed the active militia and encouraged the formation in 1868 of the Dominion of Canada Rifle Association to promote marksmanship. Canadian riflemen subsequently won such acclaim that when a similar organization was later proposed in the United States—the National Rifle Association—its representatives went to Canada for advice and information, including plans and drawings upon which to base its first shooting range in Creedmoor, New York. The Canadian government's reach to regulate long guns later in the twentieth century would alienate rural and western gun owners, energize Canada's pro-gun lobby, and result in acrimonious swings in national policy.[85]

Canada's control of handguns has been an entirely different matter from the beginning. Even before Confederation, riots and sectarian conflicts sparked misgivings about the potential for increased violence inherent in the public carrying of handguns. In the 1840s, for example, riots among canal workers and pitched battles between Orangemen (Protestant Loyalists) and Irish Catholics led to provincial bans on possessing firearms at public works and carrying "dangerous and unusual weapons" (e.g., handguns).

After Confederation, pressure increased for stronger national controls.[86] There was a surge in riots in the 1870s. Inexpensive handguns began pouring in from the United States after the end of the Civil War when American gun companies found themselves stuck with excess manufacturing capacity. To take up the slack, they began mass production of cheaper guns for foreign and domestic markets.[87] Neighboring Canada was a convenient marketing target. Canadians feared that these mass-produced handguns "increased the number of shooting accidents, encouraged suicide, and led to murder."[88] Specific cultural decisions distinguishing Canada from the United States were being made. In 1877, for example, a Canadian senator advocated "ways that Canada could avoid experiencing American levels of gun violence, noting ominously that pistols killed 312 people in the United States the previous year."[89] That number of American handgun deaths from almost a century and a half in the past was just shy of double the 172 total firearms homicides in Canada in 2012.

Concern about handguns was undergirded in part by another cultural aspect: the widely held conviction among the dominant white, propertied British-American ruling class that only its members had the proper temperament and social values to be entrusted with handguns. "The increased regulation of handguns . . . represented an exception to the generally modest system of gun control. Canadians expressed fear about the immigrants flowing into the nation. . . . Like youth, immigrants allegedly lacked mature 'British' instincts for the proper use of guns."[90] Until well into the latter half of the twentieth century, therefore, Canadian gun control efforts were carefully crafted so as not to infringe on the perceived rights of the law-abiding gentry while restricting access to handguns by members of groups deemed to be dangerous.[91] The specific outgroups varied over time. They included at various points Aboriginal People, young working-class men, Irish immigrants, Eastern and Southern European immigrants, and enemy aliens in time of war (Germans, Austrians, and Japanese).

This is a historical axis on which Canadian and American cultural lines intersected. Much the same prejudice drove early gun control efforts in the United States. "While, after the Civil War, widespread firearm ownership had become much more established, white Americans were still keen to prevent African-Americans (former slaves) and indigenous peoples amongst others from owning firearms. While firearms ownership in old Europe was overlain by restrictions of rank and religion, in America they were colored by race, ethnicity and social class."[92] The effects of racial and ethnic tensions around gun regulation remain powerful today. The shock of seeing militant members of the Black Panthers, a black nationalist civil rights group, legally and openly carrying guns into the California state capitol in 1967 frightened white America and its politicians. Then-governor Ronald Reagan—subsequently a bogeyman of progressive America—and the National Rifle Association alike supported a new law that banned the open carrying of firearms. The California legislation emboldened America's nascent gun control movement. That movement's progress in turn helped ignite a reaction among gun-rights enthusiasts that continues today.[93]

A series of laws in Canada gradually tightened the government's grip on handguns. After 1877 anyone whom authorities caught carrying a handgun had to prove to a magistrate that they had a good reason for carrying that gun. This rule of law was a sort of retroactively enforced discretionary permit system. The first Canadian criminal code in 1892 eliminated the retroactive decision. It expanded control on handguns by requiring that anyone who wanted to carry a handgun had to first get a permit, known as a "certificate of exemption." This was in effect a "may issue" licensing system for concealed carry. Finally, in 1913 the law was expanded again to cover sale as well as carry of handguns. Anyone who wanted to buy a handgun thereafter had first to obtain the certificate by showing good cause and good character. Although Canada has wobbled in its regulation of long guns, it has never looked back on its strict regulation of handguns, at least in theory and on its law books.

Modern Canadian Gun Control

The current Canadian regimen controlling handguns appears on the surface to be strict and comprehensive. It stands in marked contrast to the shambling, patchwork American system—a floor of weak federal law based primarily on background checks of limited effectiveness and a patchwork superstructure of state laws that range from nonexistent to very strict. Canada's federal system includes in the letter of its laws (if not in their implementation) most of the regulatory safeguards that American public health experts and gun violence reduction advocates would like to see adopted in America. These include deep background checks and continuous monitoring of gun owners for their involvement in any acts or threats of violence.

All "individuals and businesses that possess or use firearms must be licensed" in Canada.[94] Handguns are categorized as "restricted weapons." In order to obtain a license for a restricted weapon, the applicant must "demonstrate awareness of the principles relating to safe handling and use of firearms," specifically by having successfully completed the Canadian Firearms Safety Course and the Canadian Restricted Firearms Safety Course.

On the law books, at least, the Canadian application screening process is a discretionary licensing system on steroids. It is intended "to reduce the possibility that individuals who pose a public safety risk acquire or have access to firearms." Most applicants are supposed to "undergo thorough security screening, including interviews of the applicants and their references, as well as Internet checks." In addition to criminal checks and third-party character references, Canadian authorities "must consider whether within the previous five years the applicant has been treated for a mental illness, whether in a hospital, mental institute, psychiatric clinic or otherwise and whether or not the person was confined to such a hospital, institute or clinic, that was associated with violence or threatened or attempted violence on the part of the person against any person; or has a history of behavior that includes violence or threatened or attempted violence on the part of the person against any person."[95]

Applicants are subject to a mandatory waiting period. Records of all license holders and their firearms are maintained in a centralized data base. These records are accessible to Canadian law enforcement so that in theory they can ascertain what firearms might be held at a given location subject to law enforcement action. License holder records are also supposed to be continuously monitored, for example, to detect whether a license holder has been involved in a violent crime or become subject to court-ordered prohibitions.

Permits for legal concealed carry are rarely granted. As a general rule, handguns must be possessed in the holder's residence (or at a place authorized by a chief firearms officer), as recorded in the firearms registry. They may be transported and used under very strict and specific circumstances, including, among others, "for use in target practice, or a target shooting competition." A person can carry a handgun only in very limited circumstances and in most cases, only with a permit known as an Authorization to Carry (ATC). The permits are usually restricted to cases in which the handgun is used in connection with the licensee's lawful occupation or to protect life.[96]

On paper and in theory, the Canadian gun control system appears to be comprehensive and seamless, at least with respect to handguns. One might fairly ask, then, how it was possible that, in spite of these controls, someone like Christopher Husbands—a man with a dodgy criminal record who was out on bail awaiting trial on serious charges, including rape and firearms offenses—could obtain a handgun and shoot up a public venue?

South of the Border—Gun Trafficking into Canada

Until a few years ago, the answer would have been fairly easy. Blame the United States. "If we go back a little bit in history, there was a huge influx of weapons coming up from the United States and that was the norm for quite a period of time," Dianne Watts, a Conservative Member of Parliament, told the *Vancouver Sun* in 2016.[97] Canadian gun control activist Wendy Cukier put it this way to the *Atlantic* magazine: "Our problem is, because we share a border with you, even if we ban handguns, we would still have a problem with smuggled guns."[98] Both had a point. It is a fact that historically most of the guns used in crime in Canada came from the United States through illicit channels.[99] But the narrative got considerably more complicated in the latter half of 2016 as evidence emerged of a major change in the historic pattern.

To be sure, smuggling firearms from the United States into Canada was and still is an attractive criminal business. "A lot of people in Canada want guns," Riccardo Tolliver, a convicted gun smuggler serving a thirty-two-year sentence in a U.S. federal prison in Beckley, West Virginia, told the *Windsor Star* in 2013.[100] "Dealing with the underworld in Canada, that's what a lot of guys would ask me for, because I'm American: guns."[101]

Who else to ask but an American? "In the United States, trafficking guns is a high-profit, low-risk activity," policy analysts Sarah Kinosian and Eugenio Weigend wrote in a *Los Angeles Times* op-ed in 2017.[102] It requires a minimum of capital, is easy to get into operationally, and is lucrative. The authors of a study by the University of San Diego Trans-Border Institute noted that "the large number of guns available in the United States is facilitated by a widespread availability of retail firearm licenses, permissive import regulations, and largely unregulated, owner-to-owner 'kitchen-table' sales. This ensures that many types of low- and high-caliber firearms, ammunition, and explosives are legally available for purchase in the United States."[103]

It's not just the criminal American gun traffickers who are making money, according to Kinosian and Weigend. They cite the University of San Diego research. That study in turn showed the other half of the underlying Mephistophelian bargain between traffickers and the gun industry. "Half of U.S. gun dealers benefit financially from the U.S.-Mexico illegal gun trade, to the tune of $127.2 million in 2012."[104] Throw in Canada and you've got the art of a deadly deal.

Canadian authorities are said to believe that Tolliver smuggled more guns into Canada than anyone else in history. His is the ancient story of the push and pull of supply and demand in contraband goods—cheap at one end of the pipeline, expensive at the other. "There's a significant markup for firearms, particularly handguns," University of Toronto professor Jooyoung Lee, an expert on gun violence, told Canada's Global News. "Like any kind of illicit underground economy, people are in it to make money."[105]

The long border between the two countries is punctuated by points at which monitoring criminal traffic is difficult. Some are places—like the Ambassador Bridge over and the Detroit-Windsor tunnel under the Detroit River—where heavy volumes of traffic make routine close inspection of vehicles impossible. Others are remote wilderness or water crossings, like some areas along the Canadian border in northeastern Vermont. These wilderness spots make feasible old-fashioned smuggling by foot or boat.

But just as important as the places to smuggle guns across the border is the ease with which firearms can be obtained in large quantities in the United States. Gunrunner Tolliver bought the handguns he smuggled from a variety of American sources. They included pawn shops, private person-to-person transactions completely off of any regulatory grid, and "straw buyers"—people who have no disqualifying record, can pass the cursory American background check, and take a small commission for each gun they buy for a gun trafficker. Gun shows are also convenient markets where unlicensed sellers legally sell all manner of weapons privately without asking questions of the buyer, much less running a background check. "The same absence of regulation that characterizes private party gun sales generally is also true at gun shows. Some unlicensed vendors advertise their unregulated status; at one show, a vendor posted this sign: 'No Background Checks Required; We Only Need to Know Where You Live and How Old You Are.'"[106]

Tolliver assembled some guns from parts he bought or machined himself. He paid as little as $100 to $200 for some of the guns that he purchased. He sold those guns in Canada for $1,200 to $2,000. "A Desert Eagle, a large semiautomatic pistol, sold for up to $4,000. Mac-10 machine guns fetched as much as $5,000."[107] The gun pipeline had another criminal return leg. Tolliver smuggled high-grade marijuana back from Canada into the United States. "When pressed, Tolliver estimates he sold between 1,000 and 3,000 guns in Canada," the newspaper reported. "If he averaged, say, $1,000 markup per gun, that would mean $1 million to $3 million in gross profit—not including drug money—though he had others to cut in on the action."[108]

Other traffickers innovated. Toronto police reportedly discovered that some Canadians attending sports events in Detroit were being used as unwitting "mules," unknowingly transporting firearms into Canada. While the Canadian fans were seated inside sports arenas enjoying the games, the gun traffickers were out in the parking lots, attaching guns and GPS devices to the undercarriages of fans' cars. Using the GPS devices, the traffickers tracked down the cars after they were back in Canada. They then retrieved the guns from the vehicles and their unsuspecting "mules" were none the wiser.[109]

A Quebec man, Alexis Vlachos, pleaded guilty in 2018 to U.S. federal charges that he smuggled more than one hundred handguns into Canada through Vermont. Vlachos's American coconspirators bought the handguns from various federally licensed dealers in Florida. Some of the guns were smuggled through the Haskell Free Library in Derby Line, Vermont. The library straddles the border, with rooms on both sides of the line. The Americans left the guns in small backpacks in a restroom, from which Vlachos retrieved them. Other guns were handed over to him in a remote area of Vermont. He hiked them over the border into Canada.[110]

North of the Border—Rogue Canadians, the Dark Net, and Ghost Guns

As late as July 2016, some Canadian law enforcement officials were publicly estimating that about two-thirds of the guns used in crimes in Canadian cities like Toronto came from the United States.[111] But other officials were aware of a shocking truth. Investigations prompted by a surge in gun violence revealed that as many guns used in Canadian crimes were coming from Canadian domestic sources as were coming from the United States. It turns out that, just like some Americans, some Canadians are using their licenses to buy large numbers of guns that they then sell to criminals and traffickers. The ratio of Canadian-sourced to American-sourced crime guns in Canada is now reported to be just about 50-50.

"They go get their license for the purpose of becoming a firearms trafficker," Detective Rob Di Danieli of Toronto's guns and gangs unit was quoted as saying in July 2018. "A lot of people are so ready to blame the big bad Americans, but we had our own little problem here."[112]

In a December 2016 letter to Canada's minister of public safety, the mayor of Toronto scathed the registration system's failure to notice what was going on under its nose. "What's particularly troubling to me is cases where licensed gun owners are able to amass small arsenals of handguns and there are no red flags despite their purchases being registered in the Canadian Firearms Registry."[113]

Examples of domestic trafficking popped up all over Canada. A man in British Columbia registered forty-nine restricted firearms, mostly handguns, between 2009 and his arrest in 2013. They included ten Glock semiautomatic pistols, three of which he bought on the same day. When police raided his home, they found only seven of the forty-nine guns he was supposed to have.[114] In Toronto, a financial adviser bought fourteen guns on ten occasions over a seven-month period, a plumber bought nine guns over five weeks, a university student bought twenty-three handguns over a twenty-two-month period, and a security guard bought a whopping fortyseven handguns in six months. All of them sold their guns to criminals.[115]

An internal Toronto police memo pointed a finger at internal conflict within the Royal Canadian Mounted Police (RCMP), the agency responsible for the Canadian gun control program. "The regulatory side and the investigative side although administered by the same organization i.e. the RCMP are frequently in conflict," the memo was reported to say. "Often that manifests itself in an inability or reluctance to share information with each other, Provincial and Municipal Agencies."

The memo blamed in particular a blinkered culture within the licensing side of the RCMP. "No one is thinking 'dirty' during the review process. Only in extremely rare cases is there ever a personal interview or visit by the [chief firearms officer] or staff in Ontario. Telephone Detective would be a good description of the current process."[116]

"Telephone Detective" is not the only new culprit. Another is a surge in gun sales and registrations in Canada. In 2017, CBC News reported that the number of "restricted" firearms in Canada (mostly handguns) rose

5.5 percent in 2016, reaching its highest point in more than a decade. Tony Bernardo, executive director of the Canadian Shooting Sports Association, attributed the surge to the rise of shooting sports and shooting ranges in Canada. "It's still a continuation of the increase in popularity of target sports," he told CBC. "This has been going on now for a few years. A lot of young people getting involved, a lot of ladies getting involved." Bernardo also pointed a finger at movie companies using the guns in films being shot in Canada.[117]

The formula is more subtle than moviemakers, target shooting, and "ladies." More guns equals more leakage of legal guns into criminal hands. More leakage equals more gun crime.

Rogue Canadians are not the only recent development in firearms trafficking to Canada. Cooperative international investigations found that gun traffickers are now using the so-called Dark Web, or Dark Net, to sell guns to buyers all over the world. The procedure is structured to ensure anonymity in sales and stealth in delivery.[118]

The internet is like a global iceberg. The visible tip, the part that most people use daily, is called the Surface Web or the Clear Web. It makes up only about 4 percent of the iceberg. The other 96 percent lies beneath the surface. It is composed of the Deep Web (the largest section of the iceberg) and the Dark Web.

Websites on the Surface Web can be found with ordinary search engines like Google or Microsoft's Bing. Its content is familiar. It includes commercial marketplaces from Macy's to Amazon, news outlets, and social media. Individual users of the Surface Web can be monitored, their patterns tracked, and their histories reconstructed. For all of the frantic buzz about internet privacy, the Surface Web offers little real anonymity.

The greater part of the hidden 96 percent is called the Deep Web. Much of its content is also available to the general public. However, most of its sites are not indexed and thus cannot be found by the usual search engines. The user must know the exact URL to find a Deep Web site. These sites are often password protected. Examples of Deep Web sites include academic databases, medical records, subscription-only sites, and content specific to and accessible only by government organizations, such as law enforcement agencies.

The Dark Net's very purpose is anonymity. Knowing a Dark Net URL—lists of which can be found by searching the Surface Web—is not enough to obtain access. The content can be accessed only through specialized anonymity software, such as The Onion Router (TOR). Although there are legitimate users of the Dark Net, such as investigative journalists and their sources, the deep anonymity it offers is perfect for, and heavily exploited by, criminal networks. One recent estimate is that the division of usage on the Dark Net between legitimate usage and criminal usage is roughly even.[119]

TOR software was developed by the U.S. Naval Research Lab in 2002. It was intended for use in American intelligence operations.[120] Subsequently, illegal Dark Net arms sales facilitated by TOR came under scrutiny by the Five Eyes Law Enforcement Group (FELEG), a consortium of international law enforcement agencies from the United States, the United Kingdom, New Zealand, Canada, and Australia that shares intelligence on transnational crime.[121] FELEG is itself a spin-off from a broader intelligence-sharing group called Five Eyes, formed shortly after the Second World War by the same consortium of nations because of Cold War tensions with Soviet Russia.[122] The life cycle of TOR is thus a special case within the intelligence community of "what goes around, comes around."

The Dark Net abounds with individual vendors and conglomerate marketplaces offering access to contraband. Products and services for sale on the Dark Net include child pornography, drugs, weapons of mass destruction and classified information about them, stolen and counterfeit consumer goods, computer-hacking tools, assassins for hire, poisons, and weapons, including firearms of every variety.

Transactions in these goods and services are shrouded in layers of anonymity that protect both buyers and sellers. Payment is usually made in crypto currencies, like Bitcoin, which have no physical location and are difficult to trace. Contraband is typically repackaged and delivered hidden within ordinary consumer products. Firearms are broken down into separate parts and then packed inside of consumer products like computer games, power tools, hair dryers, and televisions. "Darknet vendors resort to very ingenious means to ship firearms and related components," Rob O'Reilly, interim director of firearms regulatory services at the RCMP, told the Canadian Press. "In the darknet community, this is known as stealth shipping, and the intent is to disguise or hide the actual contents from law enforcement and border services."[123]

The Dark Net is ideal for gun trafficking. The websites of individual vendors and conglomerate markets devoted to guns are as comprehensive and slick as many legitimate gun industry marketing sites. For traffickers in the United States, the Dark Net offers a global portal through which to move their deadly products abroad.

A team of four traffickers in the Atlanta area, for example, set up a Dark Net vendor page they called "CherryFlavor." They bought guns legally through domestic online markets on the Surface Web. Buying guns through the internet eliminates the need to pay straw buyers or to make visits to a variety of brick-and-mortar gun stores (in order to avoid arousing suspicion that might arise about repeated or large-scale purchases from any one outlet). The traffickers then sold the guns to buyers worldwide at exorbitant markups. Glock pistols that the gang bought for about $500 were sold for as much as $3,400. The group sold at least seventy guns to customers in Australia, Austria, Belgium, Denmark, France, Germany, Ireland, Kazakhstan, the Netherlands, Russia, Sweden, the United Kingdom, Zambia—and Canada.[124]

This borderless, online dark market has compounded Canada's gun-trafficking problem. A final twist is that some traffickers are now selling individual component parts that have never been assembled into a gun. "This challenge has existed for some time in regards to our neighbors to the south, however it is compounded in a borderless online market that is truly international," the RCMP's O'Reilly said. "Once imported to Canada, these components can be easily finished and assembled through online tutorials, the results of which are often completely untraceable firearms, sometimes known as ghost guns."[125]

The Consequences of One Shooter and One Handgun in Toronto

It is not known where, when, or how Christopher Husbands got his Glock high-capacity semiautomatic pistol. It was certainly not by legal means. But, however Husbands got his pistol, his use of it demonstrated the terrible firepower of a single modern handgun with its generous ammunition load.

If the public account is accurate, he pumped twelve out of the fourteen rounds he fired into his two intended targets. That 85 percent hit rate was quite high, likely because his attack was apparently a spontaneous ambush. The shooting was neither a confrontation in which both sides were armed, nor a gunfight in which shots were exchanged. No one was brandishing a gun or shooting back at Christopher Husbands, either of which conditions would almost certainly have affected his accuracy.

Trained law enforcement officers do much worse on average in their deadly force encounters. Research shows that "when police officers use deadly force, more often they miss the target than actually hit the target."[126] In 2016, for example, New York City police officers who fired their guns were reported to have hit their targets 35 percent of the time, and in 2017, 44 percent of the time.[127] Although these "hit rates" vary across police agencies, they often do not exceed 50 percent.[128] In 2005, NYPD officers achieved only a 17.4 percent hit rate.[129] Moreover, one controlled study showed that "individuals who had completed standard law enforcement academy training were not more accurate in their shooting than those who had not had any law enforcement handgun training."[130]

Christopher Husbands's high "hit rate" notwithstanding, five other innocent bystanders were struck by bullets. Given the math—twelve of fourteen bullets hit the two targeted men—some of the bullets or their fragments must have struck more than one person. The other hospital-treated casualties were a twenty-five-year-old woman and a twenty-two-year-old man who were both hit in their left legs, and a thirty-year-old woman who suffered a grazing wound to her abdomen. Those three were treated and released from the hospital. Another woman was struck in the hand but left the hospital without treatment.[131]

The fifth bystander, thirteen-year-old Connor Stevenson, was in a fight for his life. He had a bullet in his brain.

Jessica Ghawi stayed in Toronto for several days after the shooting, deeply impacted by what she had seen, heard, and felt on that spring day in Toronto. Wherever the thread of her life might lead her, she was sure of one thing.

"I was shown how fragile life was on Saturday," she wrote in her blog. "I was reminded that we don't know when or where our time on Earth will end. Every second of every day is a gift."

CHAPTER THREE
WHEN LONNIE MET SANDY

The first time Lonnie Phillips met Sandy Anglin, he didn't. The second time was magic.[1]

The first time was a comedy of errors. It was June 1994 and a mutual friend tried to connect the two at a singles bar in San Antonio, Texas. Sandy and Lonnie were both divorced. Neither was particularly anxious to meet someone new. Sandy was there for the Wednesday night happy hour dancing. Lonnie was there for the Wednesday night wet T-shirt contest. Sandy had less than zero interest in the latter event. A mutual friend thought Lonnie would be perfect for Sandy. But Sandy was skeptical. After a few minutes of arm-twisting, however, she reluctantly agreed to go meet this supposedly great guy on the other side of the bar.

The problem was that the crowded, noisy bar had a circular layout. Lonnie was at that moment making a loop in the same direction as Sandy and her friend, who were behind him in the swirling mix. As it happened, the two women never caught up with Lonnie. He decided that he was bored. He walked out of the bar and went home. The connection was missed.

The second time was what Sandy calls a "dare date." Her friend gave Sandy Lonnie's phone number and urged her to call him. Sandy was not up for that, until her friend said, "If you don't call him, I will." Sandy finally called Lonnie. But the call seemed as if it were going nowhere fast until the two learned that they had another mutual friend in common. Gingerly, cautiously, they set up a meeting, both taking care to have an easy bailout.

Lonnie brought along his stepdaughter. Sandy made sure that their meeting was in the midafternoon, around two o'clock, so that she could plausibly plead the need to cut it short and leave for a business appointment.

But magic happened on June 23, 1994.

Sandy liked the way Lonnie walked. And the way he talked reminded her of her father's slight but distinctive Louisiana-bred accent. "I just warmed up like a purring kitten," she says. Lonnie was taken with Sandy's green eyes. "And we've been together ever since."

Sandy dismisses Lonnie's suggestion that she might also have been impressed by the fact that he drove up in a 1993 Cadillac Seville. The smaller-size sedan was Cadillac's answer to the popularity of European luxury cars like Mercedes Benz. Lonnie was a successful independent car dealer, so he always had a good ride.

"I could have cared less," Sandy says and laughs. "I've never been impressed by cars. Anybody can get a fancy car and be in debt up to their eyeballs."

She takes a little less issue with another of Lonnie's recollections.

"I had her in the palm of my hand," he says. "I'm talking about the first motorcycle ride I took her on, which was the first one she'd ever been on. I had to fight her off after that."

"You are so full of it!" Sandy laughs.

The story of how the lives of these two—a California girl who was a former Disneyland Alice in Wonderland straight out of a surfer movie, and an East Texas entrepreneur who was a former hell-raising motorcycle racer—crossed half a continent and bonded in love is one of the bedrock stories of American enterprise and its restless human migration. True, some of that constant change is reflected in the polarizing sorting that divides America today. But at its best—as in the story of Lonnie and Sandy—it is the key to what makes America great, and not "great" in the twisted politician's dark sense of divisive "nationalist" slogans and hateful racist nostalgia.

Sandy grew up as an only child in Long Beach, California. Her father, Jesse Anglin, was born in Louisiana. He met Sandy's mother, Doris Redfield, while he was in military service during the Second World War. When he came back from the war, Jesse married Doris. They moved to St. Louis, Missouri, where Sandy was born. Before Sandy was three years old, they picked up and moved to Long Beach, and she thinks of herself as a California girl. It was the early 1950s and America was inching into the "silent revolution," the movement of cultural tectonic plates that Ronald Inglehart would later detect and write about. It was a time when the population was enjoying unprecedented economic well-being and starting the incremental, generational move away from "Materialist" survival values to "Postmaterialist" values of individual expression.

Jesse was a "natural engineer," Sandy says, and although he did not have an engineering degree he ended up with a successful career supervising engineers at the nearby Northrop aircraft manufacturing plant. Doris was one of the few mothers who worked out of the house in that neighborhood, in that era. She worked for a restaurant supply company and was one of the first women to learn computer programming. Jesse was able to retire when he was fifty-five years old. He and Doris then traveled the world.

"I had a very normal upbringing," Sandy says. "Southern California beach, good high school, good college, opportunities." There was one thing about her life that was ahead of the curve. Before the women's movement, Jesse was teaching Sandy a progressive lesson. "I know that your mom is with me because she wants to be, not because she has to be financially," he told young Sandy. The message was that she had every right that her male peers had. It stuck.

Sandy grew up well-acquainted with guns. Jesse owned shotguns, and he introduced Sandy to the shooting sports. "Weekends were quite often spent at the range and in tournament shooting," she recalls. In 1960, when she was ten years old, Sandy was the only girl in the NRA's Southern California firearms safety class.

"In fact, we still have the pamphlet from that class," Sandy says. She keeps it "because this is what the NRA used to be and it isn't anymore."

When Sandy was eighteen years old, she took a summer job at Disneyland. "It was supposed to be for one summer," she says. "I left eleven years later." She started out as Alice in Wonderland. The expansion of that iconic theme park to other locations—Disney World in Florida and others around the globe—opened up opportunities for the Disneyland staff, and particularly for women. Sandy moved into training and development. She became a protégée of Van France, a legendary Disney executive. France created Disney University, a mandatory school for all of the theme park "actors," who serve in many different roles at Disney park locations.[2] Sandy worked with him on the training program for Disneyland in Tokyo. From Disney she moved to a job with the Anaheim convention and visitors bureau. In that position she traveled the world promoting Anaheim and Southern California as a tourist destination.

On one of those promotional trips to Texas she met the man who was to become her first husband, Nick Ghawi, an Arab Christian who had moved from Jerusalem to Texas. Sandy moved to San Antonio. She spent four years trying to conceive Jordan, her son and first child. In 1987, when Jordan was only sixteen months old, Sandy got a surprise on April Fools Day. She was pregnant again. The doctor assured her he was not joking. Jessi was born on November 27, 1987, the day after Thanksgiving. She was named Jessica after her grandfather Jesse Anglin, who was then dying of cancer. Jessi would later take her grandmother's maiden name, Redfield, as her pen name. Her "mam-maw," as the family called her, had always wanted to be a journalist. This was Jessi's way of honoring her.

Sandy and Nick divorced. Sandy started her own business, combining her skills in training and development and tourist travel promotion. When the children were old enough for her to work outside the home, she took a job with the San Antonio convention and visitors bureau. In 2012, she won a senior position as the executive director of a Texas state tourism unit.

If opposites attract, Lonnie's early life provided the opposite of Sandy's in almost every way. He was born in Marshall, Texas, not far across the border from Shreveport, Louisiana. Marshall was the seat of Harrison County, which had the third-highest number of lynchings of black people among counties in Texas between 1877 and 1950.[3] Lonnie grew up mostly in Lake Charles, Louisiana.

"My father was the biggest redneck you could ever imagine," Lonnie frankly says. "I mean he was totally bigoted." Odis Phillips was a sheet metal worker "and a rambling man." He went where the work was. Lonnie's earliest memory is of living in a tiny trailer with his mother, Floreen, and his brother, Jimmy, "below the seawall in Galveston, Texas." Odis often took high-paying one-year contracts to work on construction projects in foreign countries. Saudi Arabia was one of them. "So he was pretty well missing during a lot of my childhood," Lonnie says.

"He was a weekend alcoholic, a mean drunk," Lonnie recalls of his father. "He was never physically abusive, but he was very mentally abusive to my brother and to my mother. He was a philanderer. I don't know how many times she found lipstick on his collar. But she stuck with him. She had an eighth-grade education, he had maybe a high school education, but he had a trade and he managed to take care of the family."

Lonnie was "pretty much" on his own from the time he was about twelve or thirteen years old. "I saved my money working for fifty cents an hour and bought my first motorcycle when I was fifteen," he says. "I was so young I had to have a governor put in it to control the speed. It took me about fifteen minutes to find the governor and take it out and terrorize the streets of my neighborhood." He eventually gravitated to motorcycle racing. His parents supported his semiprofessional racing until he finished high school. In those high school years, he was by his own admission an "absolute hell-raiser."

Like Sandy, Lonnie was introduced to guns at an early age. But it was in a very different way. It happened when Lonnie was a paperboy saving up to buy his first motorcycle. As he was riding by the house of a large black family, their dog ran out and bit Lonnie. "I went home and showed my dad," Lonnie recalls. "He threw me in the car, grabbed his gun, and went up the black guy's house and said, 'This dog bit my son. He rides by here every day. If that dog bites my son again, I am going to come and kill him.'"

About a week later, the dog bit Lonnie again.

This time, Odis grabbed his .22 rifle, put his sons in the back seat of the car, and drove over to the house. "He got out of the car with his gun," says Lonnie. "The guy's children and wife were lined up on the front porch. The dog ran under the house. My father lay down on his belly and shot the dog right between the eyes. Then he got back in the car and drove off."

Lonnie reflects on the lack of consequences for his father in the Louisiana of the 1950s. "Never heard a word about it, nothing ever happened. Not a visit from the police. Nothing."

If Lonnie was a hell-raiser in high school, he was determined to better himself. His uncle was a union business agent in Paris, Texas. When Lonnie graduated from high school his uncle got him into a job as an apprentice crane operator. By the time he was nineteen years old, before he had finished the two-year apprentice program, he was being sent out on jobs to operate cranes on his own. "I worked my way through college that way. The union called and sent me out on jobs three days a week, and I would attend school two days a week, and carry fifteen hours."

He graduated from San Antonio Community College and then went to the University of Texas in Austin. A motorcycle accident interrupted his academic progress for a while. The timing was fortuitous. Lonnie was not on the Austin campus in August of 1966.

But Lonnie in Texas and Sandy in California were, like all of America and much of the world, well aware of what happened on the first day of that month. It was broadcast live.

Deep in the Heart of Texas

There was no such thing as a federal background check for gun buyers in August 1966. Just about anybody who wanted just about any kind of gun could buy it just about anywhere in America, legally and without formality in that year of the Beach Boys, miniskirts, race riots, and the growing protests against the undeclared war in Vietnam. Those demonstrations were vexing President Lyndon B. Johnson and distracting attention from his other, declared war—the "War on Poverty," the war that Donald Trump's administration claimed fifty-two years later was over and won. We now know that in 1966 the great dealignment of Americans from their political parties was well underway. The tide was rushing out. But progressive idealism was still making changes in the American way. In June 1966, the U.S. Supreme Court overturned the rape conviction of an Arizona man named Ernesto Miranda. The court imposed a set of rules that law enforcement would henceforth be required to follow when they questioned any suspect. The rules became the obligatory stuff of police procedural dramas and were popularly labeled "the Miranda warnings."[4]

For the American gun culture, it was the good old days. Mail order catalogs spilled a cornucopia of guns, ammunition, and shooting supplies into homes from sea to shining sea and across the fruited plain. The Remington Arms catalog celebrated the company's 150th anniversary with specially commissioned illustrations of "classic shooting scenes in the history of American hunting." The catalog devoted a full-page spread to the bolt-action Remington Model 700, "designed for the real rifleman. . . . The shooter who wants the accuracy bonus of Remington's famous precision rifling and short, crisp trigger pull."[5] In New York City—now commonly disparaged as a firearm enthusiast's desert—the Bannerman Company issued its swan song, a 100th anniversary catalog. Bannerman had been the mother of all war surplus trading companies. It had a store on Broadway. Its floors sagged under the weight of disorderly piles of armament and military gear ranging from field artillery to infantry webbing. Bannerman had its own private island in the Hudson River, on which still stands a castle the company built as a warehouse. Bannerman was going out of business, and its last publication was "less a catalog from the Bannerman Company than . . . an effort by them to republish all the best articles and pictures from their catalogs published during the preceding 100 years."[6] Bannerman catalogs are still prized as "amazing gun porn."[7]

The U.S. Army had recommended adopting the ArmaLite AR-15 rifle as its main battle rifle, which became the M16. But semiautomatic assault rifles, or tactical rifles, or modern sporting rifles, or whatever one prefers to call weapons of this distinctive design had not yet won many customers in the American civilian gun market—unless you count the M1 carbine, of which more later. Most police departments and civilian handgun owners still favored six-shot revolvers over semiautomatic pistols capable of holding eight to fourteen rounds of ammunition. The assassination of President John F. Kennedy in November 1963 by a sniper using a mail order Italian war surplus rifle had inspired thoughts and prayers about tougher gun control from many of America's politicians. But this pious political posturing signified nothing and went down its dusty way to the legislative deep freeze for years. Even if the politicians' talk had resulted in action, even if there had been put into place a system of mandatory background checks for gun buyers, the beefy young man who walked into Charles Davis Hardware in Austin, Texas, looking for a few good guns on the blistering-hot morning of August 1, 1966, would have ticked easily through all of the correct boxes on the most stringent screening checklist imaginable. He might even have been able to get medical endorsement from a part-time psychiatrist, attesting to his basic mental health.

An All-American Boy

The local newspaper described Charles ("Charlie") Whitman the next day as "a good son, a top Boy Scout, an excellent Marine, an honor student, a hard worker, a loving husband, a fine scout master, a handsome man, a wonderful friend to all who knew him—and an expert sniper."[8] Dr. Maurice Dean Heatley was an M.D., but he had neither a degree in psychiatry nor board certification in that speciality. At the time, however, any licensed physician in Texas could hang out a psychiatrist's shingle, and Heatley had done just that. He served as a part-time psychiatrist at the University of Texas student health center. Dr. Heatley had counseled Charlie a few months earlier, on March 29, 1966.[9] He later coined and forever ensured the young man's personal brand with his offhand description of him at a press conference on August 2, 1966. "He was a large, muscular youth who looked every bit a professional ball player, an energetic, active Marine, which he had once been. There was something about him that suggested and expressed the All-American boy."[10]

So Charlie had no problem buying a .30 caliber Universal M1 carbine and eight boxes of assorted ammunition at the hardware store. Nor did the former altar boy have a problem at his next stop, Chuck's Gun Shop, where he bought more boxes of ammunition and some cleaning supplies. Ditto at the Sears store in the Hancock Shopping Center, where Charlie bought a Sears Model 60 semiautomatic 12 gauge shotgun. The all-American boy—six feet and 198 pounds of crew-cut congeniality—was completely at ease in gun stores. He had begun handling firearms as a toddler, and his father boasted that Charlie "could plug a squirrel in the eye by the time he was sixteen."[11] Charlie told several of those who waited on him that morning that he was planning a trip to Florida to shoot wild hogs.[12]

In fact, Charlie had a very different plan. He didn't plan to shoot hogs. He planned to shoot people. A lot of people.

The Mask

As far back as 1961 Charlie mentioned this murderous fantasy to a close friend. His friend thought Charlie was just clowning around. Charlie also described his recurring impulse to shoot a lot of people to Dr. Heatley, who of all those Charlie talked to should have known that Charlie was wearing a mask, concealing his deviant anger. But even though he thought Charlie "seemed to be oozing with hostility," Heatley wrote the young man's macabre remarks off to harmless venting, so much sophomoric hot air of the kind he regularly heard from depressed or upset students.[13] He told no one else about it. Overall, Dr. Heatley seemed to be more impressed by Charlie and his archetypal football-playing, crew cut, Marine Corps look than he was concerned about the young man's mental health.

"Today it is evident that Charlie had become a consummate actor," Gary M. Lavergne wrote in *A Sniper in the Tower*, his definitive book about Charles Whitman's life and rampage.[14] "People used the word 'nice' *ad nauseam* to describe Charlie. But for Charlie, *pretending* to be nice proved easier than actually *being* nice. He developed a benevolent facade to his inner turmoil. Patience and kindness did not come naturally."[15] What did come naturally to Charlie—raised in a gun-loving home and trained to a razor's edge by the U.S. Marine Corps—was implementing a sniper's war plan, selecting his kill zone, and carrying out the grisly fantasy that he had described to friends and therapist alike.

"Charles Whitman was a psychiatrist's worst nightmare," Lavergne wrote.[16] Behind the mask of Charlie's apparently model record and his all-American looks lay a decidedly tortured mind, nursing into life an unimaginably evil fantasy. We can look back today and trace the path of Charles Whitman's life to that broiling August morning. The details are well-documented. What is maddeningly elusive is the why of it. Why did this all-American boy choose to carry out his monstrous fantasy—he alone among all the young men whose lives were no less difficult and just as frustrating in 1966 America, many of whom knew as much or more about guns and sharpshooting as did Charlie? If society's objective is to "keep guns out of the wrong hands," what was it about Charlie's mind or character or brain that made his hands the wrong hands? And how might we see behind the masks of others like him, walking among us and pretending to be nice?

The Snares and Traps of a Tangled Life

Unwinding the tangled skein of Charlie's life begins best with his father, C. A. Whitman, an unlettered and unforgiving man who was raised an orphan and rose to middle-class wealth as a plumbing and septic-tank contractor in Lake Worth, Florida. The elder Whitman served his community as a scoutmaster, a scout commissioner, and the president of the local PTA and of the chamber of commerce. But C. A. had his own mask. "I did on many occasions beat my wife, but I loved her," he confessed. "I have to admit it, because of my temper, I knocked her around."[17] C. A.

also "knocked around" his three sons, with his fists and a paddle. "I am not ashamed of any spankings. I don't think I spanked enough, if you want to know the truth about it."[18] There was, however, one thing C. A. and the boys bonded over. Guns. "My boys know all about guns," C. A. said. "I believe in that."[19]

Charlie resented his father, whom he told Dr. Heatley was "brutal, domineering, and extremely demanding."[20] No achievement of young Charlie's was ever enough for C. A. Becoming an accomplished pre-teen pianist and the youngest Eagle Scout ever at age twelve, good grades, proven athletic prowess, and civic involvement were not enough for the stern father. He thought Charlie and his brothers were "spoiled rotten" and said they "should have been punished more than what they were punished."[21] Charlie's superficially "cordial relations with his father appeared to be an act," according to Lavergne, an act that they played out around their "mutual love of guns and hunting."[22]

To escape his father—and without his knowledge—Charlie enlisted in the Marine Corps in June 1959, straight out of high school. After boot camp he was sent to the U.S. Naval Station at Guantanamo Bay, Cuba. On April 27, 1960, he was apparently "caught in a phone booth struck by lightning."[23] Sometime later he learned of the Navy Enlisted Scientific Education Program (NESEP), aimed at providing promising sailors and marines college educations and ultimately commissions as officers. He applied for and won an all-expense scholarship. He spent two months in intensive academic and social preparation at the Naval Academy Preparatory School, which was then located at the U.S. Naval Training Center in Bainbridge, Maryland. After he completed that course, Charlie enrolled in the mechanical engineering program at the University of Texas in Austin. He later switched to architectural engineering. There he met Kathy Leissner, the young woman he married on August 17, 1962, in her hometown of Needville, Texas. Their wedding photo was as 1960s all-American as it gets, she in a lacy white wedding dress and he in a nicely fit white dinner jacket, everyone smiling. But Charlie did not settle down and work hard enough to meet the navy's expectations that he would earn a bachelor's degree, complete Officers Candidate School, and become a commissioned officer. His grades were erratic. He gambled, partied, was arrested for poaching a deer, brandished guns on occasion, and became known as something of a class clown given to practical jokes with a cruel edge.

Charlie was also fascinated by the Texas Tower, which dominates the campus. The tower was the tallest structure in Austin at 307 feet in height (because it is on a slightly higher elevation, it is two feet higher than the state capitol). The four sides of the observation deck on the twenty-eighth floor offered a commanding view of the university campus and much of Austin's city center. In September 1961, standing with a fellow student whom he had met in the marines, Charlie indicated the tower and said, "You know, that would be a great place to go up with a rifle and shoot people. You could hold off an army for as long as you wanted."[24] Charlie's friend did not believe that he was serious. It was just Charlie being Charlie. But whatever Charlie thought or meant in 1961, it was moot for the time being. Charlie was washed out of the navy's program on account of his poor grades. In February 1963 he withdrew from the university and returned to active duty to finish the rest of his enlistment in the Marine Corps, which he had extended when he entered the NESEP program.

The young marine's second tour of active duty was an undisciplined train wreck. By the end of 1963, Lance Corporal Whitman was facing a court-martial on charges of gambling, usury, and unauthorized possession of a civilian firearm. He started a diary while he was awaiting trial, "The Daily Record of Charles J. Whitman." He would console, examine, and try to explain himself by writing about his private struggles for the rest of the few years remaining in his life. After his conviction and sentence—ninety days at hard labor, thirty days confinement, and reduction in rank to private—Charlie wrote that he "seemed to have reached the pit of life's experiences."[25]

The Clinical Self-Reflection of a Troubled Mind

Something was going on in Charlie's mind, an unsettling change that he was perceptive enough to realize. As a recent chronicler remarked, he described his "personal demons" in his diary with "disturbingly clinical self-reflection."[26] For example, Charlie wrote of his inner turmoil, "I don't know if it is for better or worse or if it is real or fantasy but I feel different and I don't know if I am the cause of it all or if other circumstances are adding to it."[27] The substance of Charlie's writing, even his penmanship, paralleled the downward spiral of his life, author Lavergne observed, and "the theme of his writings became more hopeless and pathetic" over time.[28]

After his discharge from the Marine Corps on July 18, 1965, Charlie returned to Austin and again enrolled at the University of Texas. Although he seemed determined to succeed, set demanding goals for himself, worked hard, got good grades, and was liked by numerous friends and classmates, he was torn by internal pressures and prone to listless bouts of depression. A commission later concluded that Charlie "was living under conditions of increasing personal stress from which he felt he could not escape, and which he could not master. He experienced this stress essentially in increasing personal psychological isolation, and had done so for years."[29]

Charlie was swimming in another toxic current. He was abusing drugs. He regularly used dextroamphetamine, a prescription-controlled variant of amphetamine marketed under the trade name Dexedrine. Charlie had an illegal supply of the pills, which friends said he took "like popcorn."[30] Amphetamines are stimulants that speed up the body's system.[31] An estimated thirteen million Americans use various forms of methamphetamine without medical supervision today. The drugs are known on the street as Bennies, Black Beauties, Crank, Ice, Speed, and Uppers.

Amphetamines were discovered in the late nineteenth century. They were originally used to treat asthma and other breathing disorders. By the 1930s they had become popular as "pep pills" and diet pills. The world's military forces began using the stimulant during the Second World War, handing pills out to help troops stay awake and alert during sustained combat operations. Sometimes called "go" or "go/no go" pills, they are still used today by, for example, aircrews and Special Forces. They are prescribed in the civilian world to treat narcolepsy and attention deficit disorder. In the 1960s, Dexedrine was popular on college campuses as a means to stay awake during "all-nighters" before examinations. Charlie's friends described several periods of his staying awake in 1966 for as many as five days and nights.

But stimulant drugs can have seriously adverse psychiatric effects. According to one manufacturer's prescription guide, "Administration of stimulants may exacerbate symptoms of behavior disturbance and thought disorder in patients with a pre-existing psychotic disorder."[32] A U.S. Drug Enforcement Administration fact sheet provides a more detailed warning.

The effects of amphetamines and methamphetamine are similar to cocaine, but their onset is slower and their duration is longer. In contrast to cocaine, which is quickly removed from the brain and is almost completely metabolized, methamphetamine remains in the central nervous system longer, and a larger percentage of the drug remains unchanged in the body, producing prolonged stimulant effects.

Chronic abuse produces a psychosis that resembles schizophrenia and is characterized by paranoia, picking at the skin, preoccupation with one's own thoughts, and auditory and visual hallucinations. Violent and erratic behavior is frequently seen among chronic users of amphetamines and methamphetamine.[33]

Charlie's behavior was certainly erratic and violent by this time. Like his father, he "knocked around" his wife on at least two occasions. Whatever the sources of his private demons, they broke into full chorus in March 1966, near the end of the spring semester. Fed up at last with C. A.'s abuse, Charlie's mother left the marriage. The dutiful son drove to Florida and brought his mother back with him to Austin, where she found a job and her own apartment. It was around this time that Charlie told a professor who had become a friendly helper, "I just despise my father. I hate him. If my father walked through that door, I'd kill him."[34]

Life was overwhelming Charlie. At one point he was talked out of dropping out of school, leaving his wife, and either becoming a bum or going to Japan to study martial arts. His wife urged him to visit the university's student health center. Charlie was eventually referred to the Mental Hygiene Clinic and Dr. Heatley, its part-time psychiatrist. Dr. Heatley wrote a memorandum after that visit. One sentence of that note to the file shocked Austin and the world when it was publicly revealed at a press conference four months later. "Repeated inquiries attempting to analyze his exact experiences were not too successful with the exception of his vivid reference to 'thinking about going up on the tower with a deer rifle and start shooting people.'"[35] Pressed by stunned reporters, Heatley explained that Whitman's statement had not alarmed him, because patients often made such sweeping statements and the tower had inspired violent fantasies before. It was in this context that he made his remark forever branding Charlie as the epitome of the all-American boy.

One might argue that Charlie's statements about killing his father and shooting random people from the tower were "red flags." Anyone who talked like that should be—exactly what? Arrested? Committed to a mental institution? Barred from buying or possessing a gun? If so, for how long? Putting aside the threshold question of exactly who would report such talk to whom and why, the practical problem is that millions of people who say things very much like what Charlie said are indeed harmlessly venting—perhaps in passing anger, or under the influence of a mental condition, or hoping to shock with dark humor. "I could kill my boss." "I want to strangle my mother." The challenge for an effective screening system—called "threat assessment" today—is separating real threats from harmless (and free-speech-protected) venting and hyperbole.

From Fantasy to Plan

No one had to grapple with the practicalities of any such decisions on August 1, 1966, because there was no screening system at all in Texas and in most of America. And if there had been, it is unlikely that any reasonably imaginable screener would have had access to the thoughts Charlie had written down within the last twenty-four hours, after he had surrendered to his demons and his tower fantasy became a concrete plan.

> I don't really understand myself these days. I am supposed to be an average reasonable and intelligent young man. However, lately (I can't recall when it started) I have been a victim of many unusual and irrational thoughts. These thoughts constantly recur, and it requires a tremendous mental effort to concentrate on useful and progressive tasks.[36]

Charlie also made a brief reference to his visit to Dr. Heatley. There lurks in it the implication that Charlie thought that the university's health care system had failed him.

> I talked with a Doctor once for about two hours and tried to convey to him my fears that I felt come [sic, perhaps "some"] overwhelming violent impulses. After one session I never saw the Doctor again, and since then I have been fighting my mental turmoil alone, and seemingly to no avail.[37]

It was as if Charlie wished that Dr. Heatley had talked him out of the whole thing or at least more forcefully taken him in hand. And then there was this macabre, prescient request. "After my death I wish that an autopsy would be performed on me to see if there is any visible physical disorder."[38]

It is also unlikely that anyone selling Charlie a gun that morning could have known or guessed that the night before, this convivial all-American boy had stabbed to death his wife and mother, whom he also strangled for good measure. So Charlie paid for his guns and supplies with a credit card and a bad check from an overdrawn account, walked out with them, and went home. In truth, he already had more than enough guns at home, including a deer rifle that his father had paid for and with which he was to do the most damage during his rampage. But he had apparently reviewed his plan that morning and decided that he needed to improve his arsenal. Once he was back home, he sawed off the barrel and stock of his shotgun, cleaned his weapons, and packed the guns and a staggering amount of supplies into his old Marine Corps footlocker.

How Charlie got the heavy footlocker up to the twenty-eight-floor observation deck was evidence that, whatever else was going on in his brain and his mind, his tactical planning skills were in excellent working order. First thing that morning he had rented a two-wheeled mover's dolly. Next he slipped into light blue workman's coveralls and wrestled his footlocker into the back seat of the Chevrolet Impala his father had given him. He put a number of overflow items into the car's trunk. Then he headed for the tower.

The arsenal he took with him included the following weapons (he left several others at home):

- 6mm Remington 700 ADL bolt-action hunting rifle, with a 4-power scope

- .30 caliber Universal M1 carbine

- .35 caliber Remington Model 141 slide-action hunting rifle

- 12 gauge Sears Model 60 semiautomatic shotgun

- Smith & Wesson Model 19 .357 Magnum revolver

- 9mm Luger P08 semiautomatic pistol

- .25ACP Galesi-Brescia semiautomatic pistol

Charlie's supply of food and other gear clearly indicates that he planned on a long stay "holding off an army" from the tower, although his last writings indicate that he expected to die up there:

> The footlocker and trunk held the following items: cans of meat ravioli, Spam, Vienna sausage, peanuts, sliced pineapple, fruit salad, and liquid diet formula; a jar of honey, boxes of raisins, sandwiches, and a vacuum flask of coffee; vitamins, Dexedrine, Excedrin, earplugs, jugs of water and of gasoline, matches, charcoal lighter fluid, rope, binoculars, canteens, a machete, a hatchet, three knives, a transistor radio, toilet paper, a Gillette razor, and a plastic bottle of Mennen spray deodorant.[39]

Parking around the tower was restricted to university staff and faculty. Charlie had a plan for that. He convinced the parking-lot guard that he was delivering supplies to a faculty member. The guard obliged Charlie with a temporary parking pass. Once he had parked close to the tower, Charlie strapped the footlocker onto the dolly and took an elevator to the twenty-seventh-floor reception area, from which two sets of stairs led to the twenty-eighth floor and the observation deck. He inflicted fatal blows to the receptionist and hid her moribund body behind a piece of furniture. A few minutes later, he allowed a young couple leaving the observation deck to pass by him without harm. Because they were leaving and were completely unaware of what he was doing, the couple presented no threat to his plan. The two were later called the luckiest couple in Austin. But when Charlie was interrupted by a family of tourists on their way up to the observation deck, Charlie shot and killed two and wounded two of the party with his sawed-off shotgun.

Minutes later, Charlie stepped out onto the observation deck. He blocked the door by propping the mover's dolly against it. Then he opened his footlocker, took out his guns, and unfolded his fantasy.

An All-American Sniper

Charlie fired his first shot at 11:48 a.m. and, in the words of a *Texas Monthly* retrospective, "introduced the nation to the idea of mass murder in a public space."

Before 9/11, before Columbine, before the Oklahoma City bombing, before "going postal" was a turn of phrase, the 25-year-old ushered in the notion that any group of people, anywhere—even walking around a university campus on a summer day—could be killed at random by a stranger.[40]

Charlie continued shooting until he was finally confronted and shot to death at 1:24 p.m. by two Austin city policemen, Ramiro Martinez and Houston McCoy. They were armed respectively with a six-shot revolver and a shotgun. By then Charlie had killed outright fourteen victims on campus and wounded another thirty-two. One of the wounded died of his injuries thirty-five years later and is often included in the total of those killed. By that count, and including his wife and mother, Charles Whitman murdered seventeen innocent victims.

Charlie's shooting was methodical and disciplined. He took precise aim and never shot his targets more than once, following the sniper's motto, "One shot, one kill."[41] Although he fired most of his guns at one point or another (beginning with the shotgun shootings near the reception desk), the greater part of the carnage was done with his 6mm bolt-action Remington 700 ADL scoped hunting rifle, the gun his father had paid for. Remington introduced this rifle in January 1962 and it soon became one of the most popular high-powered commercial rifles in the world, according to a history of the company.[42] It was popular among deer hunters in Texas. The Remington 700 fired "a very slim, high-velocity missile over a long distance on a nearly flat plane" and had an effective range of three hundred yards even without its scope.[43] Charlie was in effect shooting downhill from the tower. Shooting uphill or downhill is a challenge for many occasional shooters. But it was no problem for Charlie, who would have learned the Marine Corps' technique for properly adjusting his aim.[44]

The toll might easily have been much higher. By the time Charlie stepped out onto the observation deck, he had just missed a regular change of class during which hundreds of students poured out onto the plaza below him. His targets were thus limited to a smaller pool of unsuspecting people moving about the campus and nearby Austin on the ordinary business of a scorching summer day.

Most of the casualties took place within the first twenty of the total ninety-six minutes. After that, students and other citizens had gone home, got their own rifles, and started shooting back at Charlie. Puffs of dust from where their bullets hit the tower can be seen in images taken on that day. Lonnie and Sandy Phillips each remember watching the horror unfold on television, she in California and he in Texas.

The return fire forced Charlie to keep his head down. "Once he could no longer lean over the edge and fire, he was much more limited in what he could do," recalled one witness. "He had to shoot through those drain spouts, or he had to pop up real fast and then dive down again."[45] Allen Crum, a retired air force officer who armed himself with a rifle and accompanied Officer Martinez to the observation desk, called the ground fire "a Godsend to us, as it got Whitman pinned down."[46]

The Tower Shooting—Baseline for Public Mass Shootings

Charles Whitman's Texas Tower rampage is a starting point, a rough baseline for assessing the phenomenon of American public mass shootings into the twenty-first century, how to prevent them, and what—if anything—has changed since then. Its several facets reflect difficult questions of law, public policy, public health, and American culture that are relevant today not only to mass shootings but to gun violence generally. These questions do not admit of easy answers. They must be grappled with. Finding answers that are both effective and politically realistic without major cultural change in America is more difficult than simply postulating theoretical "commonsense" solutions.

One aspect can be disposed of at the outset. Charles Joseph Whitman did not "flip out." He did not suddenly change from all-American boy to mass killer. He had been wearing a mask for a long time, for at least the five years from his first known mention of his fantasy of shooting people from the tower. Putting aside the important questions of how and why he came to be wearing that mask, Whitman shared an important characteristic of public mass shooters described in an FBI study of "targeted mass attacks."

> Targeted mass attacks are just that—"targeted." Forethought and planning go into the attack. These are not spontaneous, emotion-driven, impulsive crimes emanating from a person's immediate anger or fear. In

fact there is no evidence in the research to date that "snap" mass murders occur at all. The perpetrators often have a grievance and they take time to consider, plan, and prepare their attack.[47]

The type and number of Whitman's guns is a trail that ends in a policy bramble. More recent public mass shootings—Aurora, Sandy Hook, Orlando, Parkland, and many others—have focused attention on the enormous firepower of semiautomatic assault weapons and high-capacity ammunition magazines. But that sort of mass firepower was not part of the Texas Tower shooting. It was rather a classic sniper attack consisting of a prolonged series of long-range, precisely aimed single shots. Whitman did not walk into a crowded venue and cut loose with an indiscriminate spray of bullets. None of Whitman's guns fit the design profile of an assault weapon, with the arguable exception of his Universal M1 carbine.

Moreover, even if one counts the M1 carbine as an assault rifle, it was not Whitman's primary weapon. The gun with which he did the most damage was his Remington 700 ADL single-shot, bolt-action hunting rifle with a 4-power scope, the gun featured in a full-page spread in Remington's 150th anniversary 1966 catalog. With the long range and flat trajectory of its 6mm ammunition, and the aid of its optics, it was more suitable as a sniper rifle than either of his other two rifles. This includes the M1 carbine, to which combat veterans often gave negative reviews for its short range and mediocre "punch."[48] As a bolt-action rifle, the Remington 700 would be excluded from the definition of assault rifle in any past, present, or proposed law known to the author, starting with the ineffective and since-lapsed 1994 federal assault weapons ban, which specifically provided that the ban did not apply to any firearm that "is manually operated by bolt, pump, lever, or slide action."[49] That exclusion also would have exempted Whitman's .35 caliber Remington Model 141 slide-action hunting rifle and his 12 gauge Sears Model 60 semiautomatic shotgun. For good measure, the 1994 federal law included in an appendix a long list of makes and models of firearms that were specifically not covered by the law. The Remington 700 ADL was on that list.[50] The "good guns" list also included M1 carbines, albeit made by another company, Iver Johnson.

The inescapable fact is that Whitman wreaked havoc with what were then and are now garden-variety civilian recreational firearms. Looking for something to restrict or ban in that mix of guns is a largely fruit-less search. As author Lavergne wrote, "Only the confiscation of over 100,000,000 privately owned handguns, rifles, and shotguns nationwide might have prevented the University of Texas tragedy; it is a degree of gun control that, even if possible, would never find political acceptance in the United States."[51]

What about the sheer number of guns that Whitman owned? People unfamiliar with the habits of the American gun enthusiast might think that owning so many guns in and of itself signals something sinister about the owner's state of mind and violent tendencies. Flush with op-timism following passage of the 1993 Brady law, for example, the Brady organization pushed a comprehensive follow-on bill known popularly as "Brady II." Introduced by then congressman Charles Schumer, the bill would have among other things required persons possessing more than twenty firearms (defined to include ammunition magazines and gun parts as separate firearms) or one thousand rounds of ammunition to obtain a "federal arsenal license."[52]

There was nothing unusual about Whitman's arsenal in 1966 Texas. *Behind the Tower: New Histories of the UT Tower Shooting* is a "public history" website presenting the collective study and analysis of eleven University of Texas graduate students and a history professor. Their work is intended to "open up a discussion of all the issues connected with the shooting, its context, and its aftermath."[53] Among the scholarship memo-rializing and reflecting on the tower shooting is a discussion of the Texas gun culture at the time of the shooting. "In the press reports after the shooting, nobody seemed particularly fazed by the large number of armed civilians present on the UT campus that day," the writer noted. "To the contrary . . . they were treated as heroes." As to the number of guns Whit-man was found to own, "several sportsmen said afterwards that arsenals this size and even larger were not uncommon in Texas households. The secretary of the Texas Senate himself reported owning six rifles, three shotguns, and a pistol."[54] It's an open question how much, if at all, the gun culture and its politics have changed in Texas. A law allowing licensed concealed carry of handguns on Texas state university campuses went into effect on August 1, 2016—the fiftieth anniversary of the tower massacre.[55]

If Whitman's guns offer little traction, what about his mental health? From the minute the shooting stopped, experts from all of the likely disciplines have engaged in a polite free-for-all seeking to pin down exactly what drove this all-American boy off the rails. Was it the environment of his dysfunctional family and abusive father? Did he suffer from an underlying and undiagnosed psychosis? People who suffer lightning strikes, even near hits, sometimes later develop emotional problems, including personality changes and mood swings.[56] Could it have been that near miss in a phone booth while he was stationed at Guantanamo? What about his abuse of the stimulant drug Dexedrine? Or was it the interaction of some or all of these things?

The autopsy was of limited help. It was not conducted until after Whitman had been embalmed. His blood could not be analyzed, therefore, for the presence of drugs. The several shotgun blasts he suffered when the police shot him had so shredded his brain that no evidence of physical abnormality could be found among the pieces—with one intriguing exception. Charlie's suspicion that something was going on in his brain was well founded. The autopsy revealed that he had a "pecan-sized" tumor growing in his brain. It was pressing down on a small structure in the middle section of the brain called the amygdala.

The amygdala is part of the limbic system, which is strongly involved in human emotions and basic feelings. It is tied to emotional memories, aggressive impulses, and "fight-or-flight" responses.[57]

> Injury or disruption to the limbic system can produce serious problems involving basic emotional perceptions, feelings and responses to the world and oneself. One's actions, so often guided by emotions, can become uncontrollable and emotion dysregulated. A person with injury to the limbic system can become locked into patterns of over- or under-reacting to the simplest situation. One minute everything is all right, the next minute, the world seems to be crashing down. That person with a limbic system injury may feel that they no longer have any control over their actions and may become impulsive, haphazard, and disconnected from their family and friends.[58]

Whitman's lightning strike has been ignored, not even reported in the news media until its mention in a *Behind the Tower* post.[59] The tumor was largely discounted as a cause of his actions until recently, although at the time—journalist Kevin Davis writes in his recent book *The Brain Defense*—"The Texas Tower Massacre raised a debate over whether brain tumors can cause criminal behavior."[60] Studies by neurologists in recent years claim to have identified connections between criminal behavior and injury to specific parts of the brain—including the amygdala.[61] These studies have led to speculation that it was Charlie's tumor after all that drove him to his horrific attack. But to many the suggestion that some faulty switch in the brain can make us do bad things offends the notions of free will and personal moral responsibility upon which much of Western criminal law and codes of morality are based. "Brains do not commit crimes; people commit crimes," Stephen J. Morse, a professor of law and psychiatry at the University of Pennsylvania who has written extensively about culpability and neuroscience, was quoted as saying in a 2007 survey of neuroscience and the law.[62]

Threat Assessment and Threat Management

However convinced individual advocates within this scrum of causal analysis may be, it is impossible to isolate exactly what drove Charles Whitman and what drives other public mass shooters. But even if we cannot pin down the causes of their murderous behavior, we likely can be alert for objective signals that almost always slip out from behind the masks that they wear. This brings us to the world of "threat assessment" and "threat management." Known by a variety of terms, these conceptual twins are among the more promising tools for lessening the risk of public mass shootings and gun violence generally. Threat assessment is "the process of gathering information to understand the threat of violence posed by a person," and threat management is "the process of developing and executing plans to mitigate the threat of violence posed by a person."[63]

> Assessment is . . . the process of gathering information . . . [about] if, why, and how a person has formed violent goals, intentions, and behavioral plans; the extent to which these goals, intentions, and behavioral plans are stable and coherent; and how best to interrupt the goal-intent-behavior sequence in light of the person's likely future life circumstances.[64]

Putting aside the many questions of law and public policy that are raised by effective threat management—such as, specifically what to do if a given person is judged to be off the rails—we can readily see how an effective system of threat assessment likely would have picked up the signals that Charles Whitman emitted. These signals, sometimes called "leakage," may even in some cases be intentional subtle calls for help. They are, however, not useful information unless there is a system to notice them, deduce their significance, and take prompt action to intervene. "Recognizing a threat or a concern for violence is only the beginning; doing something about it is what may change the course of events."[65]

The signals that Charles Whitman sent were blatant, specific, and packed with potential information. In the absence of any systematic means of evaluation and intervention, however, Charlie's "leakage" was so much useless noise until it was too late. James Egan Holmes was also leaking signals forty-six years later in Colorado. And, although there was supposedly a system of threat assessment and threat management in place, that system also failed to adequately evaluate James's "goal-intent-behavior sequence" until it was too late.

Gary Lavergne assessed the effect of the tower shooting at the end of his book. "Charles Whitman stole from us the comfort of believing in the safety of public spaces," he wrote. Whitman and other "high-profile" killers, he concluded, "made us pay a high price for living in a free society."[66]

But the price of anything is always a negotiation, a compromise between supply and demand. Today, Americans passively endure intrusions into their lives made in the name of fighting terrorism that they would have found unacceptable before 9/11. The civil liberty price point changed after that September morning. It turned out that, yes, Americans were willing to negotiate some part of their constitutional rights in order to feel and perhaps even be safer. American society always has the (at least theoretical) option of deciding that the price of repeated public mass shootings is too high and that it is tired of paying for it with the blood of innocents. The American people might insist upon cultural change significant enough to flip the costs of gun violence away from innocent victims and the community at large and directly onto the gun industry and the consumers of its products. Through such means as stricter regulation, taxation, licensing fees, and the imposition of civil damage awards, a cultural choice could be made to make the price of possessing guns, or certain types of guns, so high that manufacturers and consumers would choose to divert their resources to other uses. This is what was done in the case of fully automatic machine guns by the National Firearms Act of 1934.[67]

In assessing the likelihood, extent, and nature of any such substantial change, however, one needs to consider the certain opposition of millions of Americans who love their guns, are unlikely to commit any crime with them, and are not inclined to give them up, or even to suffer any major inconvenience in acquiring them. This should not be considered a surrender to the gun lobby. It is rather a clear-eyed acknowledgment of reality.

Politics is also a negotiation. The recreational and security value that some Americans find in owning guns must ultimately be balanced with the pain that guns inflict on other Americans and the costs that gun violence imposes on medical and law enforcement systems everywhere in America.

An Introduction to Gunshot Wounds and Their Treatment

Public mass shootings by definition result in many gunshot injuries. The precise nature of gunshot wounds and their consequences are largely ignored by the news media. Images of exploded faces, grossly ruptured chests, and shredded stomachs leaking intestines are not considered suitable media content. But the true horror and real cost of gun violence cannot be understood without at least a basic understanding of what it means to be shot with a firearm. More interviews with trauma surgeons and less coverage of politicians emitting their "thoughts and prayers" after public mass shootings would be a start.

The first thing to learn about gunshot injuries is to forget everything you thought you learned from watching news broadcasts, films, television, and other popular entertainment media. Any victim of any shooting knows much more about the reality of gunshot wounds and their effects than all of the Hollywood film writers and news media producers put together know or care to know. The reality is bloodier, more painful, and life-changing for survivors.

A matrix of factors influence the chance of anyone surviving a gunshot injury, and the quality of their recovery if they do survive. Where did the bullet strike? How many times was the victim shot? What was the size and velocity of the bullet? What care did the victim receive on the spot? How quickly were they transported to a trauma center? Was it staffed and qualified to effectively treat their injury?

Dr. Thomas Scalea discussed these and other points about gunshot injury during a March 2018 interview at his office in downtown Baltimore, Maryland. He has performed thousands of surgeries on critically injured gunshot victims over the last three decades. As fate would have it, there was a shooting at a high school in Maryland on the morning of that interview. Dr. Scalea kept a constant eye on messages about the shooting victims in that event.[68]

Scalea is physician-in-chief at the R. Adams Cowley Shock Trauma Center. The center was founded by and is named after the doctor acclaimed in medical history as the father of trauma medicine. It is one of only a handful of "freestanding" trauma centers in the United States.[69] Freestanding centers are so named because they bypass the usual emergency room visit and take critically injured patients directly into advanced surgical suites staffed by highly trained and experienced medical staff. In addition to spending about a hundred hours every week in the trauma center, Dr. Scalea is "The Honorable Francis X. Kelly Distinguished Professor in Trauma Surgery" at the University of Maryland School of Medicine.

Dr. Scalea did not plan on becoming a doctor—he took his medical school entry boards on a dare and decided to enroll only after a graduate fellowship in another field evaporated. Today, however, he says he was born to oversee the "ballet of organized chaos" of the trauma center in action. He "can't imagine doing anything else."[70]

The Three Factors of Surviving Gunshot Injury

Surviving a gunshot wound "all depends," Dr. Scalea explained. "What happens when you get shot? Three things happen, potentially."[71]

The first of these three is direct injury caused by the bullet itself.

"The bullet goes through and, unlike a car crash where the energy dissipation can be all over your body, if you get shot, the energy dissipation is in the missile track. So what gets injured is directly related to the path that the missile took. If it goes through your liver or through a big blood vessel, that's not so good because you bleed a lot. You can get shot ten times, and if it's all in non-critical areas, then you're okay. On the other hand, one gunshot wound to the head or the heart, that's a lethal effect. Ten gunshot wounds to the extremities may break some bones, but if you don't bleed to death, then you're going to be okay. So, there is direct injury to the structures in the path, remembering that bullets don't always travel in a straight line."

The second factor is a wave effect, called "cavitation." Something like the wake of a speeding boat, cavitation rapidly expands outward from the channel the bullet makes. It compresses, tears, or otherwise damages tissues and organs. "There is a zone of injury that is larger than the missile itself."

Experienced surgeons can see the effects of cavitation on the body. They can also describe the horrific effects of the high-velocity bullets fired by modern semiautomatic assault rifles like the AR-15. "The tissue destruction is almost unimaginable," Dr. Jeremy Cannon, a trauma surgeon and military veteran told the *New York Times*. "Bodies are exploded, soft tissue is absolutely destroyed. The injuries to the chest or abdomen—it's like a bomb went off."[72]

Secondary missiles within the body add to the injury. "So, if I shoot you in the femur," Dr. Scalea explained, "I break your femur and the bone splinters, and then the little pieces of bone become missiles. And maybe the bullet doesn't injure your femoral artery, but the bone does."

Finally, there is the question of ammunition capacity—how many rounds a shooter can discharge from one loading of his firearm. Greater ammunition capacity enhances lethality. "The more times you get shot, the greater the chance that you're going to get hit in something sensitive," Dr. Scalea observed. The fourteen rounds in the ammunition magazine of Christopher Husbands's Glock were more than enough to ensure the deaths of Ahmed Hassan and Nixon Nirmalendran, and to wound five innocent bystanders.

Traumatic Brain Injury: A Canadian Teenager and an American Congresswoman

When the shooting started at the Eaton Centre food court in 2012, Jo-Anne Finney and her children dove under a table and tried to hide. As Jo-Anne tried to move around the pillar next to them, she noticed a pool of blood.

"Connor wasn't moving," she testified at Christopher Husbands's trial. "He was awake, but he wasn't moving. As we were pulling him back, I recall looking at his head and seeing it looked like something was sticking out of his head."

She put her hand up to her son's head.

"I felt at the time there was a bullet in his head."

(Finney clarified in a news interview later that she meant "felt" in the sense of "thought" or "believed," as opposed to actually touching a bullet.)

Gunshots wounds to the head are much more often fatal than not—about 91 percent of such victims die, most of them at the scene.[73] The January 2011 shooting and substantial recovery of U.S. representative Gabrielle Giffords brought national attention to the 9 percent who survive. Their survival is in part because hospital care of traumatic brain injuries (TBI) has improved. "Due to advances in surgical technique and critical care management, there has been a marked reduction [in deaths and unsatisfactory outcomes] from patients admitted with TBI over the last 30 years. However, the postoperative mortality rates for [such gunshot wounds] remains well above 20%."[74]

Even so, and even with the best of care, surviving a gunshot to the head is in essence a macabre crapshoot. "You do see people who get really lucky," Dr. Nirit Weiss told *Time* magazine shortly after Representative Giffords was shot. "When that happens, we say, wow, that guy is lucky, he won the lottery."[75]

The Injured Brain

We most often think of the brain in cybernetic terms, as a computer, the amazing command center of our central nervous system. That system of instant, sophisticated, and incredibly adaptive communications and control operates through billions of intricately integrated cells. There are about a hundred billion neurons in the brain. Neurons are communications cells, constantly processing electrical and chemical signals at lightning speeds. Virtually everything we do, think, and say depends on these neuronal interactions. Neurons are supported and nourished by between ten to fifteen times their number of glial cells.[76]

Another, complementary way to view the brain is as an industrial center, a constantly busy complex of pipelines, fluids, chemicals, and storage tanks. Blood vessels, cells, sinuses, and other structures store, transmit, and exchange not only the blood and the oxygen essential to life itself, but dozens of chemicals, waste products, and other elements supporting the brain's functions. Proper functioning of the brain's intricate hydraulic system depends on barriers that keep fluids and chemicals in the right channels and away from places where they would cause harm.[77]

When a bullet crashes through the skull and into the brain, it is like a terrorist's bomb ripping through a combined industrial and communications complex supporting a massive metropolis. It wreaks havoc. Critical flows are interrupted, fluids go where they create danger, and systems that maintain vital functions like blood pressure and temperature are all knocked askew. The metropolis—our body—in thrown into chaos. For those few who survive such an initial blow, the surgeon's immediate task is damage control.

"In a way, we can do a lot," Dr. Weiss told *Time*. "But that said, all these measures can only mitigate the damage, we can't undo it. We're just spraying a hose on the fire, but the fire has already been set."[78]

There are two distinct phases of gunshot injury to the brain, the primary injury and the secondary consequences.

"The brain is an important organ with a huge amount of blood supply," said Dr. Scalea. "The brain takes up all of the space inside the skull. So, when the brain gets injured, particularly with a missile, it bleeds, there is damage, and that is the primary brain injury."

As in other gunshot wounds, cavitation plays a significant role in the primary injury. According to the report of a study by several neurosurgeons, cavitation "causes suction of air, skin, hairs and debris into [the] brain . . . this temporary cavity collapses upon itself only to re-expand in progressively smaller undulating wave-like patterns. Every cycle of temporary expansion and collapse creates significant surrounding brain tissue injury." The cavitation effect is greater or lesser depending on the velocity of the bullet. In general, rifle bullets have much greater velocity than handguns and create a greater cavitation effect.[79]

Primary injury to the brain is irreversible. Brain cells are different from other cells in the body, such as skin, bone, and muscle. Brain cells are not replaced when they are injured. They die, and their death changes how a person's brain works, and thus how that person functions as a human being. The extent of those changes and their impact on how one thinks, talks, walks, moves, and interacts with others depends on a number of factors, including which part of the brain is injured.[80] Most commonly, however, those who survive gunshots to the brain suffer "devastating neurological outcomes."[81]

Most of us can conjure up an image of the brain, a convoluted, symmetrical gray mass. An anatomical map of that mass is divided into sections that are called lobes, a brain stem that is connected to the spine, and another small mass called the cerebellum. Each lobe—frontal, temporal, parietal, and occipital—has specific functions, as do the cerebellum and the brain stem. These functions are also distributed by sides of the brain. A healthy brain is symmetrical, but if one were to split it down the middle, the functions of the two equal sides are different. For example, the left side is the seat of analysis, logic, and language, the right of creativity and imagination. Curiously, the left side of the brain controls the right side of the body and vice versa.[82]

Gunshots that pass through more than one lobe, the deep center of the brain, the area behind the back of the mouth, or a blood vessel are almost always fatal.[83]

Representative Giffords was shot in only one lobe, the one on the left side of her brain. That lobe is the seat of our language and reasoning abilities. Fired from a Glock 19 semiautomatic pistol (with a thirty-three-round ammunition magazine), the 9mm bullet that struck her entered the left side of the back of her head, traveled through the left lobe, and exited through her forehead.[84] According to published reports, the injury left her with a condition known as non-fluent aphasia.[85] People with such a condition "have trouble speaking fluently but their comprehension can be relatively preserved," according to the National Aphasia Association. "Patients have difficulty producing grammatical sentences and their speech is limited mainly to short utterances of less than four words. Producing the right sounds or finding the right words is often a laborious process."[86] Yet some people with non-fluent aphasia can still use the musical right side of their brain. They can remember songs, and there is evidence that some can learn to improve their communications ability through the right side, for example by memorizing longer passages in the form of songs.[87]

Because Connor Stevenson's surgeons have declined interviews in the past and declined to be interviewed for this book, a firsthand clinical description of his injuries and treatment is not available. However, it is possible to assemble a well-informed description from news reports and the statements of Connor and his mother about the nature of his wound and the course of his treatment. At a press conference following her trial testimony, Finney said, "It just looked like his hair was all puffed up in one area, but when I felt it, I feel a hole. So, it really just looked like a hole in his head."[88]

Connor was struck near the center and relatively high on his forehead.[89]

"He was bleeding forever," his mother recalled. "I didn't think he would make it to the hospital."[90]

Neither did paramedic Rob Kovasci.

"I honestly didn't think he was going to live," he said in *The Survivor*, a Canadian television documentary about Connor.[91] Kovasci knew that Connor's chance of survival hinged on whether he could get the care he needed within what emergency medicine calls "the Golden Hour," a term coined by Dr. R. Adams Cowley, founder of the Shock Trauma Center in Baltimore, Maryland.

The Golden Hour

"The Golden Hour is a concept," Dr. Scalea explained. "It's not necessarily sixty minutes. Injury is a time-sensitive disease, and the clock starts ticking at the time you get injured, not at the time you get to the hospital. It speaks to a system of care that transports you as quickly as possible to the right place. If you get shot in the heart or shot in the chest, the Golden Hour may not be sixty minutes. Maybe it's six minutes."

Paramedic Kovasci knew all of the real-life factors that eat into the Golden Hour.

"You can lose a minute during the 911 call. You can lose a minute during dispatch. You can lose four minutes during transport. There's six minutes, there's 10 percent of your time gone right there. That's before you even get there. . . . It's amazing how sixty seconds here, two minutes here can add up. Those are the things that kill people."[92]

Knowing all that, and assessing Connor's condition, the first responders made a decision to go into what they call the "load and go" mode. That meant putting the injured youth immediately on a stretcher and heading straight for the Toronto Hospital for Sick Children, popularly called "Sick Kids." After wheeling Connor past Jessi Ghawi and into an ambulance, they got him to Sick Kids at 6:51 p.m.—twenty-seven minutes after the first 911 call.[93] (Representative Giffords arrived at the hospital in Tucson "within minutes" and her surgery began within thirty-eight minutes after she was shot.)[94]

Although no one knew it at the time, Connor had already "won the lottery" in terms of his primary brain injury.

"If the bullet had went in an inch to one side, it would have hit a major artery, which is almost instant death," his mother later explained. "So, he got lucky. He's a lucky little boy."[95]

Connor's luck would have to hold, however. "Only a fraction of the neurological harm arises at the moment of impact."[96] Secondary brain injury may be more life-threatening than the primary. "The worst damage is often done not by the initial wound but by the body's attempt to heal it," according to neurosurgeon Dr. Nirit Weiss.[97]

"There is secondary brain injury from swelling," Dr. Scalea said. "If it's a civilian gunshot wound, the skull is not destroyed, so as the brain swells, the pressure on the whole brain produces additional brain injury."

The first order of business in a case of gunshot wound to the head is a CT (computed tomography) scan, which provides surgeons a map of the bullet's course and the primary injury.[98] From there, Connor went into three hours of surgery. In order to relieve pressure within the brain, surgeons removed a portion of his skull.

"It's a contained space, it's not elastic at all," said Dr. Weiss. "Unless you allow for expansion of the brain by taking off some of the skull, that swelling leads to increased pressure and to cell death in areas that didn't have to die."[99]

Surgeons also cleaned up the wound, but left some fragments inside Connor's brain, a decision that Dr. Scalea describes as not unusual—trying to dig everything out of a damaged brain can do more harm than good.

"You take bullets out in cowboy movies," Dr. Scalea said. "You know, 'Oh, we gotta get the slug out.' It's not true. What you are treating is the damage that the missile did. Extracting the missile has only a little bit to do with it, and in the brain in particular, if you debride, take out all the damaged brain, it's hard to know what's good, what's bad, what will recover . . . and so, that becomes its own set of decisions."

Connor survived and eventually thrived, apparently suffering no disabling neurological damage. Along the way, he had to endure two more lengthy surgeries. One to replace the bone removed to give his brain space to swell. Another to replace that bone with a synthetic substitute after his body rejected its re-implant.[100]

Lives Interrupted

Christopher Husbands was convicted by a jury of two counts of second-degree murder. But the Ontario Court of Appeal overturned the conviction in 2017 because of a jury selection error and ordered a new trial. That trial was yet to be held at the time of this writing.[101]

Jessica Ghawi stayed in Toronto for several days after the shooting, deeply impacted by what she had seen, heard, and felt on that spring day in Toronto.

"I feel like I am overreacting about what I experienced. But I can't help but be thankful for whatever caused me to make the choices that I made that day," she wrote in her blog. "I wish I could shake this odd feeling from my chest. The feeling that's reminding me how blessed I am. The same feeling that made me leave the Eaton Center. The feeling that may have potentially saved my life."

OVER THE DOUBLE RAINBOW

L ike many who are traumatized by violent events, Jessi had trouble sleeping after her near miss at the Eaton Centre shooting.

On Monday, June 4, she wrote, "I couldn't sleep last night. I kept thinking about what I saw at the Eaton Center." She turned to the natural outlet for a writer, and at 3:00 a.m. posted on her blog about the incident. The next night was also sleepless. "4 am and I'm still wide awake. Not sure how to make this brain of mine stop thinking long enough for me to fall asleep." Eventually, Jessi's effervescent resilience carried her through the dark crisis. Her passage to the light shows in her wry comments on life around her.

"She surprised people because she was as feisty as she was," Sandy recalled. "She was very, very funny, very witty, a real wordsmith. She would take somebody saying something and run with it, change it up."[1] Jessi commented humorously on her sense of humor. "I am perfectly fine," she wrote, "with the fact that I have the humor and maturity of a 12 year old boy."

Jessi immersed herself in hockey while she was in Toronto. On June 9 she divided her time between two championship tournaments. One was broadcast from the United States and one was played in Toronto. The National Hockey League's Stanley Cup championship game between the Los Angeles Kings and the New Jersey Devils was held at the Prudential Center in Newark, New Jersey. And in Toronto the Toronto Marlins and Norfolk Admirals squared off for the American Hockey League's Calder Cup.

Jessi had a keen eye for color. She penned trenchant observations about both events. "A woman with tig old bitties who has sex on camera for a living sat behind the glass during the SCF," she tweeted about the televised Stanley Cup playoffs on June 8. "HOW IS THIS STILL NEWS 2 DAYS LATER?!" She was referring to the widely remarked and allegedly distracting presence of a Canadian porno film star named Taylor Stevens, who was seated in a prominent spot during an earlier playoff game. The woman promised to make a return appearance in the final game.

"There's a toddler behind me yelling 'you suck refs.'" Jessi tweeted during the Calder Cup playoff game. "I love that they teach them young here in Canada."

A natural event two days earlier seemed to have markedly buoyed Jessi's spirit. It was a double rainbow that she saw from the top of the CN Tower, a 1,815-foot-tall observation tower in downtown Toronto and a popular tourist site. Twice she posted pictures of the rainbow arcing across the harbor.

Rainbows are an optical illusion, the prismatic effect of sunlight through water droplets suspended in air. They have been imbued with mystical connotations of hope and connection to higher or better worlds in many cultures throughout history. To the Norse, a rainbow was the bridge from earth to the home of the gods, and it could be crossed only by the gods themselves or by humans killed in battle. The rainbow was personified in Greek mythology as Iris, a messenger between the gods and humanity. And in Judeo-Christian religious thought, the rainbow that appeared after the flood recounted in Genesis symbolizes God's promise to never send another flood to destroy all of the earth.

On that day, June 7, 2012—perhaps at the very moment that Jessi was marveling at her rainbow—a young man walked into the Gander Mountain gun store in Thornton, Colorado, 1,500 miles away. He walked out with a Smith & Wesson M&P15 Sport Rifle. He had his reasons for picking that particular type of gun, as would another young man 1,826 miles away and six months later in Newtown, Connecticut.

Both wanted an efficient killing machine.

A Well-Armed Active Shooter

After every public mass shooting, the news media find someone—a former neighbor, a family member, a coworker—who will say on camera that there was "no way anyone could have seen this coming," or "he must have just snapped." According to an FBI study of active shooting incidents between 2000 and 2013, however, these curbside assessments are flat wrong. They are not only wrong, they "can fuel a collective sense of a 'new normal,' one punctuated by a sense of hopelessness and helplessness."[2] In contrast to the popular idea that public mass shooters just "flip out" one day, the FBI found that they take time to plan and prepare for their attacks. A majority of them get their guns legally.

Inspection of the record of public mass shootings reveals another truth. Those who inflict the greatest toll in innocent human life do not simply go out and get just any gun. They often research and carefully select the most efficient killing machines available on the militarized civilian gun market. That market has changed dramatically since Charles Whitman committed mass murder from atop the Texas Tower in Austin. It is no longer necessary for the public mass shooter to be a well-trained marksman or, for that matter, to have even modest familiarity with firearms. Technology and hypermarketing have made it easy for those whose only intent is killing to acquire weapons designed for mass killing on the battlefield. One of the most significant elements of the design of these modern weapons is ease of learning and use by conscripts, partisans, and other young combatants who may never have fired a gun until one of these killing machines was put into their hands.

A Not Very Well Regulated Arm at Fort Hood

On July 31, 2009, a major wearing a U.S. Army combat uniform walked into Guns Galore, a firearms store in Killeen, Texas. He asked the salesman for the most "high-tech" handgun the store had. Both the salesman and an enlisted soldier who happened to be in the store concluded that Major Nidal Hasan knew virtually nothing about handguns. The enlisted soldier was a gun enthusiast, however. He and the salesman steered Hasan to the FN Five-seveN semiautomatic pistol.[3]

The major was vague about why he wanted a handgun and what he intended to do with it. The soldier owned one of the FN pistols himself and he sang its praises. It has low recoil and is easy to shoot. It delivers a devastating high-velocity round. The flat trajectory of the bullets it fires makes accurate aiming easy. It can be easily and quickly reloaded with standard twenty-round ammunition magazines, a load that can be increased to thirty rounds with available magazine extenders.

Major Hasan returned the next day, August 1, 2009, and bought an FN pistol. He took care to make a video on his phone of the salesman's demonstration of how to load and clean the gun.

The Belgian company FN Herstal designed the 5.7X28mm cartridge specifically to defeat body armor. Then the company designed a handgun to fire the potent round—the FN Five-SeveN that Major Hasan bought. FN and the gun enthusiast press originally coyly implied that sales of the new gun and its armor-piercing ammunition would be restricted to use by the military and special police units. A company spokesman said in 1996 that the pistol was "too potent" for normal police duties. It was designed for anti-terrorist and hostage rescue operations. In 1999, the NRA's *American Rifleman* magazine informed its followers, "Law enforcement and military markets are the target groups of FN's new FiveseveN [*sic*] pistol." The magazine discouraged consumer expectations. "Don't expect to see this cartridge sold over the counter in the United States. In this incarnation, it is strictly a law enforcement or military round." A similar line was delivered by *American Handgunner* magazine in 2000. "For reasons that will become obvious, neither the gun nor the ammunition will ever be sold to civilians or even to individual officers."

This was baloney, clever hype intended to interest potential buyers of the new gun among civilian gun enthusiasts. FN was soon selling its supposedly "restricted" firearm to the larger and more profitable civilian market. What was not baloney was the deadly new counterterror weapon's lethality.

Major Nidal Hasan spent the next three months preparing for one of the most murderous assaults by one of its own that the U.S. Army has ever suffered. He bought more twenty-round ammunition magazines and magazine extenders to increase the number of rounds in each magazine to thirty. He bought two laser-aiming devices and hundreds of rounds of ammunition, including a special armor-piercing version that was in the process of being withdrawn from the civilian market. Hasan was also a regular visitor to Stan's Outdoor Shooting Range near Fort Hood. He practiced at the range and sought specific instruction in shooting at human targets from a distance of a hundred yards. A range instructor later testified that Hasan made remarkable progress in one afternoon, advancing from a poor shot to regularly hitting paper human targets in the head and chest.

On the morning of November 5, 2009, Major Hasan opened fire with his Five-seveN in a crowded building in Fort Hood where soldiers were being processed to go overseas. Ten minutes later, twelve soldiers and one civilian had been shot dead. Another thirty-one soldiers and a police officer had been wounded.

Although a great deal of attention is properly given to the use of semiautomatic assault rifles in public mass shootings, modern semiautomatic pistols have also been used to inflict mass casualties. Incidents in which handguns were used in public mass shootings include, for example, thirty-two dead and seventeen wounded in the April 2007 shooting at Virginia Tech, and twenty-three dead and twenty wounded in the October 1991 shooting at Luby's cafeteria in Killeen. What these modern handguns have in common with semiautomatic assault rifles is their high-capacity magazines.

The American handgun market switched in the mid-1980s from being dominated by six-shot revolvers to high-capacity semiautomatic pistols capable of being loaded with fourteen, twenty, and even thirty-three rounds of ammunition. This change did not just happen. It was the result of deliberate strategies by two foreign handgun manufacturers, the Italian company Beretta and the Austrian company Glock.[4] Beretta burst onto the American scene in 1985 when it won the contract to replace the U.S. military's standard sidearm, the Colt Model 1911 .45 caliber pistol. A Beretta executive later explained that the company's strategy was to first win the military contract and, after winning that cachet, go after the much larger and more profitable civilian handgun market. Glock had the same strategy in mind when it began pitching its high-capacity semiautomatic pistols to civilian law enforcement agencies. Like Beretta, Glock successfully parlayed its cachet into the bigger market of civilian sales.

The AR-15 Rifle—History of a Killing Machine

The Bushmaster XM15-E25 rifle used on December 14, 2012, to murder twenty children and six adults in less than five minutes at Sandy Hook Elementary School was not merely a sporting rifle used in a crime. It was a semiautomatic assault rifle, the civilian version of a class of infantry rifle specifically designed for the modern battlefield. It was used exactly for what it was designed to do—killing efficiently.

The prototype AR-15 was developed by a gun company called ArmaLite, for which the "AR" in AR-15 stood. (ArmaLite produced a number of other firearm models, beginning with its AR-1.)[5] When the U.S. military accepted the AR-15 into its inventory it designated the new rifle the "M16." The military's current M4 carbine uses basically the same design, but with a shortened barrel and some related modifications. Overall, the M4 shares about 80 percent commonality with the M16.[6] Colt marketed a civilian version of the rifle as the AR-15. It no longer holds the patent for the design, but does hold the trademark on the name.[7] Accordingly, although other civilian makes and models are often referred to generically as "AR-15s," or "AR-15–type rifles," their manufacturers—like Bushmaster and Smith & Wesson—must use a different name when marketing what is basically the same gun. (The "M&P" in Smith & Wesson's M&P15 stands for "Military & Police," a marketing meme aimed at exploiting the cachet of these two institutions in the civilian gun market.)

Overview of Mass Killing by Design

When the AR-15–type rifle is used in public mass shootings, as it often has been, it is used exactly as it was designed to be used—killing and grievously wounding human beings efficiently at close to medium range. "The AR-15 was conceived as a light and handy gun chambered for a cartridge that would produce a light recoil while shooting a bullet that took advantage of the high-velocity wounding potential of a small projectile."[8] The increased firepower of assault rifles like the AR-15 "has literally provided small groups of determined men . . . the force that heretofore was reserved for battalions and regiments."[9]

The small high-velocity bullet fired by the AR-15, the large number of rounds[10] carried in its high-capacity ammunition magazines,[11] its light recoil, compact hardware, and pistol grip (for better control) are features integrated into a military design specifically intended to enable infantry soldiers to spray bullets at close to medium range in combat.[12] These features, taken together, distinguish this class of combat rifle from earlier

U.S. military rifles which, like their civilian counterparts, were designed for an entirely different purpose, namely, measured, accurate, long-range fire.

The National Shooting Sports Foundation, the gun industry's primary lobby, argues that there is nothing special about the AR-15, which it calls a modern sporting rifle. "Since the 19th century, civilian sporting rifles have evolved from their military predecessors. The modern sporting rifle simply follows that tradition."[13] This cleverly blinkered assertion ignores the fact that none of these earlier standard infantry rifles had the capacity for the high volume of fire intentionally designed into the AR-15. The semiautomatic M1 Garand rifle of World War II and the Korean War, for example, had a maximum capacity of eight rounds of ammunition. The M1 Garand also did not use removable magazines. Each charge of eight comparatively large .30 caliber rounds had to be manually inserted into an internal magazine by means of an "en bloc clip," which was ejected when all of the rounds had been fired. A new clip then had to be loaded. The process was cumbersome, especially when compared to the ease of reloading an assault rifle with a magazine containing at least two and a half times the M1's capacity.[14] Earlier military rifles had even lower magazine capacities than the M1 or were single shot. All of these earlier, pre-M1 rifles required manual manipulation of a bolt or lever with every shot, resulting in slower rates of fire.

The gun industry justifies calling AR-15–type weapons "modern sporting rifles" or "tactical rifles," instead of semiautomatic assault rifles, on the grounds that "true" assault rifles must have fully automatic capability as do machine guns.[15] That is a *semantic* argument, based on an invented definition, addressed in more detail below. There is no *substantive* question that, no matter what one calls the AR-15–type rifle, there is only one significant difference between it and the M16 and M4 military rifles. It is that the military rifles are capable of fully automatic fire and their civilian equivalents are not.[16] The military versions have a selector switch by which different modes of fire may be selected. These "selective fire" modes are semiautomatic, automatic, and in later versions, burst fire. Semiautomatic requires a separate trigger pull for each round fired. In fully automatic fire, the gun continues to fire as long as the trigger is held down until it runs out of ammunition. This is what defines a machine gun. Burst fire is a limited form of automatic fire, in which a single pull of the trigger fires three rounds.

The civilian versions are semiautomatic only because "automatic fire-arms have been severely restricted from civilian ownership since 1934."[17] Gun expert Duncan Long summed the matter up in his 1986 book surveying "the strange combat weapons to which our savage modern age has given birth," *Assault Pistols, Rifles, and Submachine Guns*:

> Marketplace considerations came into play as well. While a fully-automatic weapon has only a limited market, one manufactured in both auto and semi-auto alone will often enjoy handsome profits, thanks to a free society's inexhaustible compulsion to purchase firearms.[18]

Proponents of the civilian commerce in AR-15–type rifles also assert that those gun violence reduction advocates who advocate restricting access to them are simply uninformed people reacting to the scary "look" of the semiautomatic assault rifle. In fact, however, the AR-15 design looks as it does—as do all of the world's assault rifles—because its form follows its combat function. That function is to provide a high volume of fire over a close to medium range, and the design features that give the weapon its distinctive "look" all contribute to that lethal function.

The AR-15 has been described by one military historian as providing "the soldier's ability to spray bullets quickly over a given area a short distance away."[19] A 1962 army report, written when the AR-15 and other combat rifles were being evaluated, succinctly described the "large volume" of fire expected of the infantry rifle in modern combat.

> In rendering the enemy ineffective, the rifle squad must be capable of delivering a large volume of aimed fire in a relatively short time with minimum casualties to itself. This large volume is to kill, wound, and demoralize the enemy, force him to seek cover, and reduce his ability to return fire effectively. Rifle squad targets at times also include large masses of enemy attacking at close proximity ("human sea" attacks). Therefore, ideally all rifles should be capable of automatic fire even though not habitually employed in this mode.[20]

This army report makes clear that soldiers were expected to fight with their rifles mainly in semiautomatic firing mode—which is precisely that of the civilian version. Then as now, automatic fire is "not habitually employed," but may be used "at times," such as "human sea" attacks.

The Crucial Doctrinal History—From Musket to Assault Rifle

Although the army's 1962 report still specified "aimed fire" as a goal, the history of the army's change from a doctrine of deliberate, long-range marksmanship to one of high-volume, even random semiautomatic fire illuminates the essence of the AR-15's design.

An excellent, impartial source for this history is a paper written in 1979 by Thomas L. McNaugher for the Rand Corporation.[21] McNaugher is a West Point graduate with MPA and PhD degrees from Harvard University. He served as an active-duty army officer from 1968 to 1975, including a tour as an adviser in Vietnam. He also served as a mobilized army reservist and participated in Operations Desert Shield and Desert Storm in 1990 and 1991. He studied and wrote at Rand, the Brookings Institution, and other "think tanks" during his career. McNaugher knows what he is writing about and his paper is singularly objective. It is crucial to note that he wrote this paper well before there was any controversy over AR-15 civilian models of the M16 (and other semiautomatic assault weapons). He had no discernible ax to grind one way or another about the weapon. The focus of his paper was on the internal Defense Department procurement process that led to the adoption of the AR-15 as the army's main battle rifle. But in the course of describing that process, he simultaneously and succinctly explained the related pivot in army doctrine regarding combat rifles. Another useful source is the first chapter of gun expert Duncan Long's later book, *The Complete AR-15/M16 Sourcebook*.[22] Long's book—wholly complementary in content to McNaugher's paper—provides more detail about the development of the weapon's technology and a discussion of the internal politics around the procurement decision.

From Muskets to Rifles

A firearm is a bullet delivery system. Any bullet can kill a human being. But the design of a gun and its ammunition affect its lethality—the likelihood that in any given encounter a bullet from that gun will strike and wound or kill a human being. Design factors include ammunition capacity, rate of fire, reloading ease, range, ergonomics that affect ease of handling and therefore accuracy, and bullet size and velocity.

The standard American military arm from the Revolution to the Civil War was not a rifle at all but a smoothbore musket, essentially a pipe loaded by pouring in gunpowder and ramming a wad and a lead ball down after it. Forcing the ball down the barrel often deformed the ball, further reducing its accuracy.[23] The smoothbore musket's range was at most a hundred yards.[24] Musket balls "were really nothing more than high-speed stones."[25] Soldiers fired two to five rounds (at best) per minute.[26] Infantry tactics consisted of massing troops at close range to unleash a large volume of fire.[27] "The corollary to this was that with massed ranks of men all they had to do was take a rudimentary aim and massed firepower would do the rest."[28]

This changed in the mid-nineteenth century with the advent of the breechloading rifle.[29] (Breechloading rifles are loaded from the rear end of the barrel.) Gun makers knew as early as the fifteenth century that cutting grooves ("rifling") inside of a barrel increased accuracy by gripping the bullet and causing it to spin. The ballistic effect is like the spiral of a well-thrown football, and "dramatically increased the weapon's range and accuracy."[30] Mass rifle production was not mastered until the mid 1800s. By the 1870 Franco-Prussian War, all major armies fielded single-shot rifles with ranges of about a thousand yards—ten times that of the Civil War musket.

Paradoxically, aiming the more accurate rifle was more difficult than simply pointing a musket's barrel. "Even though the rifle musket had a hugely increased range over the smoothbore, it was extremely difficult for any soldier to take advantage of that capability."[31] Rifle bullets must travel in an arc rather than a straight line in order to compensate for gravity's downward pull over distance. Making sure that the bullet's arc intersected with a distant target demanded the skill of marksmanship. "To reap the full benefit of the weapon . . . men had to be given special instruction."[32] Rather than simply point the barrel in a straight line, riflemen raised the barrel at a specific angle that they determined by using adjustable sights.

The Advent of the U.S. Army's Marksmanship Doctrine

There was little U.S. Army marksmanship training through the Civil War. In the 1870s, however, army officers—influenced by their observations during the Civil War and the Indian Wars—embraced rifle training. National Guard officers formed the National Rifle Association in 1871 to enhance marksmanship and sponsored rifle matches among military units, later including civilians.[33] These events had a profound effect on U.S. Army doctrine. "[I]t was in these years that the Army elaborated a rifle doctrine stressing aimed fire at long range, a doctrine that became a genuine tradition of marksmanship," McNaugher wrote. "That tradition dominated the service's tactics, its training, and its approach to advancing small-arms technologies. It left a mark on the service still visible in 1960."[34] The army decided that "fire superiority" lay not in the number of shots that soldiers fired but in the number of hits they made on their targets.

The army's zeal for marksmanship led it to resist design innovations that would have increased the infantry rifle's rate of fire on the theory that slower, more deliberate fire would be more accurate. For example, the next significant improvement in infantry rifle design was adding an ammunition magazine, creating the faster "repeating rifle." The German Mauser eight-round magazine rifle appeared in 1884 and was adopted throughout Europe.[35] Instead of manually loading one round at a time into the breech, soldiers inserted a magazine into a well, fired, worked a bolt to eject the used cartridge and load a new one, and fired again until the magazine was empty. They then replaced the magazine.

The U.S. Army, however, saw the magazine rifle's more rapid fire as an unnecessary threat to the marksman's skill. Its experts were adamant in their belief that "well-aimed single shots were needed at longer ranges and at battle ranges."[36] It was only when "pressured by the Congress as well as by the knowledge that most European armies had adopted magazine rifles [that] the service finally relented." Even then, "it taught its soldiers to fire the weapon as a single-shot piece, reserving the rounds in the weapon's magazine for emergency use only."[37]

This marksmanship doctrine defined American infantry rifles until the Vietnam War and the adoption of the AR-15 as the M16.

A practical corollary and one seized upon by defenders of civilian assault rifles was that, until the advent of the assault rifle, military rifles were much like civilian rifles, since they both were designed for much the same thing—measured accurate fire over a distance, which was as useful in hunting as it was in combat. In 1935 the army adopted its first semiautomatic rifle, the M1 Garand, with a firing mechanism not different from that of a semiautomatic hunting rifle. But the M1's eight-round en bloc clip was very unlike the AR-15's easily inserted, high-capacity, ten- to forty-round ammunition magazines.

The Changing Battlefield—Industrial Firepower

Meanwhile, technology was changing the face of the battlefield, the nature of combat, and the infantry weapon. The soldiers of World War I armies carried long-range, bolt-action, magazine rifles. Machine guns swept long-range swathes, cutting down thousands of infantrymen massed in traditional formations. New artillery guns absorbed recoil instead of rolling back on their wheels. This enabled fast, accurate fire that rained high explosives and shrapnel down onto exposed troops. The soldiers "desperately dug holes in the ground to escape from the firepower."[38] The enemy was hard to see under these conditions. Raising one's head above the parapet was beyond dangerous. Yet most of the generals never came to terms with the modern technology of firepower. "Time and again they threw their men forward," with tragic results.[39]

This new battlefield inspired thinking about new tactics and new kinds of weapons among some soldiers and their officers. They thought that nineteenth-century rifles should be replaced by handier, rapid-firing side arms. German troops, for example, complained that their standard infantry rifle "was too long, clumsy, and too sensitive to dirt for close-quarter fighting in the trenches. But the underlying objection was that, being bolt-action, its operation was too slow."[40] Among the new tactics were "trench raids" by small bodies of men who slipped across "no-man's-land" to surprise the enemy. Late in the war the German army equipped its specially trained "Storm Troopers" with a new automatic weapon, the Bergmann MP-18 "machine pistol," the world's first submachine gun. It was smaller and handier than the cumbersome rifle, with many more rounds of ammunition.[41]

The submachine gun, however, was not the ultimate answer for infantry weapons in modern combat. Automatic fire—then as now—consumed ammunition too quickly. And the submachine gun fired pistol rounds, which are smaller, weaker, and of much shorter range than rifle rounds. The rifle round's longer range, however, came at a cost—it was bigger and heavier and had higher recoil than a pistol round. These big rifle rounds were not suited for portable high-capacity magazines. The challenge was to find something in between—a medium-range, high-capacity weapon suitable for the closer, episodic engagements of modern battlefields.

Design Ferment—Velocity, Mass, and the STG-44

Between the world wars, German designers grappled with the physics involved in ammunition design.[42] The energy of a bullet varies with its mass and velocity. Velocity plays a much greater role than mass in the energy equation. Velocity increases energy by its square. Thus, increasing velocity by any multiple has a greater effect on an object's energy than increasing mass by the same multiple. German designers focused on the size and weight of the bullet and its metal case. They wanted a combination of bullet size and propellant charge that would yield effective velocity and energy at medium range, yet would be light enough for soldiers to carry a great many rounds in easily inserted ammunition magazines. "What was needed was a new cartridge," expert Ian Hogg wrote. "[T]he rifle could be lighter, making it easier to handle, and the cartridges would be lighter, so that the soldier could carry more of them . . . [and] it would still be effective at ranges of 500m to 600m (550–650 yd), all that appeared to be needed."[43]

During World War II, these designers developed just such an "intermediate" round. They then built a new infantry rifle around it, capable of laying down heavy fire at close to medium range.[44] This mid-sized, selective-fire rifle had a pistol grip for control and used detachable magazines, which held many more intermediate-size rounds than they could have held full-size rifle rounds. Designated the *Sturmgewehr* 44 ("Assault Rifle 44," stamped "STG 44"), it was the world's first true assault rifle— "assault rifles subsequently became the dominant battle instrument for infantrymen around the world."[45] The STG-44 was developed late in the war and its issue was limited (about four hundred thousand were produced in 1944). But its firepower proved especially useful to German forces facing waves of Russians on the Eastern Front.

The STG-44 greatly impressed the Russians, who set about designing their own assault rifle.[46]

In 1947 Russia fielded its own intermediate-round assault rifle with selective-fire, high-capacity magazine and pistol grip, the *Automat*

Kalishnikova, or AK-47. In the 1960s, the U.S. Army faced the AK-47 in Vietnam. After a fierce internal debate, the army eventually decided to break with its marksmanship doctrine and adopt its own high-volume assault rifle, the AR-15/M16. "What is most interesting about the development of the M16 from the ArmaLite range of weapons has to be the volte face of the U.S. military."[47]

The U.S. Army Reluctantly Changes Its Doctrine

Four factors tipped the balance away from slow, deliberate marksmanship to fast, high-volume fire: (1) a faction of combat-experienced infantrymen who preferred assault rifles; (2) studies of how combat casualties in several wars actually occurred by the Army's Operations Research Office (ORO); (3) research into small-bullet lethality by the Army's Ballistics Research Laboratory (BRL); and (4) field tests by the Defense Department's Advanced Research Projects Agency (then "ARPA," now "DARPA").

Some American World War II veterans thought that the long range of the M1 rifle was not often used in combat. Their allied peers felt so even more strongly. British experts found that "few soldiers fired over about 300 yards in combat [and] fewer still bothered to aim their shots."[48] The members of the post-war North Atlantic Treaty Organization (NATO) sought to standardize military equipment, especially ammunition. The British wanted an intermediate round and an assault rifle to go with it.

But the U.S. Army prevailed. It was still wedded to its marksmanship doctrine and insisted on a higher-caliber, longer-range round as the NATO standard. For the American soldier, this "shibboleth . . . resulted in the M14, a rifle that failed to advance rifle design one iota."[49] The U.S. Army's official doctrine "continued to espouse the precepts of marksmanship. . . . Still, there existed after World War II a sizable group of U.S. infantrymen who preferred an 'assault rifle'—a lighter weapon of less power than the M1 but capable of volume fire."[50]

The assault rifle faction eventually gained significant support from the army's operations research analysts. ORO studies on casualties caused by small-arms fire, small-arms design and characteristics, and marksmanship led to several conclusions: (1) accurately aimed rifle fire was no more effective in producing enemy casualties than was volume of fire, (2) the rifle was seldom used at ranges beyond three hundred meters, and (3) most rifle "kills" were made at less than one hundred meters. ORO analysts thus found that what the army needed was a low-recoil weapon firing a number of small projectiles. The office eventually determined that the AR-15 was the best design of such a weapon.[51]

The smaller bullet concept was reinforced by BRL analysts who "showed that the bullet's velocity was in fact more important than its size in determining lethality."[52] In 1962, ARPA reported favorably on AR-15 field tests with ARVN soldiers and their U.S. Army advisers.[53] Having seen its utility, army field commanders urgently requested the new weapon, and in 1966 the army ordnance establishment surrendered and the AR-15 soon entered service as the M16.

The Gun Industry's Marketing of Semiautomatic Assault Rifles to Civilians

The AR-15's military design broke radically from civilian sporting design, but gun makers marketed it to civilians without significant change. "In an effort to capture the civilian market, Colt introduced a semi-auto only AR-15 in the mid-1970s."[54] Colt later boasted in a regulatory filing that it "distinguished itself by translating innovative military weapons into the most desired . . . recreational firearms . . . 'Colt' defines iconic firearms that first establish worldwide military standards and then become the guns every law enforcement officer and serious recreational shooter wants to own." The company stated that its M16 rifle and M4 carbine "created the 'modern sporting rifle' ('MSR') market."[55] When these combat killing machines began showing up in mass shootings and among violent criminal cartels, the gun industry was heavily criticized for selling assault rifles to civilians. Asked about such incidents in 1997, the then president of Bushmaster Firearms replied, "I guess I don't see that happening enough to feel that it's a legitimate social issue."[56] The industry knew it had a public relations problem, though, and among its responses was the invention of an entirely semantic argument: Civilian AR-15s are not "assault rifles." True military assault rifles can fire in fully automatic mode. Civilian rifles are semiautomatic only, and should be called "modern sporting rifles." Because they are not really "assault rifles," any concern about them is misplaced.

In fact, however, the gun industry knew precisely what it was selling and regularly used the terms "assault rifle" and "assault weapon" before it was criticized for selling them. "The popularly held idea that the term 'assault weapon' originated with anti-gun activists, media or politicians is wrong," gun expert Phillip Peterson wrote in his *Gun Digest Buyers Guide to Assault Weapons.* "The term was first adopted by the manufacturers, wholesalers, importers and dealers in the American firearms industry to stimulate sales of certain firearms that did not have an appearance that was familiar to many firearm owners."[57] Gun fan magazines published in the 1980s "enthusiastically and flatly used military terms and the word 'assault' to describe these guns."[58]

The Semantic Argument—Distinction without Difference

The semantic argument pivots on a theoretical distinction without a practical difference either in military combat or public mass shootings in civilian life. As far back as the STG-44—the original "assault rifle"—military leaders have instructed troops to use semiautomatic fire in most situations. After the U.S. War Department learned of the STG-44, it issued a report on the weapon in April 1945 in which it stated:

> Although provision is made for both full automatic and semiautomatic fire, the piece [the STG-44] is incapable of sustained firing and official German directives have ordered troops to use it only as a semiautomatic weapon. In emergencies, however, soldiers are permitted full automatic fire in two- to three-round bursts.[59]

Just as the Germans did in 1944, and as the U.S. Army stated in its 1962 evaluation report, the American military today continues to discourage routine use of automatic fire with its assault rifles. "The most important firing technique during fast-moving, modern combat is rapid semiautomatic fire . . . it is surprising how devastating accurate rapid semiautomatic fire can be." Consistent with this doctrine, automatic fire is in fact sparingly used in combat.[60]

An object example of the strength of the doctrine favoring semiautomatic fire over automatic in combat is provided by the recent case of an air force Special Forces sergeant alleged to have been left behind alive after being thought to have been killed during a combat engagement in

Afghanistan. Afterwards, the senior team member, a navy SEAL senior chief petty officer, reacted to an aerial surveillance video of what was said to have been the air force sergeant, still alive and fighting off insurgents. He "questioned why the man shooting in the video appeared to fire on full automatic, rather than with the single aimed shots that the sergeant would have been trained to use."[61]

Gun enthusiast and expert Duncan Long frankly called the civilian versions "semiauto assault rifles" and brutally disposed of the semantic argument: "According to the purists, an assault rifle has to be selective fire. Yet, if you think about it, it's a little hard to accept the idea that firearms with extended magazines, pistol grip stock, etc. cease to be an assault rifle by changing a bit of metal."[62]

Smith & Wesson Goes for the Gold

Smith & Wesson's decision to market a semiautomatic assault rifle was a historic turning point for the company. The M&P15 was the first rifle produced by the company, which had historically manufactured only handguns.[63] The company began shipping its first rifles in 2006. By then, AR-15–type rifles were a mainstay of the civilian gun market. Smith & Wesson executives saw the dollar signs.

"We believe the features of these tactical rifles make them strong contenders in the military and law enforcement markets," said Michael Golden, Smith & Wesson president and CEO. "We also believe that our M&P rifle series fills a tremendous gap in the marketplace by delivering high-quality, feature-rich tactical rifles that will be readily available in commercial channels."[64] In June of 2006 Golden told investors that "consumer response has been very strong" for its new semiautomatic assault rifle.[65]

Three years later, on July 20, 2009, Golden told the *Daily Oklahoman* newspaper that a "category that has been extremely hot is tactical rifles, AR style tactical rifles."[66] He also said that the company was doing so well with its assault rifle that it was introducing a variant in .22 caliber because the ammunition is much cheaper than the military-style ammunition used in the M&P15. "We have an M&P15 that shoots .223 ammo that sells extremely well," Golden said. "We have just launched an AR-style rifle that shoots .22 caliber rounds that we think will be extremely popular because of the price of ammo."[67]

Exactly three years to the day after Golden's encomium to his company's "extremely hot" assault rifle, James Egan Holmes would use the Smith & Wesson M&P15 Sport Rifle that he bought in Thornton, Colorado, to the deadly effect for which it was designed.

The Odd Case of the M1 Carbine

An interesting weapon overlooked in almost all of the extensive writing and debate about what is—and what is not—an "assault rifle" is the U.S. M1 carbine. Charles Whitman took a civilian model of the M1 carbine with him up to the observation deck of the Texas Tower.

A short rifle at just under three feet,[68] the M1 carbine should not be confused with the M1 Garand main battle rifle. The M1 carbine was developed later and separate from the M1 rifle. The carbine is not simply a short version of the rifle. They share a common prefix only because of the army's system of equipment nomenclature.

The M1 carbine was designed and developed in the two years before the attack on Pearl Harbor and the entry of the United States into the Second World War. It was first fielded in mid-1942. The design objective was to provide support troops—those not directly involved in frontline combat—a weapon of greater power and range (three hundred yards) than the pistol that they traditionally carried.[69] The original model was semiautomatic fire only. Later versions, beginning with the M2 carbine, included the option of fully automatic fire by means of a selector switch. Both the M1 and the M2 models saw service as late as the Vietnam War.[70]

The intriguing thing is that some enthusiastic gun writers make the point that "the M1 and, especially, the M2 carbine may arguably be termed the first 'assault rifles.'"[71] The German *Sturmgewehr* 44 is, as we have seen above, widely credited with being the first assault rifle. "Nevertheless," firearms historian Leroy Thompson writes, "the M1 Carbine preceded the STG 44 into production and incorporated an intermediate-power cartridge and a higher-capacity detachable box magazine. In the M1A1 version a pistol grip and folding stock were added."[72]

Semiautomatic M1 carbines were enthusiastically marketed to civilian gun enthusiasts after the Second World War. They and more refined variants are widely available today.[73] The 1994 federal assault weapons ban specifically exempted the M1 carbine from its definition of banned assault weapons. But some states have included the M1 carbine in their bans.[74]

How Many Public Mass Shootings Is Enough?

High-capacity semiautomatic pistols and semiautomatic assault rifles are used with such distressing frequency in public mass shootings that many Americans wonder if any time or place is safe. Are we safe? How many of these mass shootings can, or should, we tolerate?

The fine difference between possibility (it could happen) and probability (the odds that it will happen) bedevils the American conversation about public mass shootings and what to do about them. How many are there? Is the rate rising, falling, or staying the same? Are we and our children safe or not safe at a given time and place?

One of the perversities of public mass shootings is that "they are typically premeditated attacks that strike random, innocent victims," making them "functionally similar to terrorism."[75] Computing the likelihood that you, or I, or someone we love will be a mass-shooting victim is at least as complex as estimating whether we will be victims of terror. It depends on the definition and data that one chooses to use, what assumptions one makes about their nature, the means by which incidents are quantified and computed, and how one perceives apparent trends. Yet the uncertainties of terrorism have not stopped the U.S. federal government from having spent at this writing more than $5.6 trillion on its "War on Terror" (a figure that does not include state and local expenditures),[76] and inflicting an ever-growing number of inconveniences and incursions on civil liberties in the name of that endless war.

No matter which definition or circumstance one picks, however, the *probability* of one person being present at two mass shootings is so unlikely that it is almost impossible to calculate, according to University of Toronto statistics professor Jeffrey Rosenthal, quoted in the *Globe and Mail*. Another professor—Alan Lipman, founder and director of the Center for the Study of Violence in Washington and a professor at George Washington University Medical Center—said in the same story that attempting to avoid such a fate would be an exercise in futility. "It would be like saying, 'How would I protect myself against being hit by a flying piece of an orbiting space station?'"[77] Those incredible odds ultimately informed Sandy Phillips's assurances to her daughter, Jessi.

And yet, something more incredible than being hit with a piece of space junk has indeed happened more than once in America. Navy veteran Telemachus Orfanos was present at but escaped injury during the October 2017 public mass shooting in Las Vegas. In November 2018, Orfanos, twenty-seven years old, was shot to death by another public mass shooter at the Borderline Bar & Grill in Thousand Oaks, California. A number of other survivors of the Las Vegas shooting were also present at the Thousand Oaks shooting, but survived again.[78]

"What happened to Orfanos is, statistically, very unlikely," Vox writer German Lopez wrote. "But the fact it can happen at all—that there are even two awful mass shootings within such a close time frame—shows how out of control these tragedies are in America."[79]

Definitions, Probabilities, and the Question of Cultural Definition

The debate about the risk of mass shootings is confounded by the fact that there is no universally accepted definition of "mass shooting." Advocates on all sides and well-meaning commentators alike mix and match different phenomena, different terms, different definitions, and different "casualty thresholds."

"These definitions matter," the RAND Corporation observed in its assessment of the science of gun policy. "Depending on which data source is referenced, there were 7, 65, 332, or 371 mass shootings in the United States in 2015, and those are just some examples."[80]

The FBI—often the ultimate oracle in matters of crime—defined the term "mass murderer" in the 1980s as a person who kills four or more persons (other than himself), typically in a single location.[81] Accordingly, an event is a "mass murder" by the FBI's count only when the murderer kills at least four other persons. On the other hand, the independent research and data collection group Gun Violence Archive (GVA) "uses a purely statistical threshold to define mass shooting based ONLY on the numeric value of 4 or more shot or killed, not including the shooter. GVA does not parse the definition to remove any subcategory of shooting."[82] So a case in which four people other than the shooter were shot and injured, even if none died, would qualify as a "mass shooting" under the GVA's definition. The GVA's reference to removal of "any subcategory" refers to the practice of some other data collectors of excluding such events as gang-related or domestic shootings, and shootings motivated by religion or ideology, even when four or more are wounded or killed. Some other sources count as mass shootings events in which two or more individuals were injured, and some include the shooter in the body count.[83]

Finally, and most relevant to this book, is the category of the public mass shooter (also called the "active shooter" or "rampage shooter").[84] Iain Overton captured the essential dimension of the mass shooter in his book *The Way of the Gun.* "Death is the thing they seek. Killing not as a by-product of protection, or defense, or desire, but death as a means to its own powerful end."[85]

Professor Adam Lankford further distinguished the public mass shooter from other kinds of mass shooters. "Most acts of mass murder arise from robbery, burglary, drug trade, or gang conflict, or are explosive acts of rage against family members or acquaintances," he wrote. But public mass shooters are different. Their attacks are "often planned in advance for weeks, months, or even years, and rarely seem to be simply crimes of passion or escalation." And instead of solely killing people they know, "they often kill symbolic targets, random strangers, or innocent bystanders in public places, such as schools, workplaces, theaters, malls, churches, restaurants, shopping centers, or public streets."[86]

The U.S. Department of Homeland Security (DHS) defines an "active shooter" as "an individual actively engaged in killing or attempting to kill people in a confined and populated area; in most cases, active shooters use firearms and there is no pattern or method to their selection of victims."[87] State and local law enforcement agencies and other experts generally accept, but often tweak, this core definition. For example, the New York City Police Department has a slight variant and also excludes "gang-related shootings, shootings that solely occurred in domestic settings, robberies, drive-by shootings, attacks that did not involve a firearm, and attacks categorized primarily as hostage-taking incidents."[88]

Putting all of this together, the shooting at the Toronto Eaton Centre would qualify as a "mass shooting" under the GVA definition, since four or more people were shot or killed. But those who exclude gang-related shootings from their data sets would not count the shooting if Christopher Husbands was indeed a gang member. Eaton Centre would not meet the FBI's definition of "mass murder," because less than four people were killed. Number of victims aside, Christopher Husbands would not have qualified as a public mass shooter because his targets (as opposed to those suffering collateral injuries) were not random.

Lurking under all of this is the ultimate fact that—no matter how broadly one defines the data set—mass shootings of all kinds, including public mass shootings, only account for about 1 percent of all gun deaths in the United States.[89] This fact has caused debate about the proper order of priorities within the gun violence reduction movement and tense exchanges between that movement and gun-rights advocates.

When Is One Too Many?

Putting aside the quantitative for the qualitative, America's recent and apparently growing experience with mass shootings raises the central question of cultural self-definition. What have we become? Who are we? What are we willing to tolerate? Is an overbearing "gun culture" a necessary and ineradicable aspect of the broader American Culture? Can we not find common ground to reduce, if not eliminate, this bloodshed?

The cultural question may be crystallized this way. Suppose that we cannot agree on any of the monastic debate about what is a mass shooting, how many there are in a given time frame, or even whether the trend is to more or less over time. So what? Aside from all of the conceptual lint-pulling and argumentative data manipulation, how many Sandy Hook or Parkland murders of schoolchildren, or Las Vegas or Aurora or Orlando Pulse or Thousand Oaks murders of innocent people seeking an evening of entertainment, or the public mass shooting that happened last week or this week or will happen the next, are too many for a civilized society to tolerate? Why are we so passive about this continuing bloodshed but so aggressive about the considerably lesser toll of domestic terror victims?

If that question seems naive, look into the mirror of this argument from a prominent gun-rights advocate in another context. His argument hinges on what he perceives to be the intolerable injustice of a single person, carrying a handgun and a concealed carry license issued by State A, being arrested in State B, where his license is not recognized and his carrying a gun is therefore a crime. U.S. representative Richard Hudson, a Republican from North Carolina, described such a case on the floor of the House of Representatives in December 2017 during the debate on the Concealed Carry Reciprocity Act, which he authored. His point was that the federal law that he proposed would prevent such injustices by forcing every state in the Union to recognize every other state's concealed handgun carry permit.

Asked by a CBS *60 Minutes* host "how often does that happen," Hudson replied, "Well, it—once is too much. These are law-abiding citizens, these are not the problem."[90]

Let that sink in. "Once is too much." One arrest of anyone, anywhere for unlawfully carrying a concealed handgun is "too much." But we still can't figure out how many mass shootings are "too much," or what to do about them. There is something grotesque in that inversion of values, and pathetic about a Congress that cannot rouse itself to do something about it.

Are Public Mass Shootings Inevitable in a Free Society?

Many commentators sort through these analytical deck chairs and declare the matter of mass shootings hopeless, something to which Americans should just resign themselves. "Mass murder just may be a price we must pay for living in a society where personal freedom is so highly valued," two Northeastern University professors concluded in an article grimly titled "Mass Shootings in America: Moving Beyond Newtown."[91] That article sought to rebut a list of myths said to have arisen in the wake of the mass shootings in Aurora, Colorado, and Newtown, Connecticut, in 2012.

This fatalistic academic observation, hinged on "personal freedom," was remarkably similar to the constitutional-political argument advanced by former Fox News host, media personality, and Donald Trump confidant Bill O'Reilly after the 2017 mass shooting in Las Vegas. "Once again, the big downside of American freedom is on gruesome display," he wrote. "This is the price of freedom. Violent nuts are allowed to roam free until they do damage, no matter how threatening they are. The 2nd Amendment is clear that Americans have the right to arm themselves for protection. Even the loons."[92]

It is worth noting in the context of O'Reilly's comments that—"violent nuts" and "loons" aside—as many as 65 percent of Americans are said to believe that their right to bear arms is to make sure that they can protect themselves from tyranny. "Unfortunately, the determination of which Americans represent 'tyranny' can be very subjective, particularly for individuals who are struggling with mental health problems and considering a public mass shooting attack."[93]

University of California constitutional law professor Adam Winkler kicked off his book about the legal battle over the constitutional right to bear arms with resignation about mass shootings. He based his pessimism on the ubiquity of their means. "In America . . . guns are everywhere and easy for someone with a criminal intent to acquire. Those guns are here to stay, which means—awful as it is to admit—that mass shootings are here to stay as well."[94]

Public Mass Shootings in Other Countries Compared with the United States

If public mass shootings are truly the "price of freedom" for the United States, then we should expect that citizens of other free countries would be paying the same blood-soaked toll. Certainly at a minimum countries that share the common roots of British constitutional democracies—specifically Great Britain, Canada, Australia, and New Zealand—should be just as deeply scarred by the regular lashings that these shootings inflict on American men, women, and children. Yet they are not. There are good reasons that "perhaps no form of violence is seen as more uniquely American than public mass shootings."[95]

Because the globalized civilian gun industry has thrust its militarized tentacles into every crevice in the world, it is sadly true that few countries have entirely escaped public mass shootings. The American gun industry, the National Rifle Association, and other elements of the gun lobby seize upon relatively isolated mass shootings abroad as evidence that even stringent gun control laws don't work. But, putting aside terrorist attacks like the coordinated November 2008 attacks in Mumbai, India,[96] public mass shootings with death as their only discernible objective happen in no other country as frequently as they do in the United States. Nor have the governments of other democratic governments been as paralyzed as the United States has been in response to public mass shootings when they occur. In some countries, the types of guns that facilitate public mass shootings were not there to stay.

The most comprehensive and authoritative work on comparing public mass shootings worldwide with those of the United States was done by Dr. Adam Lankford, a criminology professor at the University of Alabama. Dr. Lankford has researched in depth mass murder, mass shootings, and terrorism. He has written several books and published an extensive list of academic papers in scholarly journals.[97]

In 2016, Dr. Lankford published the results of a landmark study that examined the differences among nations in public mass shootings. Using more than forty years of data, he did a "quantitative analysis of all known public mass shooters who attacked anywhere in the world from 1966 to 2012 and killed a minimum of four victims."[98] The study included complete data for 171 countries and found that "they averaged 1.7 public mass shootings per country from 1966 to 2012."[99]

So, yes, public mass shootings happen in other countries. And, because the world is so big and there are so many other countries, mass shooters taken in gross are more likely to strike somewhere beyond America's borders than within them—although not more likely or even as likely in any other given country on the planet than in America.[100] But that is only one dimension of the problem. Lankford's study exposed two facts that should be troubling for ordinary Americans, their friends, and their families. The first is that "firearm ownership rates appear to be a statistically significant predictor of the distribution of public mass shooters worldwide."[101] In simple terms, more guns equals more mass shootings—and America stands head and shoulders above the world in both gross numbers of guns and their rate per capita. The second is the consequence of that fact for the United States in particular.

> From 1966 to 2012, the United States was by far the global leader, with five times the total of the Philippines, which was the second highest country. The United States also had a disproportionately high number of offenders: Despite having less than 5% of the global population, it had 31% of global mass shooters. Because of its world-leading firearm ownership rate, America does stand apart—and this appears connected to its high percentage of public mass shootings.[102]

In another study using the same data set, Dr. Lankford found the United States "had by far the most offenders of any nation, with 90.

The next closest countries were the Philippines (18 offenders) and Russia (15 offenders)."[103]

A 2014 study by George Washington University professor Dr. Frederic Lemieux analyzed the relationship between public mass shootings and cultural violence on the one hand and gun regulation on the other.[104] Lemieux's study focused on international comparisons among twenty-five developed countries, members of the Organization for Economic Cooperation and Development (OECD) between 1983 and 2013.[105] Although his study was not as comprehensive as Dr. Lankford's, Lemieux arrived at significant and complementary results. He found that the United States had more than double the number of mass shootings than all of the other twenty-four OECD countries combined. "A significant finding is that mass shootings and gun ownership rates are highly correlated," even after the U.S. shootings are taken out of the data.[106]

Based on his review of existing literature, Dr. Lemieux described two fundamentally opposing views in the American debate over what can and should be done about public mass shootings. The first is that gun violence "is the result of a cultural appetite encouraged and validated by popular entertainment such as violent movies." Those who accept this claim "suggest that firearms are not the problem but that rather people are ('guns don't kill, people do')." The solutions proposed along this line of reasoning are "mainly anchored in the deterrence theory (harsher sentences for criminals) and a physical prevention paradigm (more armed guards or armed citizens in public places—'good guys with guns')." But another line is that "the availability of firearms has an impact on gun violence and mass shootings." Those who accept this premise argue that "restrictive firearms regulation can save lives by imposing background checks, stricter condition for access to firearms (e.g., mental health, required training, etc.), and banning specific weapons and/or features (clip magazine capacity)."[107]

After having examined these two views across international experience, Dr. Lemieux arrived at a number of conclusions. Among them were that "both international and national multivariate analyses show that gun control legislation reduces overall fatalities related to firearms. This correlation is true for Canada and Australia, which adopted and maintained stricter gun control laws. The same finding is also true for the United States as it relates more directly to mass shootings."[108]

America clearly is exceptional in the bloody matter of public mass shootings. To reduce the carnage, many public health experts and gun violence reduction activists argue for more and better enforcement of a variety of gun laws, including comprehensive background checks before any transfer of any firearm, and restrictions on military-style weapons and/or the high-capacity magazines that they use.

Negative Advocacy—The Gun Lobby's Answer to Public Mass Shootings

Unfortunately, the gun industry and its advocates within the NRA and among other dead-enders of unrestrained "gun rights" continue to put their fingers in their ears, close their eyes, and shout the disingenuous argument that America not only does not have a problem with public mass shootings, but is actually safer than the rest of the world. This is the sum of what Dr. Lemieux called the "status quo" argument that advances "protection of the Second Amendment and the assertion that gun violence in America is mainly a problem of violent culture with calling for more situational solutions (e.g., armed guards in public places, school, etc.)."[09] Consistent with his usual genuflexion to the religion of the NRA, for example, President Trump offered the classic "status quo" arguments when he said that the public mass shooting at a Pittsburgh synagogue in October 2018 had little to do with gun laws. "If they had some kind of a protection inside the temple maybe it could have been a very much different situation," he said. "I think one thing we should do is we would stiffen up our gun laws with the death penalty," he added. "When people do this they should get the death penalty."[110]

Fox News and other right-wing media and politicians promote this point of view. And it should come as no surprise that the go-to "expert" in support of this negative advocacy is John Lott.

Lott spun out a paper purporting to prove the gun-friendly proposition that America has only a minor problem with mass shootings compared to the rest of the world. That paper, however, was eviscerated in a detailed analysis posted at the fake-news-busting website Snopes.com, which concluded that it was "extremely misleading."

> It . . . uses inappropriate statistical methods to obscure the reality that mass shootings are very rare in most countries, so that when they do

happen they have an outsized statistical effect. Of the countries chosen by Lott for his analysis, the United States is by some distance the most consistent site of mass shootings.[111]

Angels Dancing on Pinheads

It must finally be said that abstract argument and remote example do not persuade many of those whom the violence of a mass shooting has touched. They live every day the reality of having suffered the unthinkable. For example, Jo-Anne Finney, Connor Stevenson's mother, focuses on daily possibilities rather than abstract probabilities.

"Every day when I'm out I think, does the guy next to me have a loaded gun?" she told a Canadian television interviewer. "The simplest things in life are now all looked at differently."[112]

The heartbroken mother of Telemachus Orfanos also sees the matter with a sharp edge.

"He made it through Las Vegas, he came home," she told the *New York Times* in a short telephone interview. "And he didn't come home last night, and the two words I want you to write are: Gun control. Right now—so that no one else goes through this. Can you do that? Can you do that for me? Gun control."[113]

Then she hung up the phone.

CHAPTER FIVE
TOBACCO ROAD

A war was coming to Colorado. Once Jessi Ghawi heard about it, there was about a zero chance that she would not join the fight.

It wasn't a real war. The cruel violence of a genuine war would have horrified the gentle soul that was sometimes hidden by Jessi's studiously tough veneer. Everyone who knew Jessi knew that soul was in there. It shines from the guileless thoughts that she shared spontaneously with her friends and her family. She did not like fireworks because they sounded to her like gunfire. On July 6, 2012, the day that she enlisted for the coming fight, she scourged herself for having accidentally run over a squirrel. "I was just involved in a vehicular squirrel slaughter in my car. I'm a horrible person! I might actually cry."

On the same day—perhaps inspired by her reflections on the fate of innocent animals—she posted the link to an online article, "14 Stories that Prove Animals Have Souls."[1] She captioned her post, "Daily dose of heart-warming." Just a few days earlier, on the Fourth of July, Jessi posted a link to a newspaper feature about the untimely death of a selfless Canadian woman who had touched the lives of people around her with her caring warmth. "Her daily life was a kiss of love," read the last sentence of the feature.[2]

"What an honor to live a life worth remembering like this," Jessi tweeted.

She did not see merit in the Ultimate Fighting Championship (UFC), the sport of mixed martial arts, which got its start in Denver in 1993.[3] "I don't get the UFC," she tweeted on July 12. "Is the point of sport to [be] the first person to beat someone within an inch of their life?"

No, a real war would not have attracted Jessi. "She was always about people who were hurting or were in trouble or having issues," her mother, Sandy, said. "She fought the bullies. She was just kind. She was a very loving, compassionate, kind young woman. She had been her whole life."[4]

But this was not a real war. This was a tomato war. "May or may not have signed up to be part of a giant 300k pound tomato fight and beer fest tomorrow," she tweeted.

It was called Tomato Battle. One of its founders called it "the largest food fight imaginable."[5] The plan was devilishly simple. Some three thousand people would gather at Dick's Sporting Goods Park, a complex in Commerce City, Colorado. After a beer-fueled warm-up, they would spend an hour hurling rotting tomatoes at each other. The Tomato Battle would have music and a costume contest. The resulting mess—an ankle-deep tomato puree—was to be cleaned up and turned into compost.[6]

The park is a major entertainment venue in the Denver region. It is said to be the largest of its type in the world. It boasts twenty-four full-size, fully lit sports fields, twenty-two of them natural grass and two synthetic turf.[7] It is the home of the Colorado Rapids men's professional soccer team. In 2018 it hosted Gay Bowl XVIII, the annual fall tournament of the National Gay Flag Football League.[8] The park's naming rights were bought by Dick's Sporting Goods, the Pennsylvania-based national sporting goods company.[9] In 2018, following the Parkland public mass shooting, Dick's announced it would no longer sell assault-style rifles like the AR-15 in any of its more than 675 stores, and it destroyed those that it had left on its shelves rather than return them to the manufacturers.[10]

The Tomato Battle's most distant roots lie in an annual event called La Tomatina in the Spanish town of Bunol in Valencia. What started as a spontaneous quarrel in 1945 became a grand spectacle after several decades of alternately being banned and promoted by authorities. In the end, tourists spending pesetas (later euros) won. La Tomatina was elevated to tradition.[11] A more immediate precedent was the annual Colorado-Texas Tomato War. That contest erupted in Colorado in 1982 as "playful animosity towards tourists from Texas."[12] Combatants were "killed" by being hit anywhere on the torso by a tomato. The last person standing without being hit by a tomato won the war. The wounded were attended by medics administering Bloody Mary drinks. By some accounts, outnumbered Texas tourists resorted to makeshift forts and jeeps tricked out as tanks with papier-mâché armor and guns. In the early 1990s the war became "a victim of concerns about property owners' liability and keeping their insurance coverage."[13]

The 2012 Tomato Battle followed these playful martial traditions. The improbability of it all appealed to the free-spirited side of a complex young woman. The threshold questions were obvious to Jessi. "Questions: What does one wear to a 300k pound tomato fight? Do tomatoes stain? What are the odds I might end up injured?"

One candidate was a black T-shirt that Jessi's mother had given her. Jessi posted a picture of the shirt. This message was printed on the shirt:

Top 10 Reasons Hockey Is Better than Women:

1. In hockey, everyone likes it rough.

2. You only get 5 minutes for fighting.

3. "Puck" is not a dirty word.

4. You don't have to play in the neutral zone.

5. It's possible to score a few times a night.

6. When you "pull the goalie" nobody gets pregnant.

7. Missing teeth doesn't stop you from scoring.

8. You can always get new wood if your stick breaks.

9. The Zamboni gets to clean up the mess.

10. Periods only last 20 minutes.

In the event, Jessi wore a plain white, sleeveless top to the Tomato Battle. Reporting the contest as a combination sports journalist and war correspondent, she posted a series of pictures with running commentary. Smiling with two women friends before the battle ("Pre tomato fight."). The crisscrossing arcs of scores of tomatoes hurtling overhead in the heat of battle ("During tomato fight!!!!"). Tomato-stained combatants hurling tomatoes ("Absolutely. Disgusting."). And the three grinning survivors, none of them injured ("Aftermath of the tomato fight. Sweet Jesus.").

It was all in good fun. The friendly warriors left the field of battle soaked in the blood-red gore of pulped tomatoes.

A Scholarly Mask

On the evening of that day, July 7, 2012, a young man not so far away in Aurora, Colorado, was making the first of several dry runs through his meticulous plan to kill as many innocent strangers as he could.

James Holmes would not have impressed anyone as an "All-American boy." He had neither the burly physique nor the outgoing personality of Charles Whitman. But just as in the case of Whitman, there was nothing in James's public record—the part of his life visible to clerks sorting through government records—that would trip wires and send up warning flares. That profile might fairly have been described as one of an exemplary, if shy, scholar. But, like Whitman, Holmes was wearing a mask, and the secrets behind it leaked out to a few people. They did nothing of significance about what they knew.

"Jimmy" Holmes, as he was known to his family, was born in Scripps Memorial Hospital in La Jolla, California, on December 31, 1987—one day shy of five weeks after Jessi Ghawi was born.[14] His mother, a California girl like Jessi's mother, Sandy, was a nurse. His father held a PhD in statistics and was employed as a government statistician. The family moved around a bit—although not more than, for example, a typical military family—and some have suggested that the moves disturbed Holmes. But at least externally he seemed to be fine. "Old teachers and family friends," according to the *New York Times*, "recalled a nice, if socially awkward, boy who played card games and was interested in computers and science."[15] A classmate at Westview High School, from which he graduated in 2006, remembered James as "really sweet, shy. He didn't have any creepy vibe about him at all."[16]

Holmes was smart and applied himself. He was on the elementary school honor roll. He won a merit scholarship out of high school. He attended the University of California at Riverside, where in 2010 he was awarded a bachelor's degree in neuroscience. He graduated Phi Beta Kappa, with just under a 4.0 grade average and the highest academic honors. "He had the capability to do anything he wanted academically," a university official said later.[17] What James wanted was a PhD in neuroscience. He enrolled in 2011 at the University of Colorado (UC) in Denver to pursue that objective. UC waived tuition and granted him a generous scholarship.

James had no criminal record. His only interaction with law enforcement had been a speeding ticket. He had never been committed to any institution for psychiatric reasons. Although he had been to therapeutic counseling episodically since he was a child, none of that history was a matter of public record. Neither, of course, was his descent into a plan to commit a public mass shooting. After careful study, James had by July 7, 2012, selected his "kill zone," a specific theater within a multitheater complex in Aurora, Colorado. On that evening and on each of his subsequent dry runs, he went to the theater complex and bought tickets. He was gaming how to end up in the exact theater he had selected.

James was well-armed by then. He owned two Glock high-capacity semiautomatic pistols, a Remington shotgun, and a Smith & Wesson semiautomatic assault rifle. He bought all of these guns legally from federally licensed gun dealers in Colorado. They were required to and did pass him through the federal background check system. Each found him good to go.[18]

- On May 22, 2012, Holmes bought a Glock 22 .40 caliber high-capacity semiautomatic pistol from the Gander Mountain store in Aurora.

- On May 28, he bought a Remington Model 870 Express Tactical 12 gauge shotgun and ammunition at the Bass Pro Shops store in Denver.

- On June 7, he bought his Smith & Wesson M&P15 .223 caliber semiautomatic assault rifle, three thirty-round ammunition magazines, and .223 caliber ammunition at the Gander Mountain store in Thornton, Colorado.

- On July 6, he bought a Glock 23 .40 caliber semiautomatic pistol, targets, and ammunition at the Bass Pro Shops store in Denver.

In addition to his guns, Holmes bought and stockpiled in his apartment thousands of rounds of ammunition and an assortment of battle gear, including body armor and tear gas grenades. He bought these supplies through online vendors. Neither federal nor state law required these sellers to conduct a background check on Holmes. Before 1986, mail order sales of ammunition across state lines had been banned by the Gun Control Act of 1968. Anyone "engaged in the business" of selling ammunition was required to obtain a federal license and maintain records of ammunition sales. These restrictions were repealed by the Firearm Owners Protection Act of 1986, another strategic victory of the mobilized gun-rights movement.[19]

The following are representative examples of Holmes's online purchases.

- On May 10, Holmes bought two Clear Out Tear Gas Grenades online from BTP Arms.

- On June 28, he bought 2,050 rounds of .40 caliber ammunition (for the Glock pistols) and 2,250 rounds of .223 ammunition (for the Smith & Wesson semiautomatic assault rifle).

- On July 2, he bought from three different online outlets a half-dozen pieces of body armor, an ensemble to protect his entire body.

To some observers, Holmes would be yet another lamentable example of someone who should have been intercepted but had "slipped through" the National Instant Criminal Background Check System (NICS). Blaming human error serves the interests of many players in the national drama that follows public mass shootings. Gun-rights activists use such incidents to deflect attention away from guns to alleged bureaucratic incompetence and the ultimate futility of any screening system. Politicians get a free pass to avoid grappling with substantive issues and point the finger at some hapless minor official. And the news media have a click-bait rabbit to chase, a target for the smug attention of talking heads who all too often know little or nothing about the substance of the background check system, what it is capable of doing, and its structural limitations.

The NICS system is run by the FBI. It is supposed to screen potential gun buyers, save lives, and prevent injury by "not letting guns fall into the wrong hands."[20] In fact, however, Holmes and his ilk are not the result of error by some nameless, faceless bureaucrat. They are examples of the failings of a poorly designed, superficially constructed, and overworked bit of gun violence reduction theater. NICS is just about as effective at preventing public mass shootings as cigarette filter tips are at preventing lung cancer.

Which is to say, not at all.[21]

Armed and Troubled

The Fourth of July—the day Jessi posted about the Canadian woman who lived a life worth remembering—marked an anniversary. One year before, Sandy and Lonnie had moved Jessi from Texas to Colorado on that patriotic weekend. "We saw such growth in her in that year that it was amazing," Sandy says. "To see her blossom and bloom, and find what she really loved to do. And doing it with such gusto. She was very happy."

During the year that Jessi was blossoming, the formerly accomplished honor student and PhD candidate James Egan Holmes was wilting. His mind was growing over with thorny weeds and his soul was shriveling. One of the few girlfriends he had ever had and perhaps the only one he thought he loved had broken up with him. He was having serious academic problems.

Just as Charlie Whitman had done in 1966, James was keeping a diary, a spiral-bound notebook documenting his descent into hell with spiderish handwriting and crude sketches.[22] At first glance, the notebook is laughable, a pastiche of sophomoric ruminations on the meaning of life and death, love and hate. Those superficial observations would have earned its author a withering critique and a failing grade in any university-level introductory philosophy course. But upon closer examination of its content, the text is hair-raising. James wrote about his mental demons with the same "disturbingly clinical self-reflection" as did Charlie Whitman. At an identifiable point, however, Holmes makes a decision. His focus shifts from cosmic questioning to a boots-on-the-ground assessment of alternative scenarios for killing large numbers of people. By its end, the notebook has turned into a focused field manual, a disciplined, highly detailed tactical plan for committing mass murder.

"Insights into the Mind of Madness!"

"Insights into the Mind of Madness!" With that revealing phrase, James Holmes began his devil's diary. For the next several pages, the scrawled text wanders through Holmes's puerile exploration of the value of life. "Why does the value of a person even matter?" he asks himself. At one point, he seems to reject violence and specifically murder. "Violence is a false response to truth while giving the illusion of truth," he writes. "This is widely understood with murder being unjust."

But the sigh of world-weariness better fits Holmes's narcissistic sanctimony and studied ennui. "However, mankind hasn't found a better alternative & there is still mass violence, war, and unfortunately these forms of violence are misleadingly still justified," he writes in the next sentence. "I have spent my entire life seeking this alternative so that the questions of how to live and what to live for may be addressed."

Squads of psychiatrists and other mental health experts would later do forensic battle over the nature and quality of James Holmes's mental state.[23] An entire book plumbs its depths, and arrives at the "not very satisfying" conclusion that "we can't really replicate [a mind like Holmes's] because we can't see all of it."[24] Like Charles Whitman, James thought that there was something seriously wrong with his mind. But Whitman was wearing a lay person's blindfold. He could only stumble about in the dark, trying to lay his hands on the contours of his self-evident illness. James had the benefit of an honors degree in neuroscience and was a PhD candidate in a graduate program in which were taught courses with titles such as "Biological Basis of Psychiatric and Neurological Disorders."[25] He had the intellectual tools to articulate the results of his self-examination in terms of mental health science. Whether Holmes was technically correct or simply engaged in a "sort of a psychobabble version of 'The Devil made me do it,'" is a separate question.[26] Rightly or wrongly, he catalogued his ills under the rubric "Self Diagnosis of a Broken Mind." It reads like the table of contents of a psychiatric disorder textbook.

- Dysphoric mania.

- Generalized anxiety disorder/social anxiety disorder/OCD/PTSD (chronic).

- Asperger syndrome/autism.

- Schizophrenia.

- Body dysmorphic disorder.

- Borderline, narcissistic, anxious, avoidant, and obsessive compulsive personality disorder.

- Chronic insomnia.

- Psychosis.

- Trichotillomania.

- Adjustment disorder.

- Pain disorder.

- Restless leg syndrome.

For the next four pages of his diary, Holmes described in detail the basis of his self-diagnosis.

Behind the Mask

James slipped behind his mask at an early age according to the account of Dr. William Reid, a forensic psychiatrist who examined Holmes for the prosecution and later wrote a book about him. In James's preteen years, Reid writes, there appeared "important differences between some of his inner thoughts and his outward behavior." While James appeared to be a more or less ordinary, if slightly shy and reclusive, child, "seemingly ominous fantasies soon began to appear. Jimmy was thinking about killing people."[27]

It would be fruitless to try to connect this strand of fantasies to Holmes's eventually murderous behavior in 2012 as an adult. "Holmes himself is our only witness to them," Reid warns, and "memory is a fragile, changeable thing."[28] But we do know that Holmes's parents were concerned enough about him to refer him several times to psychological counseling as a youth, none of which resulted in a diagnosis of any serious problems. In later years, James's images of violent events—people dying and being killed—became more vivid and frequent. And by about January 2012, "James's emotional problems were finding more and more foothold in his inner life."[29]

At the prompting of his ex-girlfriend, James sought help at the UC health center. On March 16 he was seen by counselor Margaret Roath.

She wrote in her notes, "He says he wants to kill other people, but no one in particular and he has never done anything to harm others." Roath concluded that James had obsessive-compulsive disorder and that—his statement about killing people notwithstanding—he was not a danger. She referred James to Dr. Lynne Fenton, an MD who was the director of the student mental health clinic. On March 19 Roath emailed Fenton about Holmes. "He is the most anxious guy I have ever seen. . . . But, most concerning is that he has thoughts of killing people, although I do not think he is dangerous."[30]

Two days later, Dr. Fenton met with Holmes. According to Reid, James told her "of his recently increased stress and girl-friend problems, which he said made his obsessive symptoms (daily, intrusive, ruminative thoughts of killing) and behavioral compulsions . . . worse than ever." Holmes denied having any specific targets, and she concluded in her notes that he "appears not currently dangerous but warrants further understanding and following."[31]

Dr. Fenton continued to see James over the next several months. She prescribed and later adjusted medication for him. After an appointment on April 17, she made a note. "No evidence of imminent threat (I'm worried about HI much more than suicidal thoughts in this patient.)"[32] The abbreviation "HI" stands for "homicidal ideation," or the formation of ideas abut killing human beings. Fenton also arranged for joint consultations with James and another psychiatrist, Dr. Robert Feinstein.

In the meantime, James had begun buying his guns. Whatever dysfunction was going on in James's mind, his ability to work through murderous alternatives and construct a precise plan was demonstrably not impaired, a point a prosecutor would later drive home in James's criminal trial.

One part of Holmes's reaction to this latter counseling seems to echo Charles Whitman's wistful allusion to his lone session with Dr. Heatley. "He never actually told Fenton or Feinstein that he had begun acquiring weapons," Reid writes of Holmes. "A part of him believed, and a part of him *hoped*, that they somehow knew his thoughts and his plans without his revealing them."[33]

But, of course, they did not know his plans. Reid argues that they did not have enough evidence to commit Holmes involuntarily on psychiatric grounds. This is separate from the question of whether or not an effective threat assessment and intervention system would have intercepted

Holmes and his murderous intent. The bottom line is that, after all was said and done, no record retrievable by the NICS background check system and relevant to the question of whether James Holmes could legally buy or possess firearms was ever created.

There was nothing to catch in the NICS net.

A House of Cards—The National Instant Criminal Background Check System

It is fair to say that many Americans think that the NICS system is a kind of black box, a methodical inquiry that takes a deep dive into the background of anyone who seeks to buy a gun. The term "background check" itself implies the kind of scrubbing that one gets, for example, before being granted clearance to access classified documents or sensitive policy papers—the sort of review to which Sheriff David Clarke was subjected when he was being considered for a high-level position in the Trump administration. The failure of such a putatively thorough system to catch some signal of evil design might be reasonably chalked up to human error.

But this popular view of NICS overstates the nature, scope, and mechanisms of the system. NICS operates more like a credit card authorization at a gasoline pump. You insert your credit card at the pump and computers exchange rote signals. Did you pay your last bill? Have you reached your credit limit? Is there a hold on your account for some other reason? Similarly, NICS computers query selected databases in other computers to see if there is evidence that a prospective gun buyer falls into one of the classes of people who are barred by law from buying or owning guns, called "prohibited categories." Are they, for example, a convicted felon? Have they been involuntarily committed to a mental institution?

No agents go out and interview anyone, much less the gun buyer, as at least theoretically happens in the Canadian licensing system. The default favors the applicant. If no disqualifying data is found in the files available for search within a specified time limit, the transaction must be approved. There are other jokers in the NICS deck. Some of the proven indicators of a person's likely propensity for gun violence are not included in the prohibited categories. The files available for the computer check are often incomplete. Their quality varies widely from state to state, and some are not connected to the system at all. Studies have found only moderate evidence that the system—as it is presently designed and operated—has any preventative effect on suicides and gun crime generally. There is little to no evidence that the NICS system has been effective at all in reducing public mass shootings.

Arguments for and against Background Checks

Why have background checks at all? Ask that question of enough people and you will get a range of more or less informed responses, tempered in the fires of polarization. The rationales advanced in favor of background checks for firearms sales sort themselves into three basic categories: (1) common sense; (2) public health and safety; and (3) market intervention.

There are also those who oppose background checks on principle. They often cite absolutist views of the Second Amendment. And, predictably enough, John Lott brings his statistical black box to the issue. He argues that the current system is so flawed in operation that it is merely an imposition on law-abiding gun enthusiasts while allowing felons to regularly slip through its net. Lott relies on his computation of the number of "false positives"—instances in which the NICS computer incorrectly links two similar names and dates of birth, one a forbidden person and the other an innocent. These false positives, according to Lott, "stop law-abiding people from getting weapons that they might need to protect themselves and their families."[34] This half-baked red herring is merely a variant of the "slipped through the net" argument served up with a number-cruncher's cocktail. Since Lott himself in the same discussion suggests that the answer is to "really fix" the NICS system, his polemic need only be noted and kept in mind when considering how to "really fix" the system.

The three approaches in favor of background checks are not mutually exclusive, but they do imply different answers to such important questions as systems costs and how to allocate them between taxpayers and gun buyers.

The "commonsense" rationale is often advanced by gun violence reduction advocates. "There's really no debate here," former New York City mayor Michael Bloomberg wrote in support of extending mandatory background checks to all gun transfers. "It's common sense."[35] Appeals to "common sense" enjoy the benefit of a good organizing slogan with which people on the gun control side can identify and support without having to dig into the details of the NICS system itself. Its corollaries are truisms like, "You need a license to drive a car, don't you?" and, "If you really are law-abiding, you have no reason to fear a background check."

The public health and safety approach is more sophisticated. It aims at reducing risk by way of evidence-based analysis of specific factors that create risk. Philip Cook and Jens Ludwig described the rationale this way:

> People with serious criminal records or severe mental illness may reasonably be deemed at such high risk of misusing firearms that public-safety concerns take precedence over gun rights. While in practice it is impossible to keep all members of high-risk groups disarmed in a gun-rich environment, a selective prohibition may cause some reduction in gun misuse and save enough lives to be worthwhile.[36]

The third way to look at background checks is a form of market intervention, an economic strategy aimed at shifting the costs of gun violence from society at large to gun consumers and the gun industry. The theory underlying this view was described in a National Academy of Science report on improving research and data about firearms violence:

> Firearms are bought and sold in markets, both formal and informal. To some observers this suggests that one method for reducing the burden of firearm injury is to intervene in these markets so as to make it more expensive, inconvenient, or legally risky to obtain firearms for criminal use. As guns become more expensive to acquire or hold, it is hypothesized that criminals will reduce the percentage of their criminal careers in which they are in possession of a gun. . . . [These interventions include] taxes on weapons and ammunition, tougher regulation of federal firearm licensees, limits on the number of firearms that can be purchased in a given time period, gun bans, gun buy-backs, and enforcement of laws against illegal gun buyers or sellers.[37]

As noted above, these ways of looking at background checks are not mutually exclusive and all play some role in shaping gun controls. What people call "common sense" will likely always be a big part of creating public policy in a democracy, whether it's the result of practical observation in life or a synthesis of culturally inspired, subjective preferences. It is invoked on both sides of many issues. Public health and safety measures routinely guard against potentially harmful people, diseases, and products in other contexts, most prominently in the so-called war against terrorism and in standard inoculations. Our daily lives are staked out by limitations dictated by public health and safety concerns. No one argues for letting airline pilots fly drunk or impaired, or letting incompetent surgeons continue to butcher patients, or giving drunk drivers free passes to enjoy their alcohol and the road at the same time. Cost shifting is common in government programs. If we want to use a national park, we pay an entry fee, we pay gasoline taxes to maintain our highways, and state and local taxes to pay for schools. Why should the public at large and taxpayers in particular get stuck with the enormous medical and economic costs of gun violence?

The Sublime Indifference Doctrine

Looming over any rationale for gun buyer background checks are legal arguments inspired and sustained by continuing conservative strategic litigation contesting the constitutionality of any government obstacle between citizens and the guns they want. Professor Glenn Harlan Reynolds—described by Adam Winkler as "the conservative law professor who coined the standard-model terminology for the individual-rights view of the Second Amendment"[38]—wrote a law review article in 1995 in which he seized the absolute-right high ground. Addressing the "popular argument" that the cost of readily available guns exceeds their benefits, he wrote:

> My usual response to such arguments is that as a professor of constitutional law I am as sublimely indifferent to the question of whether the availability of guns leads to crime as I am to the question of whether pornography causes sexual offenses. In either case, the Constitution has spoken, and that is enough. Such consequential concerns may be relevant to, say, the question of whether to repeal the First or Second Amendments, but they should certainly have no role in how we interpret or apply them.[39]

Reynolds is more widely known in some circles for his blog, Instapundit. His reputation is that of a "contrarian" and a libertarian rather than of a traditional conservative. "I like to joke that I'd like to live in a world in which happily married gay people have closets full of assault weapons to protect their pot," he told the University of Tennessee publication *Quest*.[40] Reynolds has blamed mass shootings, including Parkland, on the failures of law enforcement agencies. "Law enforcement keeps failing, and people keep dying," he wrote in an opinion piece for *USA Today*, to which he is a regular contributor. The specific failure, he opined, is law enforcement's missing "red flags" raised by prospective mass murderers, despite "having lots of warning."[41] In another column during the 2016 presidential campaign, he advised that the best way to improve the news media's "lousy job of protecting American freedoms" was to elect a "white male Republican."[42] Reynolds has also suggested nuclear strikes on North Korea ("If they start anything, I say nuke 'em"),[43] and the clandestine murder of Iranian clerics and nuclear scientists.[44]

It's not clear whether Reynolds was writing as a contrarian, libertarian, or conservative in 2016 when he tweeted about demonstrators who had blocked a road in Charlotte, North Carolina. "Run them down," he suggested. Reynolds was suspended briefly by *USA Today* and Twitter. He later apologized for the tweet, which he claimed people "misunderstood." What he really meant to say was that "drivers who feel their lives are in danger from a violent mob should not stop their vehicles."[45] It is perhaps entirely coincidental that in 2018 a man in Charlottesville, Virginia, James Alex Fields Jr., did precisely what Reynolds said that he did not mean to suggest with the explicit language of his tweet. Fields did "run them down," killing one protestor and injuring many more at a notorious "Unite the Right" rally.[46]

Sublime indifference may work well for tenured sages expounding from the ivory towers of academia. But it plays rather poorly among the millions of Americans whose bodies and souls have been mutilated by gunshots, and among the millions like Lonnie and Sandy Phillips who wake up every morning to the pain of having lost a precious person to gun violence. In any case, the U.S. Supreme Court has explicitly rejected the doctrine of sublime indifference. Justice Antonin Scalia wrote in the landmark *Heller* case confirming the individual nature of the right to guns:

> Although we do not undertake an exhaustive historical analysis today of the full scope of the Second Amendment, nothing in our opinion should be taken to cast doubt on long-standing prohibitions on the possession of firearms by felons and the mentally ill, or laws forbidding

the carrying of firearms in sensitive places such as schools and government buildings, or laws imposing conditions and qualifications on the commercial sale of arms.[47]

Even so, this area of the law is still a work in progress. Litigants continue to challenge all manner of government restrictions on the sale and possession of guns, including some aspects of background checks.

History and Structure of NICS

No one sat down and designed the American gun control background check system as a logical and evidence-based mechanism for reducing gun violence. The federal system just grew, like a home that started out as a modest cottage but expanded into a large manor house as a succession of owners nailed additions onto the structure. State systems that can supplement the federal system range from nothing at all to several that are more comprehensive and more restrictive than the federal system. Given the current gridlock in Washington, gun violence reduction advocates are focusing on expanding and improving state systems.

The foundation of any background check system is necessarily the definition of what the system should check for, that is, the categories of people who are prohibited by law from buying or possessing firearms. The federal government first set out to do this in the Federal Firearms Act of 1938 (FFA).[48] The FFA was surprisingly precise. It made it unlawful for "any person who has been convicted of a crime of violence or is a fugitive from justice" to receive or possess any firearm that was shipped or transported in interstate or foreign commerce. (Possession by any prohibited person was deemed "presumptive evidence" that the firearms had moved in such commerce.)

The FFA defined "crime of violence" and "fugitive from justice" in detail, and in terms that are hard to quarrel with.

(6) The term "crime of violence" means murder, manslaughter, rape, mayhem, kidnapping, burglary, housebreaking; assault with intent to kill, commit rape, or rob; assault with a dangerous weapon, or assault with intent to commit any offense punishable by imprisonment for more than one year.

(7) The term "fugitive from justice" means any person who has fled from any State, Territory, the District of Columbia, or possession of the United States to avoid prosecution for a crime of violence or to avoid giving testimony in any criminal proceeding.[49]

As sound as its definitions were, the FFA had a major flaw. "While it was criminal for a Federal Firearms Licensee (FFL) to knowingly sell a firearm to any ineligible person, the FFL did not have to verify the eligibility of a prospective purchaser or even check the purchaser's identification," scholar James B. Jacobs observed in his book *Can Gun Control Work?*[50] This defect led Jacobs to conclude that the FFA was "another example of an inexpensive regulatory system that, in retrospect at least, seems mostly to have been for show."[51]

1968 was "the watershed year for gun regulation in the United States."[52] Acting in the wake of the assassinations of Sen. Robert Kennedy and Dr. Martin Luther King, Congress passed the Gun Control Act of 1968 (GCA).[53] That law modified and expanded the categories of prohibited persons. It also forbid FFLs to sell firearms to minors—defined as persons less than eighteen years old for long guns and twenty-one years old for handguns.

The GCA's new categories were broader and less precise than those of the FFA. They now included any person

(1) who is under indictment for, or who has been convicted in any court of, a crime punishable by imprisonment for a term exceeding one year;

(2) who is a fugitive from justice;

(3) who is an unlawful user of or addicted to marihuana or any depressant or stimulant drug . . . or narcotic drug; or

(4) who has been adjudicated as a mental defective or who has been committed to any mental institution.[54]

The felon disqualification now went far beyond the specifically violent offenses enumerated in the FFA. Fugitives now included any fugitives from prosecution for any crime, not just for violent crimes. And the category of "mental defective" was added, even though the term had no recognized meaning in psychiatry and could only be implemented by means of clarifying administrative regulations. Gun buyers were required to sign a statement swearing that they were not in a prohibited category or otherwise barred by law from possessing a firearm.

The GCA did not fix the verification flaw of the FFA. Although FFLs were required to check a person's age and residence by means of a photo ID such as a driver's license and obtain the signed statement of eligibility, they were not required to do anything else to ensure that the purchaser was in fact eligible to buy a gun. "Thus, if an ineligible person was willing to falsely swear that he was an eligible purchaser, he could easily buy a handgun from a licensed dealer, although he would be committing a crime in deceiving the dealer," Jacobs notes. "In effect, the act relied on an honor system."[55] To state the obvious, no honor system is likely to deter violent criminals.

In 1993, "after a tortuous legislative history, Congress passed and President Clinton signed the most important gun control legislation in 25 years . . . commonly known as the Brady Law."[56] The 1993 law required for the first time that a government determination be made of a purchaser's eligibility, independent of his sworn statements. The Brady law—sometimes also called the Brady Bill or the Brady Act—also mandated that an instant check system be in place within five years, after which the requirement of a mandatory waiting period would expire. This provision was hoped to be a legislative poison pill by those who opposed the law. They thought that technology was not advanced enough to meet that deadline. The NICS system was in place by the deadline, however.

Congress has added several categories of prohibited persons since 1993, most significantly persons who are subject to a restraining order for domestic violence, harassment, or stalking, and those with misdemeanor domestic violence convictions. Record keeping and sharing has yet to catch up with the system's requirements, however. As a result, "the background check mostly amounts to a criminal records check in state and federal criminal records databases."[57]

Does the Brady Law Work?

The Brady law "would seem, at first blush, to have been an amazingly effective law," Harvard public health scholar David Hemenway wrote in his book *Private Guns, Public Health*. "As the criminal-records database has become more complete and readily available to law enforcement officials, more and more prospective gun purchasers have been denied because they had criminal histories."[58]

In the twenty years after the law's enactment, more than two million ineligible would-be gun buyers—about half of them convicted felons—were stopped from buying guns from licensed federal dealers by the NICS background check.[59] And, except for spikes in 2016 and 2017, violent crime rates, including homicides, have declined steadily in the United States since 1993.[60] To proponents of the Brady law, its success seems self-evident. Stopping all of these bad people must have stopped the violent crimes and murders that some of them would have committed had they been able to get a gun.

"But is the Brady law responsible for all, some, or even any of these crime reductions?" Hemenway asked, and answered. "We don't know." The problem, Hemenway explains, is that rates of crime in the United States, and gun crime in particular, are volatile. They "move in waves or cycles, and there are no good models that explain those waves." Factors other than the Brady law—for example, the decline of crack cocaine markets—could have also affected crime rates.[61] Cook and Ludwig caution that evaluations based only on homicide trends "would mistakenly attribute to the Brady Act the effects of all of the other forces that were driving crime rates down over the 1990s."[62]

In 2000, two events related to this question occurred. President Bill Clinton told a news conference that "the Brady Bill is saving people's lives and keeping guns out of the wrong hands." And Cook and Ludwig published their scholarly evaluation in the *Journal of the American Medical Association*. "Our conclusion was less positive—we found no evidence of a reduction in the homicide rate that could be attributed to *Brady*. We also considered the possibility that *Brady* reduced the overall suicide rate, but found no discernible impact on that outcome either."[63] Other independent evaluations have arrived at similarly restrained conclusions. A RAND study of existing gun violence research evidence found that "available studies provide moderate evidence that dealer background checks may reduce firearm homicides."[64] With specific respect to public mass shootings, RAND found that there was only "inconclusive evidence for the effects of background checks on mass shootings."[65] The National

Research Council of the National Academy of Sciences observed more broadly that "there is not much empirical evidence that assesses whether attempts to reduce criminal access to firearms will reduce gun availability or gun crime."[66] It concluded that the existing evidence "is of limited value in assessing whether any specific market-focused firearms restrictions would curb harm."[67]

All of that said, it is crucial to note that none of these evaluations concluded that the Brady law is not working. Each simply points out that, given the difficulty inherent in finding and weighing cause and effect in violent crime, the existing evidence is not up to the task of conclusively demonstrating that the Brady law has or has not been effective. "In all areas of policy, it is often quite difficult to effectively evaluate the impact of particular laws," Hemenway wrote. "The evaluator is trying to contrast actual events to a counterfactual—that is, what would have happened had the law not been passed. The latter is in some sense unknowable."[68]

RAND carefully noted that it was evaluating the quality of evidence, not the actual results. "Rather than concerning how strong a policy's effects are, our findings concern the strength of the available scientific evidence examining those effects," its report cautioned. "Thus, even when the available evidence is limited, the actual effect of the policy may be strong."[69] In large part because the NRA and its cohorts have strangled independent government research,[70] the evidence available about gun violence reduction is not comparable to that of more intensively studied areas of social science and public health. "That is, in comparison to the evidence that smoking causes cancer, the evidence base in gun policy research is very limited."[71] Moreover, RAND pointed out that even a gun violence reduction policy with "small effects" may be beneficial and worth its costs. "For instance, a policy that reduces firearms deaths by just a few percentage points could save more than 1,000 lives per year. This kind of 'small' effect might be very difficult to detect with existing study methods but could represent an important contribution to public health and safety."[72]

What these cautious conclusions really argue for is not doing away with background checks, but doing the science to make sure that they are as effective as possible. This means more and better research about what drives gun violence in the first place, a closer look at existing categories of prohibited persons, and willingness to add people in other categories that strong evidence indicates are prone to gun violence. On the one hand, for example, although there is a laborious procedure through which persons with convictions for nonviolent felonies (such as embezzlement or tax evasion) can regain their right to buy a gun, it might fairly be asked why they are in the law in the first place. On the other hand, there is evidence that a record of crimes involving alcohol or drugs is a strong indicator, so why should that not be added as a disabler?

Fixing NICS—Problems and Improvements

Even if one assumes that the existing NICS screen helps reduce gun deaths, injuries, and crime by "keeping guns out of the wrong hands," its operation is most certainly impeded by two structural defects.

One is a matter of scope. Federal law only requires background checks be made on purchases from federally licensed gun dealers. But a large proportion of guns are acquired in private transactions, perhaps as much as 40 percent of all transfers. (These are sometimes called the "formal" and "informal" markets.) Unless there is a state law requiring a background check, these private sales from unlicensed persons can legally be made across a back fence, in gun shows, and even through the internet for strictly intrastate transactions. Jacobs concluded that "Brady's effectiveness is severely undermined by its failure to cover secondary handgun transfers, including those that take place at gun shows."[73]

The other is the problem of incomplete, poorly maintained, and untimely databases—the primary sources that NICS checks. A 2018 review of the current system by the Associated Press summed up the problem in two concise paragraphs.

> It's up to local police, sheriff's offices, the military, federal and state courts, Indian tribes and in some places, hospitals and treatment providers, to send criminal or mental health records to . . . NICS, but some don't always do so, or they may not send them in a timely fashion.
>
> Some agencies don't know what to send; states often lack funds needed to ensure someone handles the data; no system of audits exists to find out who's not reporting; and some states lack the political will to set up a functioning and efficient reporting process, experts said.[74]

Perhaps the most vexing problem with the current system—as the Giffords Law Center to Prevent Gun Violence noted—is that it does not include some types of people "identified by public health researchers as being at a significantly higher risk than the general population of being dangerous."[75] The center listed, described, and cited studies indicating some categories that should be added to the prohibited categories.

- Those who have been convicted of violent or gun-related misdemeanors.

- Those with a history of abusing alcohol or drugs.

- Those convicted of juvenile offenses.

- Additional people who have suffered from severe mental illness.

Finally, the NICS system focuses almost entirely on a static indicator, that is, an applicant's past status. Convicted of a felony, or not? Committed to a mental institution or not? It is not well-designed to capture, and has failed to capture, the dynamic changes in a troubled person's psyche and any steps that person may be taking to act upon violent fantasies. It has not proven, in other words, to be an effective threat assessment system. There was no background check at all in 1966 when Charles Whitman was sliding into carrying out his fantasy. And forty-six years later, the NICS background check system could not capture James Holmes's descent into violent madness.

In sum, the background check system could clearly be improved by extending it to cover all gun transfers, including private sales, by providing enough funding and incentives to ensure complete, accurate, and timely databases, and by rigorously examining and revising the categories of persons who are prohibited from acquiring or possessing firearms.

An All-American Rifle and Its Sporting Enthusiasts

So far as any of the evidence available to the American system for screening buyers of firearms goes, on the day that James Holmes bought his Smith & Wesson M&P15 he might have been just another one of the several million nonviolent, law-abiding men and women who love their AR-15–type rifles. "He had passed the background check," the part-time clerk who sold him the rifle later testified. "We had done all the paperwork. We rang him through our system, charge him out, I had a second check on the paperwork, and, at that point, all of our protocol is met."[76]

Check, check, and check.

Neither would there have been anything remarkable about James or his guns at the outdoor shooting range that he researched and chose as the place to learn how to shoot his new weapons. The Bryce Canyon Shooting Range is located in foothills just west of the town of Hot Sulphur Springs, which lies about ninety-five miles northwest of Denver.[77] It is closed every winter after the hunting season to protect big game and re-opens in the spring, usually in April. Because of warmer weather in 2012, the range reopened earlier, on March 22.[78]

On that day Jessi tweeted her approval of Sauce Hockey, a hockey sports clothing company that had raised funds for Jack Jablonski, a high school hockey player in Minnesota who had been paralyzed by an accidental crash during a game.[79]

> So @SauceHockey has raised over $40k for Jabs . . . THIS is why the hockey community is the best around.

On the same day she posted a more impish rhetorical question, characteristic of her humor, both provoking and self-deprecating at the same time.

> Should I be a zombie or a runner? I'm already a soul stealing ginger, might as well be a zombie and take bodies too.

Even though there are other ranges closer to Denver, James was willing to make the long drive to Bryce Canyon and back because the range was unsupervised, with relatively few users on weekdays. He visited the shooting range about five times that July. First he put up life-size silhouette targets. Then he shot hundreds of holes in them. He practiced until he could smoothly empty dozens of rounds from his assault rifle and quickly reload it with his high-capacity magazines.[80] James did not grow up in a gun-loving family. He was not a marine. But what he taught himself at the Bryce Canyon Shooting Range was enough to do the job he had in mind. His killing machine was amateur friendly.

Nearly twenty-two million Americans participated in target shooting in 2012, according to a 2016 report by the National Shooting Sports

Foundation (NSSF), the trade association of the gun industry and related hunting and shooting businesses.[81] Seventy percent of those shooters were male. A 2015 NSSF report based on a sample survey estimated that more than fifty-one million Americans participated in target or other kinds of sport shooting (such as hunting) in 2014.[82] According to the same report, about 27 percent of target shooters who were eighteen to thirty-four years of age were new to shooting. As a twenty-four-year-old-male "newbie," James fit right into the target sports demographic.

What about his Smith & Wesson M&P15 semiautomatic assault rifle? Would that—should that—have attracted suspicion? Not likely. The AR-15 is, according to the NRA's scriptural proclamation, "America's rifle."[83] It may not be quite all that. But whatever else one might think of the AR-15 rifle or its clones, or however much one might wish to ban or severely restrict their sale and possession, there is anecdotal evidence and corroborating data that indicate it is widely owned and popular in America.

Visit the ordinary venues of the American gun culture (gun stores, shooting ranges, and gun shows), and you are all but certain to see examples of the guns themselves and the many accessories sold in the lucrative aftermarket. Part of the gun's appeal is that it can be easily customized by the individual owner with accessories such as sights, grips, lasers, and flashlights. "Today, gun enthusiasts consider the AR-15 the Erector Set of firearms."[84] Surf the gun-oriented media (popular magazines, industry catalogs, websites, blogs, and video posts) and you will find an abundance of repetitive but thoroughly enthusiastic commentary about the pleasures of owning and shooting the modern sporting rifle and its practical applications as a weapon of self-defense or resistance to tyranny. Like Bannerman's catalogs, there is an endless stream of banal assault rifle "gun porn" for every taste.

Chris Cerino, a former federal law enforcement officer and firearms instructor in Ohio, is among those who agree with the NRA. "It's an icon," he told the *New York Times*. "It's a symbol of freedom. To me, it is America's rifle."[85] The *Dallas Morning News* profiled several other AR-15 enthusiasts in a piece headlined "Sticking to Their Gun" on July 1, 2016.[86] One of them was Daley Laurel, who owns "an Olympic Arms AR-15 dipped in the pink and purple 'moonshine muddy girl camo' pattern. She shoots it while wearing a pair of pink goggles and pink ear protection."

"It's like riding a roller coaster, but different," Laurel told the newspaper in an email. "You don't feel scared anymore."

Another of those profiled was Colion Noir, who as the producer and star of a web series, "Noir," sponsored by the NRA, achieved note as "a newer, civilian shooter who brings a metropolitan and minority perspective." Noir's "pride and joy is displayed front and center: an AR-15 style HK MR762. The scope alone cost thousands of dollars, he said." Another was a veteran, Ben Allen, whose "favorite is a customized rifle with red, white and blue detailing and a Texas flag etched into the lower receiver."

It would be hard to outdo the enthusiasm for the rifle shown by "a group of worshippers wearing bullet crowns and toting AR-15 rifles" who gathered together at the World Peace and Unification Sanctuary in Newfoundland, Pennsylvania, to hold a "commitment ceremony" for about 250 couples. The ceremony was held scarcely two weeks after the mass murder at the Marjory Stoneman Douglas High School in Parkland, Florida. Reportedly, the rifles "were meant to represent the biblical 'rod of iron' referenced in the Book of Revelation, used by God's representative to dominate his enemies."[87]

No one knows how many Americans own AR-15–type rifles (or any other type, make, or model of gun for that matter). The federal government is forbidden to keep any kind of gun ownership registry. Although individual federally licensed gun dealers keep paper copies of the forms that prospective purchasers fill out for the federal background check, this information is nowhere centralized. Information on the form that is transmitted for the background check system administered by the FBI must be destroyed before the next day in the case of all approved transactions.

Probably the most reliable source of data is the NSSF. Although some suspect the NSSF of having a degree of hucksterism on the one hand, on the other it is in the business of providing reliable data to the gun industry itself. In any case, no one else has invested the time and effort to parse through industry production and import records to tease out the numbers. A declaration filed in a federal court case in 2017 by James Curcuruto, NSSF's director of research and market development, discussed the prevalence of "modern sporting rifles," which he defined as "a category of firearms comprised primarily of semiautomatic rifles built on the AR- and AK-platforms."[88] Curcuruto's declaration is sobering.

Figures from the Bureau of Alcohol, Tobacco, Firearms and Explosives (ATF) Annual Firearms Manufacturers and Exports Reports (AFMER) show that between 1990 and 2015, United States manufacturers produced approximately 9,309,000 AR-platform rifles for sale in the United States commercial marketplace. More than fifty different manufacturers produced these rifles, including Smith & Wesson, Colt, Remington and Sig Sauer. During these same years, figures from the U.S. International Trade Commission (ITC) show approximately 4,430,000 AR- and AK-platform rifles were imported into the United States for sale in the commercial marketplace. In 2015 alone, more than 1.5 million of these rifles were either manufactured in the U.S. or imported to the U.S. for sale.[89]

These figures suggest that by 2018—after adding another three years' supply—some fifteen million "modern sporting rifles" have been brought to the U.S. civilian gun market since 1990, and still counting. Some quantity of these guns would have been bought by some of the eighteen thousand law enforcement agencies in the United States. Others would have been exported legally or illegally. But even allowing a generous deduction for those cases, a fair and conservative estimate is that there are at a very minimum ten million semiautomatic assault rifles or modern sporting rifles in civilian hands. This is a dimension that the architects of any legislative ban must reckon with.

Who owns all of these guns? Curcuruto's filing included a profile of the owners of this class of firearm, based on an NSSF online survey published in 2013. The typical owner of a modern sporting rifle is "male, over 35 years old, married with a household income above $75,000 and has some college education. Approximately 35 percent of all owners of modern sporting rifles are current or former members of the military or law enforcement."[90]

Other people seek out modern sporting rifles, as well. People like James Holmes.

Midnight in Aurora

Jessi greeted the morning of July 19, 2012, with a series of humorous tweets. "How do people know where they want to be in 14 years?!" she asked emphatically. "This is absurd to me! I don't even know where I want to be in the morning!!" She followed this with her own answer. "Just kidding, yes i do. I wanna still be in bed in the morning #laaaazy."

Later on she riffed on an old friend who was visiting from San Antonio. "My bro is 6'2 166 pounds," she wrote. "He has hyperthyroidism. He can't gain weight. I just watched him eat 8 tacos. Why didn't I get this 'problem'?" As evening approached, she turned her attention to plans to go to the movie theater. "Never thought I'd have to coerce a guy into seeing the midnight showing of The Dark Knight Rises with me," she tweeted.

And then the very last tweet of her young life. "Of course we're seeing Dark Knight. Redheaded Texan spitfire, people should never argue with me. Maybe I should get in on those NHL talks . . ."

CHAPTER SIX
ONLY IN AMERICA

"**M**y biggest fear is that my idealism will fade beyond the walls of Bucknell," graduating senior Daniel Oates wrote in the Bucknell University yearbook in 1977, "where convocation addresses, philosophy classes and grade point averages can no longer shield me in quite the same fashion."[1]

On July 19, 2012, thirty-five years later, Daniel Oates was chief of police of the city of Aurora. Jessi Ghawi and Daniel Oates never met. But they shared two things in common. When Daniel was Jessi's age, he too set out to blaze a path into journalism. And they shared a love for ice hockey. To her it was the prime sport to immerse herself in, write about, and talk about as representing everything good and noble about athletic competition. To him it was not only a competitive and physically demanding sport. It was a great way to burn off the accumulation of private stresses that come with the loneliness of command.

"I play ice hockey, and I had a late night game," Oates, now chief of police in Miami Beach, Florida, recalls of that Thursday night. "I had a beer and I went to bed at about 11:30."[2]

He had two daughters. One of them had gone out that night to a midnight showing of the Warner Brothers' latest Batman movie, *The Dark Knight Rises*. The last of a trilogy, it enjoyed great reviews and was opening at several theaters in the area on July 19.

Within hours, Daniel Oates and his idealism would be tested in the fire of a uniquely American hell. He was about to be involuntarily inducted into what he calls "a perverse and growing community of chiefs."

The Great Adventure

Oates was born in Hackensack in northern New Jersey, but says he "totally identifies as a New Yorker, the Yankees and all that." His parents, John and Louise, had moved from New York City to New Jersey to raise a family. Daniel was the middle of five children. It was a family with a strong moral center and an unrelenting emphasis on the value of education. "My parents both grew up during the Depression in New York City, terribly poor. Their ticket out of poverty was education. We grew up hearing every day about the importance of education, and hearing stories about their poverty growing up."

Another powerful influence in young Daniel's life was the family's Catholic faith. "The church played an important role in our lives. It was the social center, Catholic Youth Organization basketball, and everything else that came with it."

Daniel was an eagle scout at age fourteen. Growing up, he heard stories about his father's athletic prowess. John Oates had played basketball at City College of New York under the legendary professional player and college coach Nat Holman. "He came off the bench one night in the Garden, scored seventeen points, and became a starter."

The Oates children did not disappoint their parents on the education front. All five of them went to college and all five earned graduate degrees. "In fact, my mother went back to school later in life and got a master's degree in education. After five children, she became a schoolteacher. James Comey [the former FBI director] was one of her students." The route Daniel took to his two graduate degrees and professional acclaim was, however, less than orthodox and may have thrown his parents "for a loop for a while." But "they were comfortable that I was serious and industrious in everything that I had done, and that I was on a great adventure, and it worked out."

It started out conventionally enough. Daniel graduated from Saint Joseph Regional High School in 1973 and enrolled in Bucknell University. "It was the height of the Watergate scandal," Oates says. "I was really taken by all that and all I wanted to be was a reporter." Oates was an intern at a variety of newspapers while he was in college. He was editor of the Bucknell newspaper and the yearbook. Although the market for beginning journalists was tough when he graduated in 1977, Oates got four job offers. "The one I took was as an entry-level general reporter at the Atlantic City *Press*."

He worked at the *Press* for one year. "It was the year that was the run-up to the opening of the first casino, Resorts International. It was a really exciting time to be in Atlantic City and I had a blast." If something sounds familiar about that, it is. A few years later, Donald Trump bulled his way into the casino business in Atlantic City, took a shellacking, but emerged with millions in hand under questionable circumstances and a trail of sordid business failure. "Though he now says his casinos were overtaken by the same tidal wave that eventually slammed this seaside city's gambling industry," the *New York Times* wrote in an in-depth review of Trump's disastrous venture into the casino business, "in reality he was failing in Atlantic City long before Atlantic City itself was failing."[3]

But Daniel Oates was in love and he wanted to get married. His future wife worked in Manhattan. They decided it made more sense for him to move to the city than for her to move to south Jersey. He got a job with Hearst Magazines, working as a copy editor for *Popular Mechanics*. Editing articles written by other people "about woodworking and auto mechanics and crap like that" was too far a remove from his writer's soul. Oates was disenchanted with the publishing business and growing restless. His sister was an attorney with a prestigious law firm in Manhattan. He was impressed with the ambience whenever he visited her at her office. Daniel decided to follow her example and pursue the legal track. He got far enough along to be accepted by St. John's University Law School.

In the meantime, Fate played a card. While in his car, Oates heard a radio ad announcing that the New York Police Department (NYPD) was hiring for the first time after years of freezes and layoffs. "I was 24 years old and never ever thought of being a police officer," he told the *Michigan Daily* newspaper. "I took a test on a whim, and they kept calling me back. I became more intrigued with the idea."[4] The NYPD offered him a job with "New York's finest" in 1980, just days before he was scheduled to attend his first class in law school. Oates cancelled his enrollment at St. John's "and began the great policing adventure."

His parents were, to say the least, surprised by their son's decision. "With their interest in education, I don't think they saw their middle son becoming a cop." But Daniel Oates was smart, hardworking, focused, and good at police work. His career took off like a rocket.

"I had an incredible policing career. I was a street cop in the eighties, when crime was out of control. Crack hit the street in '84. There is no more fun than to be a street cop when crime was out of control. It was a blast, catching bad guys. And then I became an executive in the early nineties, just before Bill Bratton arrived and changed the world of American policing. And I was present for all of that."

Oates wasn't just present. He was pursuing his graduate studies while he was on the job. He won a master of science in administration from New York University and a law degree from New York Law School. This graduate education helped propel him into two important posts in the police department's executive ranks. By the time he retired from the NYPD after twenty years of service in 2011, Daniel Oates had headed the department's legal bureau—essentially in-house counsel to a law enforcement corporation with fifty thousand employees—and commanded its intelligence division. He topped that off with a post as deputy commander of the Brooklyn South precinct and confidential adviser to the police commissioner.

When he was a younger officer, Oates dreamed of becoming chief of police of a village somewhere on Cape Cod, where he had vacationed with his family for as long as he could remember. As he matured into the NYPD's executive ranks, he raised his aim. "My aspirations got a little bit bigger than just a small town in Cape Cod."

Oates won his first appointment as chief of police in Ann Arbor, Michigan. He started in August 2001, weeks before the September 11 terrorist attacks on America. During those intervening weeks, as a natural part of what Oates calls "Precinct Commander 101," he had already reached out to Ann Arbor's significant Muslim community. After the terror attacks, he organized a public meeting of the city's religious leaders. The Muslim leaders thus had a public forum with the police chief and the mayor—open to the news media—to denounce the 9/11 attacks and distance their religion from the actions of the terrorists. "We never had any anti-Muslim behavior in our community," Oates says, in part because of that proactive outreach and community healing.

In November of 2005, Oates moved on to become chief of police in Aurora, which he describes as a "really, really challenging and interesting town." Economics, migration, and the writ of history have shaped this independent suburb of about 350,000, abutting the south and east of Denver. "It has all the classic challenges of urban poverty, probably 20 percent of the city is below the poverty line in the northwest quadrant of the city, and then as you move south and east, you get million dollar homes," Oates says. "It's divided into one of the best school districts in the state and also one of the most challenged school districts in the state." Oates brought all his executive skills to meeting the city's traditional policing challenges. He loved the community and its "really, really good police department."

Something else was on the chief's mind in late 2010—the problem of the active shooter, or public mass shooter.

"The reality is that you don't really believe that it's going to happen to you in your department, you just don't believe it, the odds are overwhelmingly that it's not going to be you," he says. "But if you are a responsible law enforcement leader you train as if it is going to happen."

Chief Oates directed that a significant amount of his department's training time be devoted in 2011 to the problem of the active shooter.

Against All Odds

When Charles Whitman started shooting from the Texas Tower in Austin on August 1, 1966, there was no organized police response. It fell to individual patrol officers and an armed civilian volunteer to make a plan, take action, confront the shooter, and stop the killing. There was no such thing as a "special weapons and tactics team" (SWAT) anywhere in America, much less in Austin. "Tactical situations, like the University of Texas sniper, had to be resolved by patrol officers who had little, if any, tactical training, and even less equipment available to them," Dr. J. Pete Blair and other experts write in their book, *Active Shooter: Events and Responses*. "Hostage situations, barricaded gunmen, and high-risk warrants were all handled by the patrol officer on the street."[5]

Contain and Wait—The Rise of SWAT

In the 1960s and 1970s, American law enforcement was confronted with an increasing number of large-scale, violent incidents that exceeded the ability of patrol officers to effectively respond. Urban riots accompanied by gunfire, looting, and the arson of entire city blocks, massive demonstrations in which protestors forcefully confronted law enforcement officers, standoffs with armed hostage-takers, and the fact that "criminals were becoming better armed through the availability of large-capacity firearms after the Vietnam War" all made it clear to police administrators that "the nature and complexity of tactical situations were changing."[6]

Another current was flowing through law enforcement. "The push for increased education, training, and professionalism for the police, coupled with the rapid integration of new equipment and technologies into the policing profession, began a new era of specialization in police functions."[7]

Among the new specialized units were tactical teams, generally called SWAT teams, whatever their formal organizational designation. Police agencies in large cities like New York, Los Angeles, and Houston created full-time units. The only functions of these teams were to train for and respond when called to critical incidents such as hostage situations, barricaded suspects, and snipers. Smaller agencies trained and equipped selected patrol officers to serve in part-time teams. They assembled and went into action on an as-needed basis.[8] SWAT teams were well-equipped. "Weapons and equipment such as automatic weapons, rifles, heavy body armor, flashbangs, tactical shields, helmets, and tear gas were standard equipment for SWAT teams."[9] The federal government supplied many of the new teams with surplus military equipment, such as armored vehicles.

Not everyone welcomed the rise of SWAT teams and the mission creep and abuses that some have engaged in. In *Rise of the Warrior Cop*, author Radley Balko documented the militarization of police forces and asked, "Are today's police forces consistent with the principles of a free society?" He concluded that it is "difficult" to say that they are. "Police today are armed, dressed, trained, and conditioned like soldiers."[10]

The rise of SWAT teams and other specialized units in the 1980s gradually eroded the role and responsibilities of officers on the beat. Patrol officers were no longer expected to confront public mass shooters like Charles Whitman on their own. Their role became one of containing the threat and waiting for the SWAT team to arrive. This protocol became known as the "Four Cs"—contain, control, communicate, and call SWAT.[11]

What seems in retrospect an obvious downside of this protocol was that "tactical operations are historically a very slow process from start to finish." An assessment and decision must first be made that the situation truly warrants calling out the SWAT team. Then the team members must be notified and assembled. Once the team arrives at the location, its members must put on their specialized gear, gather intelligence, relieve patrol officers, and brief superiors. "Depending upon the area and time of day, this process can take as little as 30 minutes or as much as several hours."[12]

In many places, the SWAT culture evolved to one "conditioned to a slow, methodical response" in which teams were "unable to work or uncomfortable working in dynamic, quickly changing environments such as an active shooter event."[13] There were disturbing instances where "instead of calling and waiting for SWAT to arrive, the quick action of patrol officers could have saved the lives of innocent people."[14] In July 1984, for example, a man armed with an Uzi semiautomatic assault rifle and several other weapons took over a McDonald's restaurant in San Ysidro, California. Patrol officers arrived within three minutes of the first call for help. Following the "Four Cs" protocol, they called SWAT and waited outside, listening as the shooter fired 257 rounds of ammunition, killing twenty-one people and wounding nineteen others. A SWAT sniper killed the shooter seventy-seven minutes after the massacre started.

After Daniel Oates took command of the Aurora police department, he regularly attended interdepartmental meetings with other chiefs in the Denver area. The subject of responding to active shooters came up from time to time. When it did, Oates was struck by what he describes as a "never again" attitude among the other chiefs. Many of them had been in midlevel ranks—sergeants and lieutenants—of the many police agencies that responded to the mass shooting by two students at Columbine High School in Littleton, Colorado, on April 20, 1999. These officers had borne the brunt of criticism leveled by a public outraged by the consequences of the Four Cs protocol at Columbine.

Critiques of the law enforcement response to the Columbine school shooting ignited major changes across the country in the police protocol for training and responding to public mass shootings.

Waiting at Columbine

After planning their attack and gathering weapons and explosives for a year, the two students who attacked Columbine High School in 1999 intended to open their assault by setting off a series of homemade bombs. They set timers on bombs inside the school to go off at 11:17 a.m. Then they went outside and waited in the school parking lot. They planned to ambush students fleeing from the building after the bombs exploded. The bombs failed to detonate, however, and at 11:19 a.m. the murderous pair started shooting students in the parking lot.[15] They then headed into the building, briefly exchanging fire with a school resource officer and a sheriff's deputy at 11:24 and 11:26 a.m. There was no more shooting from law enforcement until some of them entered the building shortly after noon.[16]

"Every cop had been trained for events like this," David Cullen wrote in his book *Columbine*. "Protocol called for containment . . . 'Setting up a perimeter,' they called it. They would repeat the perimeter phrase endlessly that afternoon."[17] Meanwhile, the attack inside on students and teachers continued unchecked. "Gunfire was audible to the first officers and continued through the arrival of hundreds more," Cullen wrote. "Deafening explosions kept erupting inside the school."[18] Officers were arriving at a rate of half a dozen every minute, eventually representing thirty-five law enforcement agencies.[19] Those hundreds of officers acted just as they had been trained to do in such an incident.

"[N]one entered or attempted to enter the school in pursuit of the gunmen shooting innocent people there," according to Blair. "SWAT had been called and this was a situation that a SWAT team should handle under the existing protocols."[20] A twelve-member team was assembled from three of the responding police agencies. It entered the school at 12:06 p.m.—forty-six minutes after the shooting started.[21] Almost three and a half hours later, at 3:30 p.m., officers found the two shooters in the library. Both were dead, having committed suicide with their guns.[22]

In the course of their uninterrupted spree, the two had killed thirteen innocent victims and wounded twenty-four others. America was faced with the horrifying fact that its children—even those attending well-regarded suburban schools—could be murdered without warning by other children wielding weapons designed for war.

Public criticism erupted. Focused on the delay in stopping the shooting and the fact that some of the injured were left unattended during the delay, the consequences of the tragic episode were widely blasted as a law enforcement failure. "Looking back historically since the creation of SWAT teams, the law enforcement profession had conditioned the patrol function to fail in an active shooter situation like Columbine," Blair wrote. "Not only was there very little or no tactical training provided to patrol officers to respond to this type of event, but also what training was provided reinforced the concept of containment and calling for SWAT teams to handle critical situations."[23]

In the wake of the uproar, law enforcement "finally woke up" and agreed that (1) some situations can't wait for SWAT; (2) patrol officers need some level of tactical training; and (3) in addition to that training, first responders need the authority and equipment to effectively stop an active shooter.[24] Training for patrol officers was overhauled with the goal of stopping the killing, a process that continues today, incorporating lessons learned after every public mass shooting. "Modern day active shooter training standards and tactical philosophies do not suggest officers run into active shooter situations with complete disregard for their personal safety," Blair explains. "To the contrary, officers today generally are better trained, equipped, and prepared to face a violent adversary than ever before."[25]

The new proactive approach has its own problems and presents difficult choices. The faster response and engagement is more dangerous for responding officers, according to a report by the Police Executive Research Forum (PERF), an independent nonprofit located in Washington, D.C. "Patrol officers who quickly move to confront an active shooter face a high-likelihood of being shot themselves."[26] An example is the death of Ron Helus, a veteran sergeant of the Ventura County Sheriff's office in California. When a gunman opened fire at the Borderline Bar & Grill in Thousand Oaks, Helus was one of two officers who arrived on the scene first. "They were prompted by their training that changed after the Columbine High School massacre: Don't wait," reported the *Washington Post*. "Confront the shooter." Helus was shot multiple times and died in the hospital.[27]

There are also questions about how much training and of what kind is appropriate for patrol officers. "Specialized teams such as SWAT units receive complex tactical training in how to respond to dynamic situations with many moving parts," PERF observed, "It is difficult to shrink this type of training to an abbreviated, short-course format suitable for all line officers."[28]

At Chief Oates's direction, every patrol officer in Aurora got about twelve hours of active shooter training in 2011. "Aurora PD has a phenomenal training section," he says. "We included live fire and classroom exercises. A big piece of that was that you go into a place where people are shot, and you still have to look for the threat first."

But there was a bigger question, bigger than what law enforcement agencies were doing to respond to public mass shootings. What was being done to stop them from happening in the first place? Was America just going to accept Columbine and what came after as just another part of its culture?

"When Columbine happened, it was like, whoa, this is really, really bad," Sandy Phillips recalls. "I remember protecting my kids from that knowledge. I think we all said, somebody has got to do something, and we were assuming that our government would do something to protect its citizens. We went about leading our normal lives again very quickly, because my kids were little and they needed attention, and I wasn't paying attention to the fact that nobody was doing anything about what happened in Columbine."

The Dark Knight

Batman first appeared in *Detective Comics* in 1939. Since then the familiar costumed character—also known as the Caped Crusader, the Dark Knight, and the World's Greatest Detective—has become a global icon and a reliable moneymaker for a range of entertainment industries, including comic books, television series, motion pictures, and a universe of costumes, action figures, other toys, and themed commercial products orbiting around the core productions.[29]

The Batman character and his backstory have morphed through dozens of creative variations, each shaped by the mood of the times and crafted by the vision of successive ranks of artists, writers, and directors. From his original dark origins as Bruce Wayne, the orphaned son of a wealthy socialite couple shot down in a street robbery by a two-bit criminal, Batman has wandered through periods of satire, comedy, square-jawed rectitude, and back again. Originally pursuing a vow to cleanse the mythical city of Gotham of its criminals—aided in part by their fear of the batlike costume he dons for action—Wayne and other personifications have battled with pulp fiction thugs, extraterrestrial beings, science-fiction adversaries, and even a few whimsical opponents. In the twenty-first century, director Christopher Nolan took Batman back to his darker, brooding roots in a series of three films that became known as the Dark Knight trilogy.

No mere action-figure, crash-bang, simple entertainment, the trilogy evoked metaphysical musings among critics and set box office records. *National Catholic Register* critic Steven D. Greydanus, for example, thought that the trilogy could be "fruitfully considered as an extended comic-book riff on the story of Abraham and God's judgment on Sodom in the Book of Genesis." It raised, he thought, recurring questions. "Is there hope for Gotham City? Are its people worth saving? Is salvation even possible? Are there good people here, or is there only corruption and amoral self-interest destroying itself?"[30]

The Dark Knight Rises, the last film in the trilogy, was set for release in July 2012. The run-up was full of strategic hype and commercial opportunism. "The current superhero glut may have something to do with the human appetite for tales of good and evil," *New York Times* film critic Manohla Dargis opined. "But there's no question that the corporate appetite for bigger returns is insatiable."[31] Warner Brothers presented a montage of scenes from the film in April 2012 at CinemaCon, the theater-owner convention, held that year at Caesars Palace in Las Vegas. The production company hoped to broaden the base of theaters showing the film on its release. The snippets "played well to the crowd, with loud hoots and hollers."[32] The following month, the *New York Times* ran a fluffy feature piece on the Specialists, a company in SoHo that supplies prop guns to movie and television productions in New York and much of the East Coast. Gun manufacturers, it reported, were "keen to know" the company's owner in hopes of getting their guns placed in films because "the power of movies to ignite firearms sales has been well established."[33]

With a few exceptions, *The Dark Knight Rises* got great reviews. Dargis enthused that Nolan "has completed his postmodern, post–Sept. 11 epic of ambivalent good versus multidimensional evil with a burst of light." She saw parallels in contemporary life in which "politics of partisanship rule and grassroots movements have sprung up on the right and the left to occupy streets and legislative seats." Perhaps this moment was like the darkest hour before the dawn that the Dark Knight brought to Gotham.[34] A few critics who panned the movie were attacked so angrily on the aggregate review site Rotten Tomatoes that it suspended user comments on critics' reviews.[35]

Dargis was not the only commentator who saw the politics of polarity in the film. Right-wing radio voice Rush Limbaugh perceived conspiratorial partisan mischief in the name of Batman's prime adversary, Bane. At the time that the movie was released, the 2012 presidential election campaign was in full swing. Barack Obama's opponent, Mitt Romney, was under attack for his connection to the corporate-raiding, private equity firm Bain Capital.[36] "Do you think that it is accidental that the name of the really vicious fire breathing four-eyed whatever it is villain in this movie is named Bane?" Limbaugh asked his audience.[37] Limbaugh was either ignorant of or did not care about the fact that the character Bane had been an opponent of Batman's since 1993, almost twenty years before the 2012 presidential campaign. The improbable dimensions of a conspiracy among comic book artists and Democratic politicians going back that far, forecasting not only that Romney would be nominated for president but that his affiliation with Bain Capital would become a campaign issue, would confound even the most determined partisan in a less polarized and more rational era.

A Fiery Redhead and Her Bro'

Jessi Ghawi was a "huge" Batman fan, Sandy says. And like Chief Oates's daughter, several thousand other fans in the Denver metropolitan area, and tens of thousands more who would stream to more than four thousand theaters in America that night, Jessi wanted to see *The Dark Knight Rises*. She was determined to be at its midnight opening in an Aurora movie theater complex the night of July 19, 2012.

Brent Lowak had been a close friend of Jessi's since she was thirteen or fourteen years old. "I guess you would say they dated for a very short time," Sandy Phillips says. "But they were more like brother and sister."[38] When Jessi tweeted about "my bro'" eating eight tacos earlier in the day, she was referring to Brent, not her biological brother, Jordan. The two young men had something in common besides their affection for Jessi. Jordan was a firefighter and an emergency medical technician, or "EMT." Brent was studying to become an EMT.

Lowak was in Aurora that day because of one of those circumstantial threads that weave together Jessi's story. A year earlier, Brent helped the Phillips move Jessi to Denver over the 2011 July Fourth weekend. "She and I went out ahead of time and he drove out with a moving truck a day or two behind us so we could get into the apartment and paint it," Sandy recalls. "She wanted a certain paint color on the walls. So, she and I did the painting and got everything ready. Then he came in with the furniture and helped move her in."

The thread of circumstance began its sinuous weave after the 2011 move. "Brent was supposed to fly back from Denver. He had a ticket from Southwest. But he decided instead to drive the truck back to Texas and save his ticket for something else later. That's why he went out the next year, in 2012, because he had one year to use the ticket and he would lose it if he did not use it."

Sandy was also planning to visit Jessi that month. "I was going to fly out the following Tuesday, and I almost changed my flight to fly out with Brent. Then I changed my mind. I thought, they haven't seen each other in a year, they deserve to just enjoy each other's company and have fun. So I didn't go."

Having fun for Jessi and Brent included going out together to see *The Dark Knight Rises*. Just before leaving for the theater, Jessi talked about gun violence with her boyfriend, Jay, who was in Canada. "Someone had been shot Monday, Tuesday, Wednesday, and Thursday here," Jay later told the *Toronto Sun*. "We were talking over Skype about how horrible it was."[39] When she went to the theater, Jessi was wearing a red Canadian hoodie that Jay had given her.

She and Brent took their seats in the middle rows of Theater 9 at the Century 16 Multiplex and waited for the movie to begin. Jessi was an avid user of social media, so she bantered with friends while they waited. One of those friends was sports journalist Jesse Spector, who had tweeted that he was not going to see the movie that night. Spector shared their exchange with the *New York Daily News*:

"You aren't seeing it tonight?!" she typed.
"Nope," Spector said.
"psh. Loser!" she jabbed.
"Which is why you're tweeting now and not at the movie?" Spector joked.
"MOVIE DOESN'T START FOR 20 MINUTES," Ghawi said.
"A real fan would be in a better time zone," Spector said.[40]

Jessi's last exchange of the evening was probably with her mom, Sandy, who was having a sleepless night in San Antonio. It was after midnight. July 20, 2012.

"I woke up and texted her and asked if she was still up. She texted me back from the movie theater," Sandy recalled. "The last thing she said to me was 'go get some rest, can't wait for your visit. I need my momma.' And I wrote back, 'I need my baby girl.'"[41]

Not if, but When

J. Pete Blair, one of the four authors of *Active Shooter*, is a professor of criminal justice and the executive director of the Advanced Law Enforcement Rapid Response Training Center at Texas State University. The center, known by its acronym ALERRT, has trained thousands of law enforcement officers in active shooter response. It works closely with the FBI, which promotes the training to law enforcement agencies and provides instructors to work with ALERRT's own staff.

Blair writes about two different mind-sets with which a law enforcement officer might approach the possibility of being involved in an active shooter event, the "if/then" and "when/then" attitudes.[42] He argues that an "if/then" attitude is destructive because it leads to denial and false hope. Denial says, "I can't believe that this is happening." False hope says, "I hope I can make this shot." Better, he says, is the "when/then" attitude. "'When' makes it a foregone conclusion that he or she will one day be faced with this situation and must therefore prepare for it. When it happens, the mind-set will be, 'I am ready, send me.'"[43]

When it happens, the responder's first two goals should be "stop the killing" by neutralizing the shooter, and "stop the dying" by giving emergency medical aid to the wounded.[44] But that's not so easy as it may sound. Even if the shooting has stopped and a shooter is down, police need to be sure that there are no other perpetrators. "Police have to do a systematic search before they can say the scene is secure," Blair told a PERF summit on active shooters. "It may take hours and what's happening during that time? People who have been shot and wounded are bleeding out and dying." And that means that "it falls upon our first responders who are inside the scene, the law enforcement officers, to provide immediate lifesaving care to people," either by stabilizing them or by getting them immediate transport to medical care.[45]

"When" arrived for Chief Daniel Oates sometime around 12:45 a.m. on the morning of Friday, July 20, 2012. He did not know at that moment that the killing had already stopped. The challenge for his officers was to stop the dying.

"I had just drifted off to sleep and Terry Jones, the deputy chief who had the duty that night, called me," Oates recalls. "He said there's been a shooting at Century 16, I'm not sure what's going on, but it sounds like several people have been shot. I'm headed in, you better head in too."

Oates quickly got dressed and set out in his car, lights flashing and siren wailing, for the eight- or nine-minute drive to the theater complex.

"I'm listening on the radio, and I know it's big," he says. "But I'm comforted that my people are completely in charge, in other words, it's clear that the supervisors are giving good instructions over the radio. I can't really understand what's going on, because I'm coming into the event late, but I'm comforted to know that there are good people on the radio, I recognize the voices, and they are handling it well."

It was "chaos" when Oates got to the theater. The parking lot was jammed with police cars, emergency vehicles, people fleeing, and others drawn to the scene. "I parked my car some distance away because it was so chaotic, and walked up."

He saw immediately Mike Dailey, another police lieutenant. "Mike said to me, 'We have ten dead in the theater. We have one guy with an AR and a gas mask and we're looking for a second gunman.'"

There was in fact no second gunman. But reports of there being more than one gunman are common in public mass shootings. People are in shock, disoriented, and hear and see things from different places and angles.

"I remember being so stunned that I said to Mike, 'Mike, you've got to give that to me again,'" Oates says. "'Are you saying that there are ten dead in the theater?' And he said, 'Yes.' I remember being absolutely stunned."

As it happened, a large number of officers were on duty at the moment the call for help came in. "We had some extra coverage on because it was a summer night and we were experimenting with a summer task force," Oates recalls. "So there were an extra sixteen cops working, we had narcotics working the same hour as the summer task force, and we had SWAT working the same hours. So we had healthy coverage." It was also just at the change of shifts. Officers going off duty and officers coming on duty were in the process of debriefing and handing off responsibility.

"Had this shooting occurred twenty minutes later, some of those cops would have gone home. But every single one of them responded to the theater. Everybody went, and we needed everybody."

The responding officers, Oates says, did exactly what they were trained to do.

"After the shooting, I spent at least forty-five minutes with every cop who was working that night, and got briefed on what they saw and did," he says. "Many of them said that the training from the year before came back and kicked in. And a big piece of that was that you go into a place where people are shot and you still have to look for the threat first. You know that you are going to have to step over the dead, you're going to have to step over the wounded, to get to the threat."

In the crush of the moment, Oates had forgotten that his daughter had gone out to see *The Dark Knight Rises*.

The Fifth Phase

In the world of violence prevention, "risk" and "threat" are two different but related concepts. Assessing the risk of violence is a longer-term and more generalized problem that does not necessarily focus on any given individual. What is the risk that polarized, mobilized, and armed ideological groups will take violent action? Threat assessment focuses on the more immediate problem of protecting an individual or institution from the current threat of a violent attack. A necessary corollary is identifying and intercepting specific persons who intend to make such an attack.

Theorists and practitioners of the relatively new science of threat assessment agree roughly on several basic principles. The devil is in the details of translating these principles into effective real-life models to intercept public mass shooters before they start killing people. This requires not only scientific expertise. Constitutional and legal guardrails must be observed or changed. Law enforcement agencies, courts, leaders of public and private institutions, and the public at large must be educated—what concerning behavior to look for, to whom to report it, and what to do about it.

The November 2018 Thousand Oaks shooting again provides an object lesson. The gunman in that public mass shooting was a veteran who may have been suffering from PTSD. He lived near his mother's home.

His mother's neighbors reported several occasions when they heard shouting and sometimes gunfire from inside the house. In April 2018, sheriff's deputies responded to such a complaint and engaged in an hours' long standoff, during which the officers drew their guns. After the confrontation was resolved, mental health specialists talked to the subject. "They determined that he was not an immediate danger to himself or others and that he could not be involuntarily taken to a mental hospital."[46]

No one took advantage of California's "Gun Violence Restraining Order" law, commonly known as a "red flag" law, which prevents people deemed a danger to themselves or to others from possessing a gun. Triggering the law requires a family member or law enforcement official to file a petition with a court. It is possible that neither the police nor the family even knew about the 2014 law. "I know from personal experience that whether law enforcement knows about it really depends on the jurisdiction," Allison Anderman, managing attorney at Giffords Law Center to Prevent Gun Violence, told VICE News. "I think that implementation has been a struggle in California."[47]

In September 2018, only two months before the Thousand Oaks shooting, Governor Jerry Brown vetoed a bill that would have expanded the law to allow teachers, professors, principals, coworkers, and employees, as well as mental health professionals, to petition for a gun removal order. "We talk all the time about taking guns out of the hands of the wrong people," one sponsor said. "This is exactly what that does." But Brown bowed to the argument of gun-rights advocates that the law would have denied gun owners their due process rights. "I think law enforcement professionals and those closest to a family member are best situated to make these especially consequential decisions," he wrote in his veto message.[48]

One of the emerging principles is that static variables—a person's specific psychiatric diagnosis or criminal history—are "robust predictors of general violence risk over time." On the other hand, dynamic factors—what a person is doing or saying now, such as yelling and firing guns in one's mother's home—"are most salient in the assessment of short-term risk of violence."[49]

Another generally accepted principle is the idea of a "pathway to violence."[50] Experts have constructed a number of different but roughly similar models describing the stages of this pathway. Some models articulate two parallel paths: what is going on in the inner world of a person moving along the path, and what warnings in the person's behavior may be observable by others in the external world around the subject.[51] "Warning behaviors are not linked to a particular psychiatric diagnosis but instead focus on accelerating patterns of concern. . . . They can be observed whether the attacker is mentally ill or not."[52]

Susan Riseling, then University of Wisconsin police chief, discussed the question of early detection at the PERF summit. "The key is information sharing," she said. "People become concerned about a fellow student, or a co-worker, or a neighbor. To put the pieces together, we need to share information."[53] Riseling also presented her studied conclusions about the five phases an active shooter goes through along the pathway to violence:

- "First, shooters seem to fantasize or are obsessed with other shooters. . . . Phase 1 is the fantasy phase, where they fantasize about what they can do."

- "The second thing they do is plan. . . . This is a highly premeditated action."

- "The third thing they do is prepare. It takes time for a shooter to acquire guns, ammunition, in some cases Kevlar or IEDs, and figure out how to pull all that together."

- "The fourth stage is practice. . . . They go to the location and study where they will park, where the doors are, whether doors are locked, the floor plan, and so on."

- "Then you have the fifth phase. Some call it the Event Horizon; I just call it implementation."[54]

James Holmes had methodically worked his way down the pathway, passing the stations of each of the first four phases. He had "leaked" information about his fantasy and clues to his progress to several people, including a mental health counselor, a psychiatrist, and even his former girlfriend. He recorded all of this progression in his notebook.

As midnight arrived, July 19 turned into July 20, and hundreds of innocent moviegoers settled in to watch *The Dark Knight Rises*, Holmes reached his "event horizon." He threw a tear gas grenade into Theater 9, pulled a trigger, and fired the first of 235 bullets that would rip into his helpless victims.[55]

A Farewell Prayer

"Call 911!" Jessi shouted when the first shots were fired. After she was hit several times in the legs, Brent Lowak said, her tone changed to one of pained screaming. Even though he was also shot, he applied his medical training and tried to stop the bleeding in Jessi's legs. Bullets continued to hit Jessi. When her voice stilled, Brent looked up and saw blood in her hair and evidence of a grievous injury.

One of the high-velocity bullets fired from the Smith & Wesson M&P15 semiautomatic assault rifle had struck Jessi on the left side of her face. The high-velocity round had realized the terrible wounding potential for which it was designed. It had blown away half of her face and much of her brain.

When Sandy described this wound in testimony before a Senate committee, she simply placed her left hand over the left side of her face to indicate its magnitude.

Brent realized from his EMT training that Jessi could not survive such a wound, even though she was still gasping for breath. He said a prayer over her.

"I just gave her the best sendoff I could," he said.[56]

Sandy and Lonnie's baby girl was gone.

Two Phone Calls

When Chief Oates arrived on the scene, he made two phone calls right away. "The first was to Jim Yacone, special agent in charge of the local FBI office," Oates recalls. "I said, 'Jim, I don't know if this is happening simultaneously all over the country, but I need to be coordinating with you, because this is big, and it could be, it could be a terrorist attack.' I was still considering that possibility."

The second call was to Aurora city manager George "Skip" Noe. "Can you imagine being a city manager and getting that call? I'll never forget it. He says to me, 'Okay, Dan, I understand. You manage the incident, and I'll keep the electeds off your back.' It was exactly what I wanted to hear."

It was just about this time, maybe a bit later, that two other phone calls were made.

One was to Chief Oates.

"Sometime around 1:20 it suddenly hits me that Natalie, my daughter, went to the same opening, but at the other major theater complex in town," he says. "I realized we better notify every police department in the Denver Metro area that this occurred, and that all the theaters where this movie was being premiered should be checked. That's when it hit me. I was just about to call, when my wife called me and said, 'Don't worry, Natalie's safe.' I remember feeling guilty that I hadn't thought about Natalie sooner."

The other call woke up Sandy Phillips in San Antonio.

When her phone rang, Sandy assumed that Jessi was calling to tell her about the movie. But it was not Jessi on the line. It was Brent Lowak.

For a moment all Sandy could hear was Brent's labored breathing and chaotic sounds of terrified people screaming in the background. Sandy asked Brent what was going on.

"There's been a shooting," he said. "It's random."

Sandy asked Brent if he was all right.

"I've been shot twice," he answered.

Sandy could feel the panic rising within her.

"What about Jessi?" she asked.

"I think Jessi's been shot twice, too," he said.

"Please tell me she's not dead," Sandy pleaded.

Brent just said two words.

"I'm sorry."

Sandy collapsed, sobbing, screaming, struck down by the horrible news that her beautiful, funny, loving young daughter had been ripped from life, torn forever from her friends and family. No more funny tweets. No more penetrating observations about hockey. No more sassy, loving exchanges with her mom.

Nothing but grief-stained memories would be left.

Stopping the Dying

"Our officers went directly toward the threat first," Chief Oates says. "They went directly to Theater 9. The suspect was immediately caught in the rear parking lot. Then subsequent teams formed up and went through the complex looking for any other bad guys. Then they went through a second time and a third time."

"It was horrendous," Officer Justin Grizzle, one of the first on the scene, later testified. "It was a nightmare. It looked like a war zone."[57]

Floors ran with blood, so much blood that one officer later testified that he almost slipped on it and fell down. Walls and seats were splattered with gore. Grizzle had to step over the body of a dead child. The film played loudly on and fire alarms screamed throughout much of the original response.[58]

There were wounded everywhere. Some of the injured had crawled out the back door. Because the parking lot in the front of the theater was jammed with cars and over a thousand people who had fled the theater, officers began taking the wounded out the back door and into the rear parking lot. It was then and there that a young police sergeant, Stephen Redfearn, made a command decision that made another change in police protocols.

"The story of our shooting and the lesson for our profession is to evacuate the injured by patrol car if you have to," Oates says. "Everybody with a potentially survivable gunshot wound lived, and that was a direct result of the transport of twenty-seven critically wounded by patrol car. And the story behind that is young Steve Redfearn."

Redfearn had called at least ten times for ambulances to transport the critically wounded in the back. None came.

"So Redfearn makes a decision to throw them in patrol cars and start sending them directly to the hospital," Oates explains. Redfearn himself testified that he made the decision, "quite honestly, out of desperation in what I thought was people passing right in front of our eyes."[59]

"That decision by that young sergeant, Steve Redfearn, is the critical decision of the entire night," Oates says. "It saved lives. And the number one finding of the after-action report was that that decision saved lives."

Redfearn's decision became the police version of "load and go" in the race with the Golden Hour clock.

Officer Aaron Blue found Jessi and took her to the hospital in his car. "Every time she moved she stopped breathing," he told the court.[60] Sandy is deeply grateful to Blue. "That was a comfort. I didn't want to think about my baby lying in chalk," Sandy later said.[61]

Imagine a World

Well-meaning people often say at this point when they hear stories of victims and survivors of public mass shootings, "I just can't imagine . . ."

Well, try, some survivors have said. Just try.

Try really hard to imagine that horrific moment when volleys of bullets fly into scores of innocent people. Try to imagine that you are there. Try to imagine that you are Sandy or Lonnie Phillips, or one of the thousands of others who have lost loved ones in mass shootings.

Ask yourself, Is this what we are at the end of the day? Are thoughts and prayers and memorials and half-staff flags all that America and Americans can do? Have we, as a society and a culture, tangled ourselves into a knot of polarized debate about gun rights, and itchy-fingered self-defense, and fear, and cheap partisan victories? Have we only taught ourselves more learned helplessness?

Or can we rally to change?

Lonnie and Sandy Phillips decided that they would throw themselves into the gun control movement to make a difference and bring about change. What they did not know then was that, although a few high-profile national gun control organizations regularly got attention after a public mass shooting, there was virtually no on-the-ground movement behind the talking heads and press releases of these organizations. Not only that, they were to learn in a painful way, gun control organizations had no idea how to use the potential of victims and survivors to build a real movement. Some of their leaders even thought that, beyond dutiful service as a grieving backup chorus at press conferences and hearings, victims and survivors were more trouble than they were worth.

CHAPTER SEVEN
THE RIGHT NOT TO BE SHOT

O n May 23, 2014, a bitter, mentally troubled young man went on a rampage in Isla Vista, California. He murdered six innocent victims and left fourteen others injured. One of the people he shot to death with his Sig Sauer P226 9mm high-capacity semiautomatic pistol was twenty-year-old Christopher Martinez.[1] On the next day, the heartbroken young man's father, Richard Martinez, spoke at a news conference. He posed a question that cut to the heart of the American debate on gun violence.

"They talk about gun rights," he said. "What about Chris's right to live?"[2]

The question resonated with Jonathan Lowy, the director of the Brady Center's Legal Action Project in Washington, D.C. Lowy has spent over twenty years in courts all over America, challenging gun industry practices and defending gun control laws. So he and Kelly Sampson, one of the project's staff attorneys, wrote a law review article that was published in the *Georgetown Journal of Law and Policy*.[3]

"'America's First Freedom' is not the right to firearms," they argued. "[I]t is the freedom that the Founders, in fact, announced first: the right to life, liberty, and the pursuit of happiness. The right to life—or to live—is protected by the Constitution and is the bedrock principle on which our government and civil society are founded."[4] The authors summed up their point:

> In sum, there is constitutional relevance to the question posed by Richard Martinez, and by the ever-growing list of gun violence victims. Americans do enjoy a right to enjoy a club in Orlando, Florida; to watch

a movie in Aurora, Colorado; to go to church in Charleston, South Carolina, or temple in Oak Creek, Wisconsin; to meet one's elected representative at a strip mall in Tucson, Arizona; to go to work in Washington, D.C., Minneapolis, Minnesota, or Kennesaw, Georgia; to ride a bus in Chicago; to teach or attend a college in Roseburg, Oregon, or Blacksburg, Virginia, or a high school in Littleton, Colorado, or an elementary school in Newtown, Connecticut—without getting shot and killed. When considering the breadth of the RKBA [right to keep and bear arms], courts must minimize infringement on individuals' right to live and to public safety.[5]

Lowy does not have at his disposal the light-industrial law factories of the conservative strategic litigation complex. Generously funded, these legal mills crank out volumes of law review articles. The articles are intended to be cited by sympathetic judges as "authority" to support pro-gun opinions finding an almost unrestricted right to possession of any gun, at any time, by anyone. There is no equivalent of the NRA on the gun control side to hand out generous grants to worker bees churning out ideological pamphlets garbed in a thin cloak of scholarship.[6]

But, as an intellectual challenge, Lowy's article is a sword in the stone. It addresses directly the fundamental cultural questions underlying the gun control debate. Who are we Americans? What is the sum of American culture? And more specifically, what do we ultimately stand for if the formulary enshrinement of one fiercely ideological right diminishes the most basic of all human rights—the right to live?

Sandy and Lonnie Phillips would meet Jonathan Lowy in Washington after they were induced to go to work for the Brady organization. The result would be financial and emotional disaster for the Phillips. In the view of many observers, the tragic episode left a festering blemish on the face of the Brady organization.

The tale fits perfectly the cynical adage that no good deed ever goes unpunished.

Blood, Tea, and Crumpets

In the early 1990s the husband of a young woman who was murdered during a public mass shooting on the West Coast testified—while holding his infant daughter in his lap—before several committees and subcommittees of the U.S. Congress about the impact of the shooting on his family. The bereft husband grabbed the media's attention during one hearing when he held up a picture of his late wife. Camera operators swarmed like bees on honey to the well of the hearing room to take photos and videos of the witness holding that picture. The chairman of the subcommittee leaned back in his chair, covered his mouth with his hand, and muttered to the staff attorney sitting behind him, "Don't ever have that guy at one of my hearings again."[7]

The media was paying too much attention to the wrong person. The grieving husband was slicing into the chairman's chances of getting a fifteen-second clip on the nightly news, or a photo in the next morning's newspapers.

Later in the 1990s, a survivor of gun violence made a presentation at the annual summit of several gun control organizations in Washington. When the survivor finished the talk, a senior official of one of the gun control organizations at the summit turned to the top official of another organization and said sarcastically, "Next year these people can have their own summit—in the McDonald's across the street."[8]

The survivor was "too emotional," and definitely not qualified to sit at what another gun control expert once called "the grown-up's table."

These real-life snippets illustrate a dark side of what Professor Kristin Goss dispassionately calls the failed "rational-national," expert-leader model that national gun control organizations have followed throughout most of their history.[9] For a variety of reasons, the leaders of those organizations not only did not mobilize the grassroots assets of victims and survivors, they affirmatively rejected such an on-the-ground approach. Their strategy was all about inside baseball in the big leagues of Washington. Victims and survivors had their place. They were useful as sympathetic witnesses and talking heads at press conferences. But they too often did not understand big-picture policy or the "sophisticated strategy" of inside-the-Beltway politics, much less the arcane details of social science and epidemiological studies supporting gun control. They were tiresome, emotional baggage when the real political work had to be done.

The lack of accountability to a base of active grassroots supporters had another destructive effect on relations between gun control leaders and the politicians that they were supposedly lobbying or educating. At times, the game to the gun control leaders appeared to be more about getting a coveted invitation to the White House, or a first-rank chair at a "policy meeting" at the Justice Department, or standing right behind the Speaker of the House while the cameras rolled, than it was about actually getting anything done or holding political leaders' feet to the fire. These glittering moments of "access" help drive fund-raising.

In mid-June of 2009, for example, Sarah and Jim Brady visited the White House. They met with Robert Gibbs, the new president's communications director. They had a short visit with President Barack Obama himself. Mrs. Brady's emailed report of the meeting shocked members of the board of the Brady organization, the gun control group that she guided to prominence after her husband was shot in the head during a failed assassination attempt on President Ronald Reagan in 1981. Taken in full, the email report provides a textbook example of calorie-free Washington-insider tea and crumpets, an opportunity that some of its outraged recipients thought was wasted:

> The visit to the briefing room was fun and very nostalgic—lots of old friends—the entire visit was great—I've never had that kind of service in all the years of visiting the White House—parking on West Exec.—total run of the place—a very nice visit with Gibbs—the two comparing stories—and then Gibbs told us the President wanted us to stop over on our way out—so we had a five minutes or so with him in the Oval office. He was very gracious—then on our way out we ran into Joe—Vice President and an old friend—so you might say it was a perfect visit.

So far, so good. A perfect visit. It just doesn't get much better in Washington than parking on West Executive Avenue—a closed street on the grounds of the White House—and talking directly with the president and the vice president. One minute is enough to deliver a message. Five minutes is time enough for a determined activist's thesis. But then came a shocking curve ball over the home plate of inside baseball.

> I never brought up the gun issue—as I know that our presence there was a huge reminder of what we do. I think now I can get us into [sic] see others through Gibbs.
> Joe [Biden] did say he was doing what he could—he brought it up and asked what the President had said—I responded that I hadn't brought it up that it was just a meet and greet.

> I believe this was the best strategy as I think both Gibbs and the President appreciated not being put on the spot upon our first meeting.[10]

This strategy would most likely have resulted in an angry internal revolt had there been a grass roots, and had its members learned of the meeting—which they most certainly would have given the reaction of some of those who got this email, forwarded to them by then Brady-organization-president Paul Helmke about twenty minutes after Sarah Brady sent it to him. The Brady organization had no such grass roots.

If this insider "meet and greet" strategy worked, if anybody in the Obama administration got the hint of an unspoken "huge reminder" or felt that they were then or ever "on the spot" during his first term, it certainly did not show. On the contrary, a May 2009 op-ed by *New York Times* editorial board member Dorothy Samuels—published just one month before Jim and Sarah Brady visited the White House—excoriated the Democrats' "timidity about standing up to the National Rifle Association." She blamed the "paralyzing myth" and "erroneous conventional wisdom" that the 1994 federal assault weapons ban had cost the Democrats control of the House of Representatives. In fact, Samuels wrote, "there were other major factors in the Democrats' 1994 loss, starting with perceived Democratic arrogance and corruption" and including "unhappiness with Mr. Clinton's budget, [and] his health care fiasco." Moreover, she noted, the Republicans' 1994 national campaign-organizing document—the "Contract with America"—did not mention guns at all.[11]

Two years later, the White House had still not gotten the hint. On March 15, 2011—two months after Representative Gabrielle Giffords was shot in the head at a public mass shooting—"the nation's leading gun-control activists took seats in Room 4525 at the Department of Justice," according to the *Washington Post*. This was the so-called grown-ups' table. An assistant attorney-general "went around a long conference table soliciting views from representatives of the major advocacy and law enforcement groups." (Political insiders call this form of superficial engagement "stroking.") But one person in the room kept his silence. He was Steve Croley, "the White House's point man on gun regulation policy." His silence, the newspaper noted, "echoes the decision by Democrats to remain mute on guns as a national issue. . . . Democrats have no plans for serious gun-control initiatives, and the Gabrielle Giffords tragedy, as heart-rending as it was, hasn't changed their minds."[12] *Tactical Life* magazine ("We deliver quality content produced by and for serious firearm enthusiasts") approvingly posted the news report on its website a month later.[13]

Two weeks after the political stroking at the Justice Department meeting, the *Washington Post* published an op-ed by Sarah Brady, in which she lamented that the "reluctance of congressional Republicans—and many Democrats—to support effective gun restrictions made it excruciating to watch history repeat itself outside Tucson in January." But, Brady concluded optimistically, "President Obama has begun the conversation."[14]

Whatever the conversation was that President Obama supposedly had begun, it was sotto voce. It changed nothing. On the day before the November 2012 presidential election, in the interim between Aurora and Sandy Hook, "gun-control crusaders" were counted by the *Washington Post* among the "nudgers, buttonholers and prodders" whose hopes were dashed because "they couldn't get the presidential nominees from either major party to embrace their passions as election-season centerpieces."[15]

Not present at the conversation among old friends and insiders were Lonnie and Sandy Phillips and millions of others like them, a powerful dynamo of victims and survivors that had never been turned on, never fired up, and in fact had been consigned to cold storage by the experts of the "rational national" approach.[16]

Rational National

Polarization has certainly made the politics of gun control difficult. But why should America's national schism have benefitted only one side, the gun-rights side, of the debate? Is there something organic within the issue itself, an imbedded sociopolitical virus that makes futile any attempt at progress? On the other hand, if gun control is not inherently doomed to fail, why have national organizations devoted to the issue made such little progress in reducing gun violence and public mass shootings in particular?

Kristin Goss examined in scholarly detail both of these questions and concluded that the problem is not a virus-infected patient, but doctors prescribing the wrong medicine. Her book is an issue-specific complement to the work of scholars who have charted the American political slide into polarization. "The contemporary gun control campaign, which began to coalesce in the early 1970s," she writes, "coincided with the beginning of a decades-long decline in popular trust in the federal government, the discrediting of the government-led social policies of the 1960s, and the erosion of key allies such as federated women's organizations and mainline Protestant churches."[17]

Goss maintains that most of the conventional arguments that gun control is futile "are at best incomplete and at worst flat-out wrong."[18] She argues that "the opponents of gun control have accommodated themselves better to the stubborn realities and political inconveniences of a fragmented, federalist system." In contrast, the strategies of gun control supporters "may have been rational in a policy sense but were politically naive."[19] The result is that there is no real gun control "movement."

The Usual Excuses of Conventional Wisdom

Raise gun control at any social gathering, Goss writes, and you are likely to hear the conventional wisdom that "gun owners and their main interest group are culturally and politically invincible, while the pro-control majority are indifferent or otherwise unmotivated."[20] Goss analyzed the principal arguments for futility and found them singly and collectively an inadequate explanation for the lack of a true gun control movement. While critiquing these excuses, she convincingly points out that the same conditions faced other more successful social movements.

Intensity Gap

At the top of the list is the claim that "anti–gun control forces care passionately enough to organize but gun control supporters do not." Goss dismisses this excuse. "While some gun owners are intense—as anyone who has seen them at gun control hearings can attest," she writes, "there is no reason to believe that they are more passionate than those affected by gun violence: the mothers, fathers, siblings, and spouses who show up to plead for gun control laws and in some cases devote their lives and fortunes to volunteer groups lobbying for the cause."[21] Sandy and Lonnie Phillips are examples of the latter case.

Gun-rights groups appear to be more committed because they are better organized at their roots, not because of an intensity gap. Goss demonstrates that successful mass movements don't require that everyone be committed to their agenda. But they do require "a committed core of activists and a wider circle of individuals who will show up at demonstrations and take part in other ways." The NRA has such individuals in every congressional district in America. Commitment to a cause does not necessarily precede organization, but "good organization will nurture commitment."[22]

Racism

Another often-advanced theory is that "white Americans do not feel any personal connection to gun violence or do not think anything can be done to change what they may see as minorities' proclivity for violence."[23] While Donald Trump's election exposed a strong vein of racism in America that was not apparent to most people when Goss wrote her book, her observation that "in fact, lots of whites are personally affected by gun violence" remains a strong rebuttal to the argument that subtle white racism breeds indifference.[24] Even though racial attitudes still exist, millions of white survivors and victims have a very real personal connection to gun violence reduction.

Attention Cycles

Could the problem be the "cyclical" nature of gun violence? Does interest wax after a spike and wane when things calm down? In the first place, gun violence in America is endemic and not cyclical at all. What may appear to be cyclical are the more spectacular and well-publicized events, such as public mass shootings. Given the recent and apparently lasting spike in mass shootings, even that phenomenon can hardly be called "cyclical" any more. Goss points out that other mass movements either were born or "took off" even as the problems that they addressed were declining—liquor and tobacco consumption were actually declining in America when movements to regulate them became stronger.

And, in any case, "the endemic level of violence alone should produce enough primary and secondary victims to fill movement ranks."[25] Not every victim or survivor cares to get involved in gun control activism. Some even oppose it. But the number of people living in America who have been shot or who have lost loved ones to gun violence—after the country's decades of world-leading gun violence rates—should be enough to kickstart any movement, given the right leadership.

Even if only a small proportion of those victims and survivors get involved, there could be tens of thousands more activists in every state of the union than have been effectively mobilized today.

The Futility of It All

The "futility" theory has two parts, Goss writes. One is that the gun-rights faction is so politically strong that gun control can never win. The other is that even if gun control measures are passed, they may not be effective in stopping gun violence. As to the first point, Goss answers that "almost by definition" social movements start from a position of weakness. As to the second point, she notes that few informed activists think that gun control alone is the perfect solution, but rather that it is an important part of a comprehensive strategy to reduce gun violence.

Goss considers and rejects a number of other clichés hanging in the cabinet of conventional wisdom. These excuses are not the reason that "the nation has never witnessed a vigorous, nation-spanning social movement to control access to firearms." It is rather, she writes, "in part because the leaders of the pro-control majority have lacked external resources to underwrite such a movement and in part because these leaders have chosen political strategies anathema to movement building."[26]

Good Policy, Bad Politics

Goss identified at least five times when resources were available and social conditions ripe for gun control advocates to have mobilized a national mass movement. The most recent of these was in the late 1980s and early 1990s when they had "the richest set of cultural and political opportunities in at least fifteen years."[27] Passage of the Brady law and the since-expired federal assault weapons ban appeared to validate the inside baseball strategy of the gun control leaders. In retrospect, it appears that these were hollow victories from the point of view of movement building. There was "very little movement for gun control on the ground." Although it appeared that state and local groups were proliferating, they were in fact "little more than letterhead organizations, run by a handful of dedicated volunteers, often relatives of gun violence victims." Many of them were short-lived and all of them "had little support from above or coordination among themselves."[28]

What went wrong?

Goss found that most gun control leaders "attribute their nonmovement status to factionalization within their ranks, including deep conflicts over personality, donors, philosophy, and tactics."[29] But history books are packed with stories of the internal divisions and personality fights of social movements from the beginnings of civilization to the 2018 by-elections in the United States and the machinations around the Brexit deal in Britain. Putting aside petty quarrels and funding vendettas, Goss pinpoints several more powerful factors that have impeded the coalescence of a national gun control movement. At the top of that list is the fundamental error of surrendering to "the seductive lure of elite politics" and eschewing bottom-up movement building. She points to the civil rights movement as an apposite example.

Although civil rights legislative victories in the 1960s appeared to some to be the result of elite insider politics at the national level, Goss argues, they actually came only "after decades of local organizing around modest measures—changing seating patterns on a bus route or at a soda fountain, for example." That movement, she says, "stands for the proposition that there are no quick fixes in American politics." The Founding Fathers, she argues, "meant for political reform to be slow and difficult. Movements that adapt their strategies to that reality will expand; movements that do not adapt will falter."[30] The leaders in gun control drew the wrong conclusions from the civil rights successes.

> Perhaps the most important reason that gun control has never generated a mass movement is that gun control advocates spurned incrementalism in favor of a "rational national" strategy of policy change. The rational-national strategy favored bold, comprehensive, nation-spanning gun control laws that offered little opportunity for broad-based participation. The alternative—incrementalism—is significantly more conducive to movement building.[31]

In terms of specific policy objectives, Goss argues that the gun control movement's emphasis on such "broad and severe" proposals as outright bans of handguns "would have imposed direct costs on tens of millions of gun owners, as opposed to burdening the far smaller universe of dealers and manufacturers."[32] Top-down leaders framed the issue of gun violence in ways that effectively threw a wet blanket on grassroots initiatives. "Seeing their cause as self-evidently good, gun control advocates have framed their policy arguments in terms that appeal more to policy experts than to everyday citizens."[33] The leaders' sweeping policy reforms "depressed, in indirect and unforeseen ways, public participation in the gun control cause."[34] Proposals to ban guns or require registration of all firearms and their owners in particular, Goss argues, did not generate widespread support, but they did motivate a broader spectrum of gun owners than had previously been involved in the gun-rights cause.

"When gun control advocates pushed a handgun ban," Goss writes, "they handed the NRA a golden opportunity to arouse the politically important rural interests, who are heavily represented in most state legislatures and over-represented in the U.S. Congress." The so-called "slippery-slope argument" that gun controllers secretly want to ban all guns "made many Americans suspect that gun control advocates really were extremists, thereby making moderate gun control sympathizers less likely to become active participants in the cause."[35]

The rational-national strategy also suffered from a structural defect. "Beyond writing a letter to one's senator or congressperson in Washington," Goss writes, "there was little for the ordinary gun control supporter to do." On the contrary, "by design, gun control became an expert issue in the hands of a small group of policy professionals in Washington-based interest groups." This opened up a flank in the culture wars. Pro-gun activists could argue that gun control leaders were "out-of-touch tyrants whose ideas posed a grave danger to American values."[36]

There were certainly other obstacles. They include the lack of reliable funding and government allies. Charitable foundations are restricted by federal tax laws from funding political activism: lobbying or influencing constituents to pressure their legislators. But most of them—with the exception of a few like the Joyce Foundation, based in Chicago—shied entirely away from funding anything at all related to the gun violence issue, including even basic research. Institutionally conservative to begin with, focused on funding efforts to change the "root causes" of social problems, most foundations have seen gun control as the third rail of philanthropy. Neither have gun control advocates been able to rely on the support of government allies as have other movements such as reducing smoking and curing epidemic diseases—federal public health organizations like the Centers for Disease Control, law enforcement agencies, and consumer product regulatory agencies. In its superior practice of insider politics jiujitsu, the gun-rights movement has gone with a vengeance after any federal agency, and many state and local ones, that appear in the least supportive of gun control.

None of this makes gun control leaders bad people or fools. They are in the cause because they believe in it. The dimensions and direction of the fight are not always clear to those in the ring or on the battlefield. Nevertheless, the fact is, Goss argues, "Gun control became an issue for and by elites." These elites have "pursued an inside game without an outside game."[37]

Some national leaders have in recent years attempted to reorient their efforts away from the sweeping-ban strategy and to be more supportive and proactive on grassroots organization and state and local activism. One good example is the Coalition to Stop Gun Violence, whose executive director, Joshua Horwitz, told Goss that his organization had begun to think of itself as "a little trade association for the groups we work with."[38] Another is the Giffords Law Center, which has begun to emphasize local action and to use victims and survivors in serious roles. Most other organizations—according to an off-the-record conversation with an experienced staffer in the office of a well-known senior congressional leader—"are scrambling to catch up with their grass roots." Whether they can or will remains to be seen.

In any case, when Lonnie and Sandy Phillips were invited by the leader of the Brady organization to come to Washington and get involved in the fray, neither Brady nor the other national entities had a handle on or a vision for the role of victims and survivors.

A Transient Killer

On the afternoon of February 23, 1997, a middle-aged man asked the help of several tourists among the many who were crowded onto the eighty-sixth-floor observation deck of the Empire State Building. Could they please point out for him the Statue of Liberty?[39]

"I love America and Americans," he said.

Then he pulled out a .380 caliber Beretta high-capacity semiautomatic pistol and opened fire. In a matter of seconds he shot to death one sightseer, wounded six others, and committed suicide. The man—a

Palestinian English teacher on a tourist visa to the United States—left a muddled note in a pouch around his neck explaining his rampage. At the top of his list was his anger at American support for Israel.

Investigators soon learned that the shooter had made a short trip to Melbourne, Florida. He stayed there for a few days in a cheap motel, where he attracted some attention by occasionally standing naked outside of his room. Based on that transient stay, he secured a Florida resident ID card. On the same day he got his ID card, he visited a Florida gun dealer, presented his new ID, passed the Brady law background check, paid $500, and walked out with his Beretta pistol. This transaction infuriated the then mayor of New York, Rudolph W. Giuliani, who was then a vocal gun control advocate.

"What sense is there in handing a murder weapon, an attack weapon, which is what this is, over to a man who is a transient living in a motel which I think could be described as a fleabag motel?" Giuliani asked. "I mean, that is totally insane."[40]

But like many other politicians, Giuliani's position on gun control has been at least as flexible as that of NRA congregant Donald Trump, who in a past iteration said that President Obama spoke for him and all Americans on the need for stricter gun control laws. Giuliani has tailored his rhetoric to fit the times and political ambition. In 2015, he focused his outrage on President Obama for having suggested tougher gun controls after a public mass shooting. "I think the president has very little knowledge of what causes crime or how to reduce crime," Giuliani said on Fox News. "The reality is gun control laws control the behavior of legitimate people. People who rob stores, people who rob banks and people who are insane and want to go ahead and murder don't follow the gun control laws."[41]

One of the casualties at the Empire State Building shooting was Matthew Gross, "the charismatic and creative frontman for the Bushpilots, a rock band that was playing to critical reviews in New York City and being scouted for a record contract."[42] Like Gabrielle Giffords, Connor Stevenson, and James Brady, Matthew was shot in the brain and survived. The bullet that struck him went through his frontal lobe from right to left. But like virtually all survivors of traumatic brain injury, his life was changed forever.

"You get rehabilitated," he told CBS News in 2011. "You don't recover. You don't get to where you were before."[43] In the same year, he told the *Los Angeles Times,* "You are a different person, and you have to accept the fact that you're a different person."[44]

Matthew's best friend, a guitarist in the rock band, was shot in the back of the head. Like Jessi Ghawi, he had no chance of surviving his wound. He died on the spot.

The shooting changed the life of Matthew's older brother, Daniel, who was then a partner in the J. Walter Thompson advertising agency.

"Something like this colors everything you do the rest of your life," Daniel Gross told the *New York Times* in 2000. "Not a day or an hour goes by when I don't think back."[45]

One year after the shooting, Matthew Gross, Daniel Gross, and a gathering of gun control leaders—including James Brady—announced the formation of a new group named PAX, the Latin word for "peace." The new group's objective, the newspaper reported, was "to unite other grassroots efforts against gun violence, and to teach citizens how to speak out on the issue."[46] Daniel gave up his well-paying job in advertising to devote himself to the new group, which changed its name in 2011 to the Center to Prevent Youth Violence.

"I found I couldn't go back to my everyday life," Daniel Gross told the *New York Times.* "It really was an opportunity to do something about gun violence using exactly the skills and background I'd gotten in advertising. That's what's missing from the gun violence issue." According to the newspaper's 2000 profile, "He draws a modest salary now instead of a partner's income, lives in Manhattan with his bride, who works in advertising, and uses his skills to sell gun control instead of Listerine."[47]

Daniel Gross found that he could do well by doing good. In February 2012 he was hired to head the Brady organization,[48] from which in that year he received a total of $233,606 in compensation, according to the organization's tax filings.[49] It was Gross who wooed the Phillipses, inviting them into their disastrous relationship with Brady. In 2016, when that relationship soured and would soon result in the Phillipses' bankruptcy, Brady paid Daniel Gross $409,637, which was perhaps not as much as he would have made selling Listerine.[50] In 2017, Brady parted ways with Gross and installed a curious new form of leadership, promoting two of its senior staff to be "co-presidents."[51] Meanwhile, the Phillipses had been reduced to living out of a travel trailer. They were driving around the country on their own, trying to stitch together a victims and survivors grassroots movement. The new leadership at Brady said it was sympathetic. But, in the end, the Phillipses were left to fend for themselves.

The path to that sad circumstance began in 1999 at Columbine High School, which was named after Colorado's state flower.

After Columbine—A Poisoned Flower

When three Harvard Business School scholars analyzed the impact of mass shootings on gun control policy, they came up with some interesting conclusions about the relationship between those shootings and legislation.[52] A single mass shooting generates a 15percent increase over the next year in the number of firearms bills introduced in the legislature of the state where the shooting occurred. "This effect is largest after shootings with the most fatalities—and holds for both Republican-controlled and Democrat-controlled legislatures."[53] Although mass shootings are a relatively small percentage of overall gun deaths, "they have an outsized influence relative to other homicides."[54] The "per-death impact" of mass shootings on the number of bills introduced is about eighty times greater than the impact of individual gun homicides. In sum, the researchers said they found "empirical evidence that sporadic events such as mass shootings can lead to major policy changes."[55]

So what happens to this flurry of legislative activity? What policy changes come about? That depends on which political party is in power. "A mass shooting increases the number of enacted laws that *loosen* gun restrictions by 75% in states with Republican-controlled legislatures," the scholars—two professors and a PhD candidate—wrote in their 2016 paper. "We find no significant effect of mass shootings on laws enacted when there is a Democrat-controlled legislature."[56]

On its face, this finding turns conventional wisdom on its head. Democrats are generally perceived as favoring gun control. Therefore, one might expect that more restrictive gun control measures would be enacted in states where a mass shooting occurred and Democrats controlled the legislature. On further reflection, however, and putting aside the false "third rail" mantra that the national Democratic leadership has embraced for many years, these conclusions provide evidence of the impact on gun policy of the lack of a grassroots gun control movement.

In contrast to the NRA, for example, the efforts of gun control proponents in most states have been ad hoc affairs. They have not had well-organized, adequately funded cadres of boots-on-the-ground activists to walk halls, make lobbying calls, develop lasting relationships with news media, and generate public support for stricter gun control measures. The actions of the Colorado state legislature after the mass shooting at Columbine High School are a case in point.

The False Dawn of Public Outrage

The nation seemed to be galvanized after the Columbine shooting. "Newspapers and talk radio featured impassioned testimonials about the historically tragic role of guns in America," Goss observed.[57] At the federal level, Robert Spitzer wrote, "national shock and outrage put unprecedented pressure on Congress to respond."[58] Donations poured in to gun control groups. Students demonstrated. There was a mass protest at the NRA's annual convention, held in Denver two weeks after the shooting.

Most descriptions of the reaction to the Columbine shooting, however, overlook the activities of the conservative side of the great American political divide. "Just as in the Virginia Tech case, a variety of right-wing groups and pundits exploited the tragedy to push their own political agendas," Professor Douglas Kellner wrote in his book *Guys and Guns Amok*.[59] Right-wing-politician Patrick Buchanan "blamed the tragedy on America's youth, calling them 'godless' and 'an immoral generation adrift.'"[60] Gary Bauer, a Christian fundamentalist activist and unsuccessful politician, "organized his presidential campaign around the Columbine shootings and used the issue to promote the return of prayer to schools."[61] This religious ferment could be mocked and ignored by the rational-national elite in Washington, but it played well in the religious grass roots of American conservatism. It helped divert attention from the proliferation and easy availability of guns as the primary cause of gun violence to a wide range of other things, including godless youth, absence of prayer in schools, the collapse of the American family, bullying, the internet, and video games.[62] What support there was for gun control after Columbine withered away.

"The aftermath of Columbine looked a lot like the aftermath of many other high-profile shootings in American history," Goss wrote. "Collective outrage, followed by a momentary flurry of unorganized calls and letters and donations from thousands of individuals, and then a quick return to the status quo."[63]

The "status quo" meant that after the Congress hemmed and hawed and did nothing, after the cameras dashed off to chase other media rabbits, and after the disorganized muddle of ad hoc gun control proponents went home, the well-oiled and thoroughly organized machinery of the gun-rights movement clicked on and went to work. The strategic target the gun-rights machine aimed to obliterate in Colorado was a growing movement among some lawyers and national gun control organizations to bring the gun industry to account by means of lawsuits brought on behalf of the victims and survivors of gun violence. The model these lawyers wanted to follow was successful litigation against the tobacco industry.

A Legal Earthquake

Suing gun companies was not new. If a gun blew up in one's face because of faulty manufacture, or went off unexpectedly because of a poorly designed trigger mechanism, the manufacturer could be and sometimes was held liable for the resulting damages to an unfortunate gun enthusiast or someone else in the line of fire. A group of lawyers was determined to take that practice to a more ambitious level of liability. Some of them saw civil lawsuits as a strategic scythe to cut the gun industry off at its knees.

"An earthquake shook the landscape of gun litigation in the late 1990s and early 2000s in the form of a series of lawsuits filed by more than thirty cities and counties, the District of Columbia and the state of New York against gun manufacturers and distributors," the authors of a modern legal text on guns and the law observed. "These government plaintiff suits sought to recover the costs of certain public services incurred in connection with gun violence, such as police and emergency services."[64]

The municipal lawsuits were founded on tort law, the sturdy branch of Anglo-American common law that has for centuries provided a legal path to remedies for persons who are harmed by the negligent civil (as opposed to criminal) conduct of another. The remedy may be monetary damages, correction by the wrongful party of the condition that caused the harm, or both. The two types of tort cases that are probably best known to laypersons are personal injury claims (a driver jabbering on a cell phone runs down a pedestrian in a crosswalk) and product liability cases (a defective part in a household appliance causes it to explode into flames in ordinary use).[65]

In any case, the plaintiff (the person suing) must prove two elements of negligence by the defendant to be successful. The first is that the defendant was the "proximate cause" of the injury. This is a murky concept intended to cut off argument about the potentially infinite chain of things going back to the Big Bang that might theoretically cause any factual event. It has been summed up as a situation in which "the injury was a foreseeable consequence of the actor's negligent conduct."[66] Or put more pungently, "once one cuts through all the verbiage, proximate cause is simply a tool used by courts to decide whether it is fair and appropriate as a matter of public policy to impose liability."[67]

The second element is that the defendant owed a "duty" to the defendant, another murky concept that "focuses on the foreseeability of the injury" to that plaintiff by that defendant.[68] These arcane concepts rarely rise to more than formulaic recitation in "garden variety" tort cases, and when they do, "there is proximate cause if the court says there is proximate cause and there is a duty if the court says there is a·duty."[69]

There is another traditional legal channel for fashioning fair and appropriate public policy. It is the trial jury. The results of tort litigation often depend as much on a jury's collective feelings about what is right or wrong in a given fact situation as on the charge to the jury by the judge or the abstractions of legal scholars. This collective wisdom of juries is a good thing, according to Heidi Li Feldman, a professor at Georgetown University Law Center. Jury verdicts "preserve popular sovereignty over the appropriate balance between safety and freedom," she wrote in a law review article in 2000. "Eliminating the negligence standard and the jury's role in applying it would sacrifice something of political and social importance: the opportunity for popular, collective judgments about how each citizen should conduct herself or himself when the pursuit of her or his own objectives creates the risk of injuring somebody else."[70] One might think that the idea of preserving popular sovereignty to the citizenry would appeal to the conservative mind. One would be wrong as that mind is made manifest in the polarizing ideology of gun rights.

It was no coincidence that the first municipal lawsuit against the gun industry, and a number of others that followed, was brought by a group of lawyers that called itself the Castano Safe Gun Litigation Group. Its predecessor, the Castano Group, was founded by a phenomenally successful Louisiana tort lawyer, Wendel Gauthier. It was named after his friend, Peter Castano, a smoker who died of lung cancer at age forty-seven. "Gauthier gathered over sixty of the nation's top plaintiffs' firms into a coalition to pursue a nationwide class action . . . [the group] amassed a huge war chest and wealth of legal talent."[71] Although that class action lawsuit ultimately foundered, the facts it helped uncover lay the groundwork for a comprehensive tobacco industry settlement with the states in 1998. Gauthier persuaded about half the Castano Group to join him in going after the gun industry.

Private tort lawyers are, as Gauthier himself said in connection with his tobacco litigation, often motivated by the possibility of winning large fees contingent on damage awards. "I'm not a good Samaritan," he said in an interview in 1993. "I'm in it to make money."[72] But gun control activists joined the fray on principle. They included Dennis Hennigan of the Brady Center's Legal Action Project, Joshua Horwitz of the Educational Fund to Stop Gun Violence, and Temple Law School professor David Kairys.[73] According to the 1997 U.S. Economic Census, the combined value of firearms and ammunition shipments amounted to $2.2 billion that year. This was dwarfed by the $28.3 billion reported the same year by cigarette manufacturers and the $27.7 billion reported by distillers, wineries, and brewers.[74] Moreover, aside from major manufacturers, the gun industry was built on a relatively fragile structure of retailers and distributors that was fragmented and not well-enough capitalized to fight lengthy and expensive legal battles. The private lawyers soon figured out that the gun industry was not a "deep pockets" target and many lost interest, while activists like Jonathan Lowy at Brady and Joshua Horwitz at the Educational Fund soldier on to this day.

The NRA and the Industry Respond

Recognizing that the litigation earthquake was an existential threat to the very existence of the gun industry, "the NRA launched a nationwide lobbying campaign in state legislatures and Congress to secure statutory immunity for the industry."[75] In 2000, after the Columbine fever waned, the Republican-controlled state legislature passed, and the Republican governor signed, a law that effectively forbid lawsuits against the gun industry. For good measure, the new law provided that any plaintiff who was bold enough to seek his or her day in court by bringing such a lawsuit would be required to pay the defendant's legal fees.

Many other states followed with similar laws. The state "roadblock grew into a mountain in 2005," when after several misfires, the NRA succeeded in getting a federal immunity law passed by a Republican Congress and signed by President George W. Bush. The Protection of Lawful Commerce in Arms Act (PLCAA, pronounced "plack-uh" by those who discuss it) "bars most lawsuits against gun makers or sellers in either state or federal court for injuries arising from intentional misuse of guns."[76]

This singular immunity—not enjoyed by any other consumer product industry in America—was a breathtaking and audacious refutation of centuries of common law. Congress tossed out with one sweep the traditional judgments of juries and closed the courthouse doors to the tens of thousands of innocent victims injured and more tens of thousands of survivors of innocent victims killed by guns in America—no matter what in fact the industry's design and marketing practices contribute to the misuse of guns and gun violence in America. There are some, including Jonathan Lowy, who argue that locking people out of the courthouse and preventing them from pursuing long-established common law remedies is unconstitutional. However, so far every court that has considered the question has ruled that PLCAA is constitutional.[77]

This was the shell-cratered no-man's-land of tort law into which the Brady organization thrust the Phillips. There is plenty of "he said, she said" disagreement about who said exactly what to whom and when along the way to a courthouse in Colorado. But the bottom line is that Lonnie and Sandy Phillips were a grieving, legally unsophisticated, middle-aged couple.

As it turned out, they did get hurt. And no one had their back.

The Competition for Pain

On a rainy day a few weeks after the memorial for Jessi, Lonnie was lost in the memory of a happy day with her. Sandy's voice broke through his reverie.

"You do know that we are going to get involved in gun violence prevention don't you?" she said.

"Yes," he answered.

They were naive. They especially did not understand the competition among the national gun control elite for the painful stories of victims and survivors. At the very moment that Sandy and Lonnie decided to get involved, national gun control groups were competing in this market of pain to sign on celebrities and gun violence victims and survivors. The groups in effect "franchised" any such human assets they recruited and used them in media events tied closely to fund-raising appeals. The heinous acts of 2012 were a macabre windfall and the money poured in.

Given the tragedy at Aurora, the potential value of franchising the Phillips was high. In spite of its consistently mediocre ratings by Charity Navigator, an independent guide to charitable giving,[78] Brady has high name recognition and has been regarded as a leader in gun control by the general public, many outside observers, and friendly politicians. It seemed an ideal organization to the Phillipses.

Sandy and Lonnie were invited to appear at a press conference in Washington with Dan Gross, Brady's president. While the three relaxed over drinks that night, Gross offered Sandy a job—with the benefit that she could work from home in San Antonio. A few weeks later, Lonnie was hired as Brady Campaign Manager for Gun Owners. Unaware that the bloom would be off of the rose when the novelty of Aurora and Jessi's murder wore off, the Phillipses quit their jobs and went to work for Brady. No one has ever publicly challenged their value or the vigor with which they worked.

It was during the honeymoon period that the Phillipses say Brady's lawyers asked them to join in a plan to overturn PLCAA.

The Phillipses are not lawyers. They had no reason to doubt the good faith or strategic wisdom of Brady's lawyers, or of the lawyers at the Denver branch of the Arnold & Porter law firm, who offered their help in the case pro bono. (The Arnold & Porter lawyer on the case never answered an emailed request from the author to be interviewed for this book.)

As it turned out, no other survivors would join the lawsuit. They were concerned about possible financial liabilities. "Sandy and I decided to go it alone because of our desire for justice for Jessi and to see the critical change in gun laws that Brady's lawyers said that they were pursuing," Lonnie says. "We trusted that Brady, our employer, would have our back if the lawsuit failed. In the end, an unsympathetic federal judge likewise assumed that Brady would cover us if their plan failed."

He and they were both proven wrong.

The Phillipses were hired by Brady in January of 2013.

The Phillipses' federal lawsuit was still pending when Brady fired them on December 12, 2014, less than ninety days after Brady filed the federal lawsuit against Lucky Gunner. The final blow landed on June 17, 2015, when the federal judge assigned to the Brady lawsuit threw it out of court. It was clear to him that Colorado's law passed after Columbine squarely blocked any path through any chink in PLCAA's armor. He acidly suggested that it should have been clear to Brady's lawyers that the lawsuit would be dead on arrival:

> It is apparent that this case was filed to pursue the political purposes of the Brady Center and, given the failure to present any cognizable legal claim, bringing these defendants into the Colorado court where the prosecution of [the killer] was proceeding appears to be more of an opportunity to propagandize the public and stigmatize the defendants than to obtain a court order which counsel should have known would be outside the authority of this court. By employing the mandatory word "shall," those statutes require that fees be awarded. It may be presumed that whatever hardship is imposed on the individual plaintiffs by these awards against them may be ameliorated by the sponsors of this action in their name.

The judge slapped the Phillipses with the defendant's legal fees, an amount approaching a quarter of a million dollars. Lucky Gunner promised to turn all of the fee money over to the gun lobby. This placed Brady and the Phillipses squarely on the horns of a dilemma. Neither wanted to fund the gun lobby. If Brady had raised the money to pay the legal fees, it and the Phillipses would in effect be funding the NRA and the gun-rights movement. Nothing, however, would have prevented Brady from hiring the Phillipses back—except that it had no real plan or competence for mobilizing grass roots in the aggressive manner the Phillipses wanted to pursue and seemed to have dug in against them.

Out of work and grieving, the Phillipses eventually were forced to file bankruptcy on January 27, 2017. After that, scraping by on their own and with the occasional donation, they set out to travel around America, visiting other victims and survivors of public mass shootings, trying to weld those missing voices together into a movement.

The Phillipses sought help from Brady, whose new leaders promised to "make things right." They even submitted a detailed proposal to create a new organization to start a grassroots movement of victims and survivors with significant financial aid from Brady. Brady turned them down, deciding after all not to "make things right."

In a final phone call with Brady board chairman Kevin Quinn, the Phillipses got what was in effect an "oh, well" blow-off. According to Quinn their cruel termination was just a case of bad management. He relayed the results of a board meeting in a May 29, 2018, phone call with the Phillipses, essentially laying the matter off to poor management by Dan Gross.

As to their proposal, that too was rejected. "The board is not presently prepared to find an economic resolution to the matter beyond trying to find a way to work together in some fashion," Quinn told them.

Sandy and Lonnie were out in the cold and on their own.

Rise of Another Rainbow

Miraculously, however, days after Brady finally dismissed the Phillipses' proposal in 2018, the Giffords Law Center—another organization with a bigger vision—offered them a contract to pursue exactly what they had envisioned doing on that rainy day in 2012. It was for the Phillipses a promising rainbow at the end of a long and tragic road.

"We're not looking for political friends," Sandy and Lonnie say today. "We want political champions. We are on the offensive. We will not back down."

NO EASY ANSWERS

There are no easy answers to America's gun violence problems. No simple remove and replace legislative wizardry can make it go away. And if there were easy legislative answers, the impotence of a locked-horn Congress, the tradition of a politically opportunistic White House, and an increasingly gun-rights-friendly federal judiciary make it unlikely that those answers could be enacted and implemented in the near term.

There is, however, a single difficult answer. It is a path of blood, sweat, and tears. That path is the pursuit of cultural change. It starts in the grass roots, deep down in America's heart. Change is already stirring there. This path to change is now tangled with obstructions. But with mindful organization, dedicated people, and uplifted vision, it can be cleared and grow into a highway.

America is not Canada. But neither is America a nation that once enshrined slavery, denied women the vote, and relegated people of color to lives of servitude and fear of capricious violence. Cultural change is a constant. It can and will happen. We can hear it in the voices of young Americans and in the tearful crying of gun violence victims and survivors. We can see it in the different views about guns held by different ethnicities in an increasingly multicultural nation. This potential for cultural change is what so frightens the gun-rights movement.

The path to cultural change and effective action to reduce gun violence does not go through Washington. It does not require yet another elite expert's report documenting yet again the ways in which essentially unfettered access to guns makes possible epidemic gun violence and public mass shootings. It goes through the heart and soul of Sandy and Lonnie Phillips and tens of thousands more like them. It goes through every state capitol and every city hall in America. It will require the creation of what has never before existed in America—a true grassroots gun control movement. It will require Americans in every town turning to each other to build lasting, deep-rooted networks, rather than relying on the disengaged experts of a remote political elite.

It is not as if we do not already know many things that would help reduce and contain gun violence. These are not "commonsense" measures. They are measures backed by solid research. A few examples include:

- Comprehensive background checks, coupled with effective threat assessment and threat management systems to provide ongoing means of intervention—taking away guns—when gun owners leak signs of pending violence.

- Restricting access to assault weapons. The National Firearms Act of 1934 provides a good model to start with.

- Banning high-capacity magazines.

- Revisiting the question of defining prohibited classes—people forbidden access to firearms—to take better account of the dynamics of violent tendencies.

None of these measures would take away the rights of gun enthusiasts to own and use firearms. The "slippery slope" of gun confiscation exists only in the fevered imagination of the NRA, extremists like Ted Nugent, and feckless politicians like Donald Trump. Taking away guns outright would be logistically impossible, and the idea has been proven politically counterproductive.

What is required is to so well organize the grass roots that the selfish fetishes and bizarre ideology of gun-rights extremists can be ignored and the right to live, the right not to be shot, can be raised to the first cultural principle of a nation that cares about its children, its mothers, its fathers, its friends, its neighbors, and its coworkers more than it cares about guns.

NOTES

Introduction

1. Dan M. Kahan, Donald Braman, and John Gastil, "A Cultural Critique of Gun Litigation," in Timothy D. Lytton, ed., *Suing the Gun Industry: A Battle at the Crossroads of Gun Control and Mass Torts* (Ann Arbor: University of Michigan Press, 2006), 107.

2. David Ariosto, "Gabrielle Giffords Resigns from Congress," CNN, January 25, 2012, https://www.cnn.com/2012/01/25/politics/gabrielle-giffords/index .html.

3. Fernanda Santos, "Life Term for Gunman after Guilty Plea in Tucson Killings," *New York Times*, August 7, 2012, https://www.nytimes.com/2012/08/08/us/loughner-pleads-guilty-in-2011-tucson-shootings.html.

4. Lizette Alvarez and Cara Buckley, "Zimmerman Is Acquitted in Trayvon Martin Killing," *New York Times*, July 13, 2013, https://www.nytimes.com/2013/07/14/us/george-zimmerman-verdict-trayvon-martin.html.

5. Ed Payne, "Chardon School Killer TJ Lane: Tightlipped about Motive, Escape," CNN, September 12, 2014, https://www.cnn.com/2014/09/12/justice/ohio-school-shooter/index.html; Chris Anderson, "Tuesday Marks 6-year Anniversary of Chardon High School Shooting," Cleveland 19 News, February 27, 2018, http://www.cleveland19.com/story/37599489/tuesday-marks-6-year-anniversary-of-chardon-high-school-shooting/.

6. Angela Ruggiero, "Oikos Nursing School Massacre Shooter One Goh Sentenced to Life in Prison," *Mercury News*, July 14, 2017, https://www.mercurynews.com/2017/07/14/oikos-nursing-school-massacre-suspect-one-goh-to -face-life-in-prison/.

7. "Jason Todd Ready, Reputed Neo-Nazi, among Five Dead in Arizona Murder-Suicide," CBS News, May 3, 2012, https://www.cbsnews.com/news/jason-todd-ready-reputed-neo-nazi-among-five-dead-in-arizona-murder-suicide/; Michael Muskal, "Border Guard Founder J. T. Ready Blamed in Arizona Murder-Suicide," *Los Angeles Times*, May 3, 2012, http://articles.latimes.com/2012/may/03/nation/la-na-nn-arizona-shooting-20120503.

8. Tom Diaz, *The Last Gun: How Changes in the Gun Industry Are Killing Americans and What It Will Take to Stop It* (New York: New Press, 2012), 218.

9. Casey McNerthney, "Shooting Suspect Visited Bar before; Gave Off a 'Bad Vibe,'" *Seattle PI*, May 31, 2012, https://www.seattlepi.com/local/article/Seattle-shooting-two-killed-three-wounded-3595992.php.

10. Casey McNerthney and Scott Gutierrez, "Police: Seattle Shootings Were Like an Execution," *Seattle PI*, June 2, 2012, https://www.seattlepi.com/local/article/Police-Seattle-shootings-were-like-an-execution-3599900.php.

11. Katherine A. Fowlera et al., "Firearm Injuries in the United States," *Prev. Med.* 2015 October; 79: 5–14, doi:10.1016/j.ypmed.2015.06.002.

12. See, for example, letter from Dr. Philip J. Cook et al., in response to an article titled "The Hidden Epidemic of Firearm Injury: Increasing Firearm Injury Rates during 2001–2013," and the original authors' reply to Cook in *AmJEpidemiol.* 2017; 186(7): 896–97.

13. Sandy Phillips (as told to Abigail Pesta), "My Daughter Was Murdered in a Mass Shooting. Then I Was Ordered to Pay Her Killer's Gun Dealer," *Mother Jones*, July 20, 2017, https://www.motherjones.com/politics/2017/07/my-daughter-was-murdered-in-a-mass-shooting-then-i-was-ordered-to-pay-her-killers-gun-dealer/#.

14. David Nakamura, "After Aurora Shootings, Obama Again Takes on Role as Healer in Chief in Colorado," *Washington Post*, July 22, 2012, www.washingtonpost.com/politics/after-aurora-shootings-obama-again-takes-on-role-as-healer-in-chief-in-colorado/2012/07/22/gJQAdEO92W_story.html?

15. "President Obama's Remarks on Sunday, July 22, 2012," *Denver Post*, July 22, 2012, https://www.denverpost.com/2012/07/22/president-obamas-remarks-on-sunday-july-22-2012/.

16. "Wisconsin Temple Gunman Wade Page 'Shot Himself in Head,'" BBC News, August 8, 2012, https://www.bbc.com/news/world-us-canada-19183359.

17. Brandt Williams, "A Year after Accent Signage Shootings, Debate Shifts from Gun Control to Mental Health," Minnesota Public Radio, September 27, 2013, https://www.mprnews.org/story/2013/09/27/news/accent-signage-shooting-one-year.

18. State of Connecticut, Sandy Hook Advisory Commission, "Final Report," presented to Governor Dannel P. Malloy, March 6, 2015, x.

19. Sandy Phillips, "My Daughter Was Murdered in a Mass Shooting."

20. Sandy Hook Advisory Commission, "Final Report," 10–11.

21. Mark Landler and Peter Baker, "'These Tragedies Must End,' Obama Says," *New York Times*, December 16, 2012, https://www.nytimes.com/2012/12/17/us/politics/bloomberg-urges-obama-to-take-action-on-gun-control.html.

22. Jake Tapper, "Rahm to Holder in 2009: STFU on Guns," *ABC News 20/20*, July 27, 2012, https://abcnews.go.com/blogs/politics/2012/07/rahm-to-holder-in-2009-stfu-on-guns/.

23. Tapper, "Rahm to Holder."

24. Sarah Childress, "What's Obama's Record on Gun Control?" *PBS Frontline*, December 17, 2012, https://www.pbs.org/wgbh/pages/frontline/government-elections-politics/whats-obamas-record-on-gun-control/.

25. Landler and Baker, "'These Tragedies Must End.'"

26. Landler and Baker, "'These Tragedies Must End.'"

27. Michele Gorman, "Donald Trump in 2012 on Sandy Hook Shooting: 'Obama Spoke for Me and Every American,'" *Newsweek*, May 20, 2016, https://www.newsweek.com/donald-trump-sandy-hook-shooting-obama-spoke-me-462131.

28. Peter Applebome and Jonathan Weisman, "Obama Invokes Newtown Dead in Pressing for New Gun Laws," *New York Times*, April 8, 2013, https://www.nytimes.com/2013/04/09/us/politics/obama-in-connecticut-to-push-for-gun-control.html.

29. Applebome and Weisman, "Obama Invokes."

30. Sabrina Siddiqui, "Connecticut Senator 'Embarrassed' at Political Inaction since Sandy Hook," *Guardian*, December 13, 2017, https://www.theguardian.com/us-news/2017/dec/13/sandy-hook-fifth-anniversary-gun-control-chris-murphy.

31. See generally, Christopher H. Achen and Larry M. Bartels, "Democratic Ideals and Realities," in *Democracy for Realists: Why Elections Do Not Produce Responsive Government* (Princeton, NJ: Princeton University Press, 2016), 1–20.

32. Las Vegas Metropolitan Police Department, "Criminal Investigative Report of the 1 October Mass Casualty Shooting," August 3, 2018, 19.

33. Alex Yablon, "One Year after Las Vegas, a New Texas Company Is Selling Bump Stocks," *Trace*, September 28, 2018, https://www.thetrace.org/2018/09/bump-stocks-las-vegas-mass-shooting-slide-fire-rw-arms/; Debra J. Saunders, "Justice Department Proposes Banning Bump Stocks," *Las Vegas Review-Journal*, September 28, 2018, https://www.reviewjournal.com/news/politics-and-government/justice-department-proposes-banning-bump-stocks/.

34. David J. Neal and Charles Rabin, "Grand Jury Indicts Parkland School Shooter on 17 Counts of Murder and 17 of Attempted Murder," *Miami Herald*,

March 7, 2018, https://www.miamiherald.com/news/local/community/broward/article203931034.html; Skyler Swisher and Paula McMahon, "Nikolas Cruz Passed Background Check, Including Mental Health Question, to Get AR-15 Rifle," *Sun-Sentinel*, February 15, 2018, http://www.sun-sentinel.com/local/broward/parkland/florida-school-shooting/fl-florida-school-shooting-guns-20180215-story.html.

35. "Florida Student Emma Gonzalez to Lawmakers and Gun Advocates: 'We Call BS,'" CNN, February 17, 2018, https://www.cnn.com/2018/02/17/us/florida-student-emma-gonzalez-speech/index.html.

36. Author's notes of interview with Dr. Liza Gold, MD, Clinical Professor of Psychiatry, Georgetown University School of Medicine, March 15, 2018.

37. David Hogg and Lauren Hogg, *#Never Again* (New York: Random House, 2018), 107.

38. The words "gun control" have fallen out of favor among the organized activists whose focus is on reducing death and injury from firearms. "Gun violence reduction," or the acronym GVR, is currently preferred. The change is an example of modern political rhetoric. Arguably the phrase "gun violence reduction" is less off-putting to open-minded gun owners and encompasses a broader range of policy initiatives, some of which have nothing to do directly with guns, such as improved mental health services or monitoring domestic violence offenses. It is the author's subjective opinion that people not directly involved in activism and many in the news media tend to use the term "gun control" anyway. The phrases are used interchangeably in this book.

39. See, for example, Wayne LaPierre, "Democrats Make Gun Control a 'Litmus Test'—A Test They'll Fail," *Shooting Illustrated*, October 2018, 12 ("Obama may be gone but their utopian dream for a Euro-style socialist state of America marches on. I'm not just talking about Bernie Sanders, a self-avowed socialist. Think about Nancy Pelosi, Kamala Harris, Elizabeth Warren, Bill de Blasio, Andrew Cuomo, Cory Booker, Keith Ellison, and Christopher Murphy."), https://www.americas1stfreedom.org/articles/2018/9/24/standing-guard-democrats-make-gun-control-a-litmus-test-a-test-they-ll-fail/. *Shooting Illustrated* describes itself on its contents page as "the official journal of the National Rifle Association."

40. Michael D. Shear and Sheryl Gay Stolberg, "Conceding to N.R.A., Trump Abandons Brief Gun Control Promise," *New York Times*, March 12, 2018, https://www.nytimes.com/2018/03/12/us/politics/trump-gun-control-national-rifle-association.html.

41. Jordain Carney, "Schumer Unveils Democratic Gun Control Plan with Plea for Trump Support," *Hill*, March 1, 2018, https://thehill.com/homenews/senate/376286-schumer-unveils-democratic-gun-control-plan-with-plea-for-trump-support.

42. Michael D. Shear, Sheryl Gay Stolberg, and Thomas Kaplan, "N.R.A. Suggests Trump May Retreat from Gun Control," *New York Times*, March 1, 2018, https://www.nytimes.com/2018/03/01/us/politics/trump-republicans -gun-control.html.

43. Jeffrey Schweers, "NRA Sues Florida over Gun Bill Same Day Gov. Scott Signed It into Law," *Tallahassee Democrat*, March 9, 2018, https://www.tallahassee .com/story/news/2018/03/09/nra-sues-florida-over-gun-bill-same-day-gov-scott -signed-law/412365002/.

44. Eric Lipton and Alexander Burns, "The True Source of the N.R.A.'s Clout: Mobilization, Not Donations," *New York Times*, February 24, 2018, https://www.nytimes.com/2018/02/24/us/politics/nra-gun-control-florida.html.

45. Quoted in Tom Diaz, *The Last Gun: How Changes in the Gun Industry Are Killing Americans and What It Will Take to Stop It* (New York: New Press, 2013), 197.

46. Kim Parker et al., "America's Complex Relationship with Guns," Pew Research Center, June 2017, 4, http://www.pewsocialtrends.org/2017/06/22/ americas-complex-relationship-with-guns/.

47. Kristin A. Goss, *Disarmed: The Missing Movement for Gun Control in America* (Princeton, NJ: Princeton University Press, 2006), 28.

48. Goss, *Disarmed*, 191.

49. Alan I. Abramowitz, *The Great Alignment: Race, Party Transformation, and the Rise of Donald Trump* (New Haven, CT: Yale University Press, 2018), 1.

50. See, "Has the American Public Polarized?" in Morris P. Fiorina, *Unstable Majorities: Polarization, Party Sorting, and Political Stalemate* (Stanford: Hoover Institution Press, 2017), 17–42.

51. Abramowitz, *The Great Alignment*, 101.

52. Abramowitz, *The Great Alignment*, 117.

53. See, for example, Pew Research Center, *The Partisan Divide on Political Values Grows Even Wider*, report released October 5, 2017, 7 ("The gap between the political values of Democrats and Republicans is now larger than at any point in Pew Research Center surveys dating back to 1994, a continuation of a steep increase in the ideological divisions between the two parties over more than a decade."), http://assets.pewresearch.org/wp-content/uploads/ sites/5/2017/10/05162647/10-05-2017-Political-landscape-release.pdf; Michael Scherer and Robert Costa, "'Rock Bottom': Supreme Court Fight Reveals a Country on the Brink," *Washington Post*, October 6, 2018 ("Public polling showed . . . a tribal response that tracks other evidence of increasing polarization."), https://www.washingtonpost.com/politics/rock-bottom-supreme-court-fight -reveals-a-country-on-the-brink/2018/10/06/426886e2-c96f-11e8-b1ed-1d2d 65b86d0c_story.html?

54. Henry Fountain, "Indonesia Tsunami's Power after Earthquake Surprises Scientists," *New York Times*, September 30, 2018, https://www.nytimes.com/2018/09/30/world/asia/indonesia-tsunami-science.html; Helen Lambourne, "Tsunami: Anatomy of a Disaster," BBC News, March 27, 2005, http://news.bbc.co.uk/2/hi/science/nature/4381395.stm.

55. See "What Causes a Tsunami?," March 10, 2011, VOA News, https://www.voanews.com/a/what-causes-a-tsunami-117813908/167170.html; Lambourne, "Tsunami: Anatomy of a Disaster."

56. Ronald Inglehart, *The Silent Revolution: Changing Values and Political Styles among Western Publics* (Princeton, NJ: Princeton University Press, 1977).

57. Ronald Inglehart, Jon Miller, and Logan Woods, "The Silent Revolution in Reverse: Trump and the Xenophobic Authoritarian Populist Parties," paper presented at American Political Science Association Meetings in Boston, August 31, 2018, 1, 3.

58. Inglehart, Miller, and Woods, "The Silent Revolution in Reverse," 9.

59. Bill Bishop, *The Big Sort: Why the Clustering of Like-Minded America Is Tearing Us Apart* (Boston: Mariner Books, 2009), 86.

60. Bishop, *The Big Sort*, 86–87.

61. Bishop, *The Big Sort*, 87.

62. Bishop, *The Big Sort*, 87. (Italics in original.)

63. Bishop, *The Big Sort*, 88.

64. Robert D. Putnam, *Bowling Alone: The Collapse and Revival of American Community* (New York: Simon & Schuster Paperbacks, 2000), 16.

65. Putnam, *Bowling Alone*, 42.

66. Putnam, *Bowling Alone*, 64.

67. Bishop, *The Big Sort*, 89.

68. Bishop, *The Big Sort*, 96.

69. Abramowitz, *The Great Alignment*, 21.

70. Bishop, *The Big Sort*, 93.

71. Bishop, *The Big Sort*, 102.

72. Abramowitz, *The Great Alignment*, xii.

73. Lilliana Mason, *Uncivil Agreement: How Politics Became our Identity* (Chicago: University of Chicago Press, 2018), 33.

74. Douglas Kellner, *Guys and Guns Amok: Domestic Terrorism and School Shootings from the Oklahoma City Bombing to the Virginia Tech Massacre* (Boulder: Paradigm Publishers, 2008), 92.

75. Bishop, *The Big Sort*, 103.

76. Bishop, *The Big Sort*, 103.

77. Abramowitz, *The Great Alignment*, 119.

78. Bishop, *The Big Sort*, 101.

79. Abramowitz, *The Great Alignment*, 27.

80. Bishop, *The Big Sort*, 68.

81. Bishop, *The Big Sort*, 245.

82. Bishop, *The Big Sort*, 57.

83. Greg Bluestein and Tyler Estep, "Meet the Two Georgia Counties with the State's Biggest Partisan Shifts," *Atlanta Journal-Constitution*, October 5, 2018, https://politics.myajc.com/news/state—regional-govt—politics/meet-the -two-georgia-counties-with-the-state-biggest-partisan-shifts/IW2xbxGH KOpimeIfXvKhiO/.

84. Bluestein and Estep, "Meet the Two Georgia Counties."

85. Bluestein and Estep, "Meet the Two Georgia Counties."

86. Bishop, *The Big Sort*, 226.

87. Mason, *Uncivil Agreement*, 42.

88. Steven M. Teles, *The Rise of the Conservative Legal Movement: The Battle for Control of The Law* (Princeton, NJ: Princeton University Press, 2008), 274.

89. Teles, *The Rise of the Conservative Legal Movement*, 9.

90. Teles, *The Rise of the Conservative Legal Movement*, 3.

91. Teles, *The Rise of the Conservative Legal Movement*, 12.

92. Mason, *Uncivil Agreement*, 3.

93. Mason, *Uncivil Agreement*, 47; Abramowitz, *The Great Alignment*, 17.

94. Tamar Hallerman, "Perdue Apologizes after Comparing Dems' Kavanaugh Resistance to Nazi Group," *Atlanta Journal-Constitution*, October 5, 2018, https:// politics.myajc.com/blog/politics/perdue-apologizes-after-comparing-dems -kavanaugh-resistance-nazi-group/8rmJdOpueyGszREOe4PxpN/.

95. Caleb Parke, "Georgetown Professor Who Wished Death to GOP Senators Supporting Kavanaugh on Leave," Fox News, October 5, 2018, https://www.foxnews.com/us/georgetown-professor-who-wished-death-to-gop -senators-supporting-kavanaugh-on-leave.

96. Mason, *Uncivil Agreement*, 42.

97. Mason, *Uncivil Agreement*, 44.

98. See Kevin Breuninger, "Barnes & Noble Says Political Book Sales Have Skyrocketed and It Released a Map that Shows How Polarized the Sales Are," CNBC.com, October 9, 2018, https://www.cnbc.com/2018/10/09/barnes-and -noble-map-of-book-sales-shows-polarized-readers-across-us.html.

99. Mason, *Uncivil Agreement*, 13.

100. Bishop, *The Big Sort*, 75.

101. Bishop, *The Big Sort*, 69.

102. Mason, *Uncivil Agreement*, 86.

103. Scott Melzer, *Gun Crusaders: The NRA's Culture War* (New York: New York University Press, 2009). Another history is Osha Gray Davidson, *Under*

Fire: The NRA and the Battle for Gun Control (expanded edition) (Iowa City: University of Iowa Press, 1998). A useful book is Edward F. Leddy, *Magnum Force Lobby: The National Rifle Association Fights Gun Control* (Lanham, MD: University Press of America, 1987).

104. Melzer, *Gun Crusaders*, 15.

105. For a concise summary of the NRA's early history, see chapter V, "History of the National Rifle Association," in Leddy, *Magnum Force Lobby*.

106. Leddy, *Magnum Force Lobby*, 93.

107. Leddy, *Magnum Force Lobby*, 94.

108. Leddy, *Magnum Force Lobby*, 97.

109. Melzer, *Gun Crusaders*, 37.

110. Melzer, *Gun Crusaders*, 16.

111. Leddy, *Magnum Force Lobby*, 29.

112. Melzer, *Gun Crusaders*, 2.

113. Leddy, *Magnum Force Lobby*, 48.

114. Melzer, *Gun Crusaders*, 11.

115. Melzer, *Gun Crusaders*, 66–67.

116. Goss, *Disarmed*, 194.

117. Abramowitz, *The Great Alignment*, 4–5.

118. Goss, *Disarmed*, 194.

Chapter One: Prelude

1. See, for example, Christopher Ingraham, "American Toddlers Are Still Shooting People on a Weekly Basis This Year," *Washington Post*, September 29, 2017, https://www.washingtonpost.com/news/wonk/wp/2017/09/29/american-toddlers-are-still-shooting-people-on-a-weekly-basis-this-year/?noredirect=on&utm_term=.1102088ea331; "At Least 111 Unintentional Shootings by Children in 2018," Everytown for Gun Safety, https://everytownresearch.org/notanaccident/, accessed July 24, 2018.

2. See, for example, Mark Berman, "Las Vegas Police End Investigation into Massacre without 'Definitively' Determining What Motivated the Gunman," *Washington Post*, August 3, 2018, https://www.washingtonpost.com/news/post-nation/wp/2018/08/03/las-vegas-police-end-investigation-into-massacre-without-definitively-determining-motive/?noredirect=on&utm_term=.041bf71e2514; Sheri Fink, "Las Vegas Gunman's Brain Exam Only Deepens Mystery of His Actions," *New York Times*, February 9, 2018, https://nyti.ms/2BPCAbR.

3. For an overview of the structure of the American gun industry and its design changes, see Tom Diaz, chapter 3, "The American Gun Industry: Designing

& Marketing Increasingly Lethal Weapons," in Timothy D. Lytton, ed., *Suing the Gun Industry: A Battle at the Crossroads of Gun Control and Mass Torts* (Ann Arbor: University of Michigan Press, 2006), 84–104.

4. Aaron Karp, "Estimating Global Civilian-Held Firearms Numbers," Briefing Paper, Small Arms Survey, Graduate Institute of International and Development Studies, Geneva (June 2018), 3. PDF downloaded from http://www .smallarmssurvey.org/publications/by-type/briefing-papers.html.

5. For a detailed history of Canada's gun control efforts, see R. Blake Brown, *Arming and Disarming: A History of Gun Control in Canada* (Toronto: University of Toronto Press, 2012). For in-depth scholarly and journalistic examinations of the global aspects of gun violence respectively, see Peter Squires, *Gun Crime in Global Contexts* (New York: Routledge, 2014), and Iain Overton, *The Way of the Gun* (New York: HarperCollins, 2016).

6. "Overall Firearm Gunshot Nonfatal Injuries and Rates per 100,000." Source: U.S. Department of Health and Human Services, National Center for Injury Prevention and Control, Centers for Disease Control and Prevention. Computed by author using WISQARS data base, https://webappa.cdc.gov/ sasweb/ncipc/nfirates.html. For an ongoing collection of stories about survivors of gunshot wounds in the United States, see the Trace's "Shot and Forgotten" project, https://www.thetrace.org/projects/shot-and-forgotten/.

7. Scott Clement, "44 Percent of Americans Know Someone Shot by a Gun, and They're Just as Divided about Guns as the Rest of Us," *Washington Post*, June 22, 2017, https://www.washingtonpost.com/news/the-fix/wp/2017/06/22/44 -percent-of-americans-know-someone-shot-by-a-gun-and-they-are-just-as -divided-about-gun-restrictions-as-everyone-else/?noredirect=on&utm_term= .fdbb91a0bb81.

8. Sukhada Tatke, "99.9% of Americans Will Know a Victim of Gun Violence in Their Lifetime," Quartz, October 26, 2016, https://qz.com/819003/99-9 -of-americans-will-know-a-victim-of-gun-violence-in-their-lifetime/.

9. Chelsea Bailey, "More Americans Killed by Guns since 1968 than in All U.S. Wars—Combined," *NBC Nightly News*, October 4, 2017, https://www.nbc news.com/storyline/las-vegas-shooting/more-americans-killed-guns-1968-all-u-s -wars-combined-n807156.

10. For one object example among many, see the case of Long Island, New York, father John White, reported in Selim Algar, "I Didn't Mean to Shoot Him," *New York Post*, December 15, 2007, https://nypost.com/2007/12/15/i -didnt-mean-to-shoot-him/; Corey Kilgannon, "Man Convicted for Shooting Teenager," *New York Times*, December 23, 2007, https://www.nytimes .com/2007/12/23/nyregion/23trial.html; "Man Set Free in Teen's Racially

Charged Death," CBS News, December 23, 2010, https://www.cbsnews.com/news/man-set-free-in-teens-racially-charged-death/.

11. The narrative of Todd Irvine's discovery and rescue of Christopher Husbands is based on the following sources: telephone interview with Todd Irvine, March 7, 2018; Sam Pazzano, "Eaton Centre Trial Hears of Husbands' 2012 Stabbing," *Toronto Sun*, November 19, 2014, http://torontosun.com/2014/11/19/eaton-centre-trial-hears-of-husbands-2012-stabbing/wcm/94a70774-68ff-4127-bd97-9d85890bc644; Niamh Scallon, "Eaton Centre Shooting: I Really Wanted Him to Live," *Star*, June 6, 2012, https://www.thestar.com/news/crime/2012/06/06/eaton_centre_shooting_i_really_wanted_him_to_live_recalls_the_man_who_helped_a_dying_christopher_husbands_one_cold_night_in_february.html; Jennifer Yang, "The Charmed Climb of Toronto's Tree Whisperer," *Toronto Star*, May 1, 2010, https://www.thestar.com/news/gta/2010/05/01/the_charmed_climb_of_torontos_tree_whisperer.html.

12. The description and discussion of the Regent Park and Cabbagetown neighborhoods is based on the following sources: telephone interview with Todd Irvine, March 7, 2018; "Cabbagetown, Toronto," *Wikipedia*, https://en.wikipedia.org/wiki/Cabbagetown,_Toronto; Heather Loney, "Background: Toronto's Regent Park," Global News, June 13, 2012, https://globalnews.ca/news/243057/background-torontos-regent-park/; Timothy Appleby and Adrian Morrow, "Alleged Stabbing Incident Prompted Fatal Toronto Shooting: Source," *Globe and Mail*, June 5, 2012, updated March 26, 2017, https://www.theglobeandmail.com/news/toronto/alleged-stabbing-incident-prompted-fatal-toronto-shooting-source/article4231218/.

13. Squires, *Gun Crime*, 32.

14. For a description of the role of poverty in fomenting terrorism, see the story of Mohammed Youseff Hammoud and his odyssey out of Beirut's Bourj al-Barajneh neighborhood in Tom Diaz and Barbara Newman, *Lightning out of Lebanon: Hezbollah Terrorists on American Soil* (New York: Ballantine Books, 2006), 7–16. For a description of the role of marginalization in the creation of gangs and their continuing attraction to some youth, see the discussion of the academic work of Dr. James Diego Vigil in Tom Diaz, *No Boundaries: Transnational Latino Gangs and American Law Enforcement* (Ann Arbor: University of Michigan Press, 2011), 43–45.

15. Philip J. Cook and Kristin A. Goss, *The Gun Debate: What Everyone Needs to Know* (New York: Oxford University Press, 2014), 59.

16. David Taylor, "Chicago's Deadly Summer: Guns, Gangs and the Legacy of Racial Inequality," *Guardian*, August 12, 2018, https://www.theguardian.com/us-news/2018/aug/12/chicago-gun-violence-racial-inequality-segregation-activism.

17. Albert W. Alschuler, "Two Guns, Four Guns, Six Guns, More Guns: Does Arming the Public Reduce Crime?," 31 *Valparaiso University Law Review* 365 (1997), 371, http://scholar.valpo.edu/vulr/vol31/iss2/3.

18. Squires, *Gun Crime*, 23.

19. Edward F. Leddy, *Magnum Force Lobby: The National Rifle Association Fights Gun Control* (Lanham, MD: University Press of America, 1987), 46.

20. Jeff Cooper, "Cooper's Corner," *Guns & Ammo*, April 1991, 104, cited in Tom Diaz, *Making a Killing: The Business of Guns in America* (New York: New Press, 1999), 191.

21. Los Angeles Almanac, "Racial/Ethnic Composition, Los Angeles County, 1990–2010 Census," http://www.laalmanac.com/population/po13.php.

22. Yamiche Alcindor, "Ben Carson Calls Poverty a 'State of Mind,' Igniting a Backlash," *New York Times*, May 25, 2017, https://www.nytimes .com/2017/05/25/us/politics/ben-carson-poverty-hud-state-of-mind.html.

23. Tom LoBianco and Ashley Killough, "Trump Pitches Black Voters: 'What the Hell Do You Have to Lose?'" CNN, August 19, 2016, https://www.cnn .com/2016/08/19/politics/donald-trump-african-american-voters/index.html.

24. "Full Transcript: Donald Trump Speaks in Michigan," *Politico*, August 19, 2016, https://www.politico.com/story/2016/08/donald-trump-michigan-speech -transcript-227221.

25. Jim Tankersley and Margot Sanger-Katz, "Declaring War on Poverty 'Largely Over,' White House Urges Work Requirements for Aid," *New York Times*, July 12, 2018, https://www.nytimes.com/2018/07/12/us/politics/white -house-war-on-poverty-work-requirements.html.

26. Lynda Kinkade, "America's Poor Becoming More Destitute under Trump, UN Report Says," CNN, June 22, 2018, https://www.cnn.com/2018/06/22/us/ america-poverty-un-report/index.html.

27. Interview with Dr. John Nicoletti, May 21, 2018.

28. Rosie Dimmano, "Christopher Husbands Tells Trial of Brutal Beating That Led to Eaton Centre Shooting," *Toronto Star*, November 24, 2014, https:// www.thestar.com/news/crime/2014/11/24/christopher_husbands_tell_trial_of _brutal_beating_that_lead_to_eaton_centre_shooting.html.

29. The discussion of Christopher Husbands's potential gang affiliation and drug dealing is based on the following sources: "Eaton Centre Shooting May Be Gang-Related, Police Say," CBC News, June 3, 2012, http://www .cbc.ca/news/canada/toronto/eaton-centre-shooting-may-be-gang-related-police -say-1.1160457; Jennifer Pagliaro and Curtis Rush, "Eaton Centre Shooting: Gangs 'Changed Everything,' Says Suspect's Father," *Toronto Star*, June 4, 2012, https://www.thestar.com/news/crime/2012/06/04/eaton_centre_shooting _gangs_changed_everything_says_suspects_father.html; Appleby and Morrow,

"Alleged Stabbing Incident"; Jennifer Pagliaro, Jim Rankin, and Sandro Contenta, "Eaton Centre Shooting: Sic Thugs of Regent Park and the Allure of Gangs," *Toronto Star*, June 9, 2012, https://www.thestar.com/news/gta/2012/06/09/ eaton_centre_shooting_sic_thugs_of_regent_park_and_the_allure_of_gangs.html; Steve Mertl, "Toronto Eaton Centre Shooting Shines Light on Canada's Gang Problem," Yahoo News, June 12, 2012, https://ca.news.yahoo.com/blogs/daily brew/toronto-eaton-centre-shooting-shines-light-canada-gang-202058661.html.

30. Sam Pazzano, "Accused Eaton Centre Shooter Christopher Husbands Guilty of Sex Assault," *Toronto Sun*, October 11, 2012, http://torontosun .com/2012/10/11/accused-eaton-centre-shooter-christopher-husbands-guilty -of-sex-assault/wcm/09e67bbb-93eb-4a0b-aba0-5eb9bbf9efef; "Eaton Centre Shooting: Alleged Killer Had Firearms Offences Dropped in Hamilton Weeks Earlier," *Waterloo Regional Record*, August 3, 2012, https://www.therecord .com/news-story/2609601-eaton-centre-shooting-alleged-killer-had-firearms -offences-dropped-in-hamilton-weeks-earlier/.

31. See Liza H. Gold, M.D., ed., *Gun Violence and Mental Illness* (Arlington, VA: American Psychiatric Association Publishing, 2016), 20–22; Garen J. Wintemute, "Broadening Denial Criteria for the Purchase and Possession of Firearms," in Daniel W. Webster and Jon S. Vernick, eds., *Reducing Gun Violence in America* (Baltimore: Johns Hopkins University Press, 2013), 77–93. For an object example, see Peter Hermann, "Man Shot and Injured in D.C. by Maryland Officer Was Already Awaiting Gun, Drug Trial in Maryland," *Washington Post*, July 28, 2018, https://www.washingtonpost.com/local/public-safety/man -shot-and-injured-in-dc-by-maryland-officer-was-already-awaiting-gun-drug -trial-in-maryland/2018/07/27/ef188d78-91bc-11e8-8322-b5482bf5e0f5_story .html?utm_term=.9e935e7c3f97.

32. Dimmano, "Christopher Husbands Tells Trial."

33. Dimmano, "Christopher Husbands Tells Trial."

34. Unless otherwise noted, quotes of Jessica Ghawi's observations on the events at the Eaton Centre are from her essay "Late Night Thoughts on the Eaton Center Shooting," posted June 5, 2012, https://jessicaredfield.wordpress .com/2012/06/05/late-night-thoughts-on-the-eaton-center-shooting/.

35. Cheryl Bradley, "Meet Jay Meloff: Heart and Soul Player with NH: Aspirations," *SBNation*, July 20, 2012, https://denver.sbnation.com/denver -cutthroats/2012/7/20/3168850/jay-meloff-denver-cutthroats-hockey.

36. "I Like My Hockey How I Like My Men," posted on the blog "A Run On of Thoughts," August 8, 2011, https://jessicaredfield.wordpress .com/2011/08/08/i-like-my-hockey-how-i-like-my-men/.

37. Victoria Ptashnick, "Canadian Boyfriend of 'Batman' Shooting Victim Devastated," *Toronto Sun*, July 20, 2012, https://torontosun.com/2012/07/20/

boyfriend-of-batman-shooting-victim-devastated/wcm/0ffd64d2-4148-4d78
-92ca-0b8202ce19d8.

38. Allison Cross, "Toronto Hockey Player Tells of Grief over Death of Sportscaster Girlfriend, Jessica Ghawi, Killed in Colorado Shooting," *National Post*, July 20, 2012, http://nationalpost.com/news/toronto-hockey-player-tells -of-grief-over-death-of-sportscaster-girlfriend-jessica-ghawi-killed-in-colorado -shooting.

39. Cheryl Bradley, "Meet Jay Meloff."

40. Allison Cross, "Toronto Hockey Player."

41. Telephone interview with Sandy and Lonnie Phillips, February 12, 2018. Jessi described herself on her Twitter page as, "Southern. Sarcastic. Sass. Class. Crass. Grammar snob." https://twitter.com/jessicaredfield?lang=en.

42. Telephone interview with Sandy and Lonnie Phillips, February 12, 2018.

43. See, "Eaton Centre," Canadian Encyclopedia, http://www.thecanadian encyclopedia.ca/en/article/eaton-centre/; "Toronto Eaton Centre," Wikipedia, https://en.wikipedia.org/wiki/Toronto_Eaton_Centre; "Toronto Eaton Centre," Zeilder, https://zeidler.com/projects/CF-toronto-eaton-centre/. For a video tour, see "Tour Toronto Eaton Centre," Fartur, https://www.youtube.com/ watch?v=BPbvI1YEDHk.

44. Unless otherwise specifically noted, the description of the Eaton Centre shooting in this chapter is based on Jessi's blog and the following sources: email to author from Mary Humphrey, General Counsel, Ministry of the Attorney General, Toronto, Ontario, February 12, 2018; "Toronto Eaton Centre Shoot-ing Kills 1, Injures 7," CBC News, June 3, 2012, http://www.cbc.ca/news/ canada/toronto/toronto-eaton-centre-shooting-kills-1-injures-7-1.1160460; "Eaton Centre Shooting May Be Gang-Related, Police Say," CBC News, June 4, 2012, http://www.cbc.ca/news/canada/toronto/eaton-centre-shooting-may -be-gang-related-police-say-1.1160457; Pagliaro and Rush, "Eaton Centre Shooting: Gangs 'Changed Everything.'"; Rosie DiManno, "Timeline of Christopher Husbands' Deadly Eaton Centre Attack Displayed Frame by Frame," *Toronto Star*, October 15, 2014, and accompanying video surveillance clip, https://www.thestar.com/news/gta/2014/10/15/timeline_of_christopher _husbands_deadly_eaton_centre_attack_displayed_frame_by_frame_dimanno .html; Dimanno, "Christopher Husbands Tells Trial"; Lisa La Flamme, "The In-side Story: How a Trip to the Toronto Eaton Centre Turned into Horror," CTV National News, February 1, 2013, and video "The Survivor, Part One," posted at https://www.ctvnews.ca/w5/the-inside-story-how-a-trip-to-the-toronto-eaton -centre-turned-into-horror-1.1139769.

45. "Eaton Centre Shooting May Be Gang-Related, Police Say," CBC News.

46. "Toronto Eaton Centre Shooting Kills 1, Injures 7," CBC News.

47. Pagliaro and Rush,"Eaton Centre Shooting: Gangs 'Changed Everything.'"

48. The description of Connor Stevenson's shooting, his treatment, and his recovery is based on the following sources (in addition to sources cited above describing the Eaton Centre shooting): La Flamme, "The Inside Story," and a series of documentary videos accompanying the story, titled collectively "The Survivor"; "Connor Stevenson 'Pretty Dizzy' after Being Shot at Eaton Centre," CBC News, and accompanying news video, http://www.cbc.ca/news/canada/toronto/connor-stevenson-pretty-dizzy-after-being-shot-at-eaton-centre-1.2834051.

49. The popular .40 S&W is a caliber of handgun ammunition jointly developed by the Smith & Wesson and Winchester gun-manufacturing companies in the late 1980s. It was intended to provide a powerful, more user-friendly large-caliber alternative to the .45 caliber handgun round, which many thought difficult for the average shooter to control. Husbands threw the pistol he used into Lake Ontario sometime after the shooting. The gun was never recovered. However, a firearms expert called by the Crown examined the shell casings left at the scene. He determined from unique firing pin indentations and markings on the cases that the gun was a Glock chambered in .40 S&W caliber. Email to author from Mary Humphrey, General Counsel, Ministry of the Attorney General, Toronto, Ontario, February 12, 2018.

50. Natasha Rudnick, "Why Canada's Gun Culture Is Different—And Why Its Shootings Shock America," *Washington Post*, October 23, 2014, https://www.washingtonpost.com/news/storyline/wp/2014/10/23/why-canadas-gun-culture-is-different-and-why-its-shootings-shock-america/?utm_term=.c8fb4776fc72.

51. Brown, *Arming and Disarming*, 79.

52. David B. Kopel, *The Samurai, the Mountie, and the Cowboy: Should America Adopt the Gun Controls of Other Democracies?* (Buffalo: Prometheus Books, 1992), 14.

53. See, for example, Charlotte Davis, "USA Has Been Taken Over by Tidal Wave of European-Style Socialists, Says NRA Chief," *Daily Express*, February 23, 2018, https://www.express.co.uk/news/world/922628/NRA-Donald-Trump-Twitter-President-gun-control-debate-Florida-shooting.

54. Seymour Martin Lipset, *Continental Divide: The Values and Institutions of the United States and Canada* (New York: Routledge, 1991), 2.

55. Erin Grinshteyn and David Hemenway, "Violent Death Rates: The US Compared with Other High-Income OECD Countries, 2010," *American Journal of Medicine* 129 (2016), 269, doi: 10.1016/j.amjmed.2015.10.025.

56. Grinshteyn and Hemenway, "Violent Death Rates," Table 4, 271.

57. Canada, Ministry of Industry, Canadian Centre for Justice Statistics, "Firearms and Violent Crime in Canada," Adam Cotter, author. Catalogue no.

85-0020-X, 2014, 8 (raw number of firearm homicides in Canada), Text box 4 at 10.

58. Canadian Centre, "Firearms and Violent Crime," 4.

59. Garen J. Wintemute, "The Epidemiology of Firearms Violence in the Twenty-first Century United States," *Annu. Rev. Public Health*, 2015, 35:5–19, doi: 10.1146/annurev-publichealth-031914-122535, 6. For a general discussion of the problem of guns and suicide, see E. Michael Lewiecki and Sara A. Miller, "Suicide, Guns, and Public Policy," *J. Public Health*, 2013, 103:27–31, doi:10.2105/AJPH.2012.300964, https://www.ncbi.nlm.nih.gov/pmc/articles/PMC3518361/.

60. Nell Greenfieldboyce, "CDC: U.S. Suicide Rates Have Climbed Dramatically," National Public Radio, *All Things Considered*, June 7, 2018, https://www.npr.org/sections/health-shots/2018/06/07/617897261/cdc-u-s-suicide-rates-have-climbed-dramatically.

61. Michael D. Anestis, *Guns and Suicide—An American Epidemic* (New York: Oxford University Press, 2018).

62. Canadian Centre, "Firearms and Violent Crime," 4.

63. Cook and Goss, *The Gun Debate*, 63–64.

64. Lipset, *Continental Divide*, 8.

65. Aaron Karp, "Estimating Global Civilian-Held Firearms Numbers," Briefing Paper, Small Arms Survey, Graduate Institute of International and Development Studies Geneva, 2018, 3.

66. Christopher Ingraham, "There Are More Guns Than People in the United States, According to a New Study of Global Firearm Ownership," *Washington Post*, June 19, 2018, https://www.washingtonpost.com/news/wonk/wp/2018/06/19/there-are-more-guns-than-people-in-the-united-states-according-to-a-new-study-of-global-firearm-ownership/?utm_term=.a82b56e93943.

67. Karp, "Estimating Global," Table 1 at 4.

68. Kim Parker et al., "America's Complex Relationship with Guns," Pew Research Center, June 2017, http://assets.pewresearch.org/wp-content/uploads/sites/3/2017/06/06151541/Guns-Report-FOR-WEBSITE-PDF-6-21.pdf, 6.

69. Robert J. Spitzer, *The Politics of Gun Control: Sixth Edition* (Boulder, CO: Paradigm Publishers, 2015), 8.

70. See Idil Mussa, "Spike in Gun and Gang Violence in Canada Has Experts Worried," CBC News, March 7, 2018, https://www.cbc.ca/news/politics/spike-in-gun-and-gang-violence-in-canada-has-experts-worried-1.4564643; Sigal Samuel, "Canada Is Raging against Gun Violence—But Not Like America," *Atlantic*, July 2018, https://www.theatlantic.com/international/archive/2018/07/canada-gun-control-debate/566102/.

71. Daniel Fisher, "Canada Tried Registering Long Guns—And Gave Up," *Forbes*, January 22, 2013, https://www.forbes.com/sites/danielfisher/2013/01/22/canada-tried-registering-long-guns-and-gave-up/#7c32e4995a1b.

72. Kopel, *The Samurai*, 137.

73. Lipset, *Continental Divide*, 1.

74. Lipset, *Continental Divide*, 8.

75. Lipset, *Continental Divide*, 14.

76. Kopel, *The Samurai*, 138.

77. Lipset, *Continental Divide*, 3.

78. Kopel, *The Samurai*, 137.

79. Lipset, *Continental Divide*, 91.

Chapter Two: The Maple Leaf and the Eagle

1. Unless otherwise noted, quotations from Jessi are taken from her Twitter feed.

2. Unless otherwise noted, quotes from Sandy Phillips in this chapter are from telephone interviews with Sandy and Lonnie Phillips on February 12 and October 20, 2018.

3. See Regional Heart Center, University of Washington Medical Center, "Supraventricular Tachycardia (SVT) and Catherer Ablation: Treating Your Abnormal Heart Rhythm," June 1, 2014, available at https://healthonline.washington.edu/health_online/show_details.asp?item=4250.

4. Nahum M. Sarna, *The JPS Torah Commentary: Genesis* (New York: Jewish Publication Society, 1989), 221.

5. Michelle Graff, "The History behind Mizpah Jewelry," nationaljeweler.com, July 23, 2014, https://www.nationaljeweler.com/independents/2059-the-history-behind-mizpah-jewelry.

6. "Talking to Children about Violence: Tips for Parents and Teachers," National Association of School Psychologists (2016).

7. Robert J. Spitzer, *Saving the Constitution from Lawyers: How Legal Training and Law Reviews Distort Constitutional Meaning* (New York: Cambridge University Press, 2008), 130.

8. *District of Columbia v. Heller*, 554 U.S. 570 (2008). In striking down the District of Columbia's ban on private ownership of handguns, the case settled that the right to bear arms under the Second Amendment is a personal right. A later case, *McDonald v. Chicago*, 561 U.S. 3025 (2010), extended the scope of that personal right beyond federal entities to protection against state and local government restrictions as well. For histories of the American gun regulations and cultural forces that led to these decisions, see Brian Doherty, *Gun Control*

on Trial: Inside the Supreme Court Battle over the Second Amendment (Washington, DC: Cato Institute, 2008), and Adam Winkler, *Gun Fight: The Battle over the Right to Bear Arms in the United States* (New York: W.W. Norton, 2013). For a different view than these two, see chapter 2, "Supreme Nonsense and Deadly Myths," in Tom Diaz, *The Last Gun: How Changes in the Gun Industry Are Killing Americans and What It Will Take to Stop It* (New York: New Press, 2013), 37–60.

9. Society for Personality and Social Psychology, "Why Do Americans Own Handguns? Fear of Crime and a Broader Sense of Danger," *Science Daily*, June 8, 2017, www.sciencedaily.com/releases/2017/06/170608072909.htm.

10. Philip J. Cook and John J. Donohue, "Saving Lives by Regulating Guns: Evidence for Policy," *Science* 358 (6368), December 8, 2017, 1259–61, doi: 10.1126/science.aar3067, 1260.

11. Cook and Donohue, "Saving Lives," 1260.

12. Ann E. Marimow, "Hundreds Apply to Carry Loaded, Concealed Handguns in D.C. Most Don't Live There," *Washington Post*, January 26, 2018, https://www.washingtonpost.com/local/public-safety/hundreds-apply-to-carry-loaded-concealed-handguns-in-dc-most-dont-live-there/2018/01/18/566236c2-f0ab-11e7-b3bf-ab90a706e175_story.html?; Ann E. Marimow and Peter Jamison, "D.C. Won't Appeal Court Ruling Striking Down a Portion of the City's Gun Control Law," *Washington Post*, October 5, 2017, https://www.washingtonpost.com/local/dc-politics/dc-will-not-appeal-gun-law-to-supreme-court/2017/10/05/e0e7c054-a9d0-11e7-850e-2bdd1236be5d_story.html?

13. "The Showdown over the Concealed Carry Reciprocity Act," CBS: *60 Minutes*, February 11, 2018, https://www.cbsnews.com/news/concealed-carry-reciprocity-act-showdown/.

14. Cook and Donohue, "Saving Lives," 1260–61.

15. Albert W. Alschuler, "Two Guns, Four Guns, Six Guns, More Guns: Does Arming the Public Reduce Crime?" 31 *Valparaiso University Law Review* 365 (1997), 373, http://scholar.valpo.edu/vulr/vol31/iss2/3.

16. Alix M. Freedman, "Pocket Pistols Grow Smaller, Deadlier and More Popular," *Wall Street Journal*, September 12, 1996, https://www.wsj.com/articles/SB842479592434263000.

17. For a narrative of these campaigns and their consequences, see Diaz, *The Last Gun*, chapter 5, "The Third Wave: Beyond the Gunshine State," 108–40.

18. John R. Lott, Jr., *More Guns, Less Crime—Understanding Crime and Gun-Control Laws*, third edition (Chicago: University of Chicago Press, 2010).

19. Michael Siegel et al., "Easiness of Legal Access to Concealed Firearm Permits and Homicide Rates in the United States," *American Journal of Public*

Health 107:12 (December 2017), 1923–29, doi:10.2105/AJPH.2017.304057, 1923; Cook and Donohue, "Saving Lives," 1260.

20. "NRA: 'Only Way to Stop a Bad Guy with a Gun Is with a Good Guy with a Gun,'" CBSDC/AP, December 21, 2012, https://washington.cbslocal.com/2012/12/21/nra-only-way-to-stop-a-bad-guy-with-a-gun-is-with-a-good-guy-with-a-gun/.

21. Chris Mooney, "Double Barreled Double Standards" *Mother Jones*, October 13, 2003, https://www.motherjones.com/politics/2003/10/double-barreled-double-standards/.

22. Louis Klarevas, *Rampage Nation: Securing America from Mass Shootings* (Amherst, NY: Prometheus Books, 2016), 149.

23. Evan DeFilippis and Devin Hughes, "Shooting Down the Gun Lobby's Favorite 'Academic': A Lott of Lies," *Armed With Reason*, December 1, 2014, https://www.armedwithreason.com/shooting-down-the-gun-lobbys-favorite-academic-a-lott-of-lies/.

24. Ted Goertzel, "Myths of Murder and Multiple Regression," http://www.crab.rutgers.edu/~goertzel/mythsofmurder.htm. (Originally published in the *Skeptical Inquirer*, volume 26, no. 1, January/February 2002, 19–23.)

25. Julia Lurie, "When the Gun Lobby Tries to Justify Firearms Everywhere, It Turns to This Guy," *Mother Jones*, July 28, 2015, https://www.motherjones.com/politics/2015/07/john-lott-guns-crime-data/.

26. National Research Council of the National Academies (2005), *Firearms and Violence: A Critical Review*, Committee to Improve Research Information and Data on Firearms, 150.

27. Lurie, "When the Gun Lobby Tries."

28. Lurie, "When the Gun Lobby Tries."

29. Klarevas, *Rampage Nation*, 148.

30. Peter Moskowitz, "Inside the Mind of America's Favorite Gun Researcher," *Pacific Standard* magazine, June 1, 2017, https://psmag.com/magazine/inside-the-mind-of-americas-favorite-gun-researcher; Lurie, "When the Gun Lobby Tries"; Klarevas, *Rampage Nation*, 152.

31. Lurie, "When the Gun Lobby Tries."

32. Cook and Donohue, "Saving Lives," 1260–61.

33. Siegel et al., "Easiness of Legal Access," 1927.

34. Form 990, "Return of Organization Exempt from Income Tax, 2016," for Crime Prevention Research Center, Inc., dated May 4, 2017.

35. Moskowitz, "Inside the Mind."

36. See Lloyd Sealy Library, John Jay College of Criminal Justice, "What Is a Peer-Reviewed Article?" http://guides.lib.jjay.cuny.edu/c

.php?g=288333&p=1922599; "What Is Peer Review?" https://www.elsevier.com/reviewers/what-is-peer-review.

37. Moskowitz, "Inside the Mind."

38. Olivia Exstrum, "The Guy behind the Bogus Immigration Report Has a Long History of Terrible and Misleading Research," *Mother Jones*, February 7, 2018, https://www.motherjones.com/politics/2018/02/the-guy-behind-the-bogus-immigration-report-has-a-long-history-of-terrible-and-misleading-research/.

39. On the commission's demise and discrediting, see Eli Rosenberg, "'The Most Bizarre Thing I've Ever Been a Part of': Trump Panel Found No Widespread Voter Fraud, Ex-member Says," *Washington Post*, August 3, 2018, https://www.washingtonpost.com/news/politics/wp/2018/08/03/the-most-bizarre-thing-ive-ever-been-a-part-of-trump-panel-found-no-voter-fraud-ex-member-says/; Eli Rosenberg, "Kris Kobach Used Flawed Research to Defend Trump's Voter Fraud Panel, Experts Say," *Washington Post*, August 7, 2018, https://www.washingtonpost.com/news/politics/wp/2018/08/07/experts-say-kris-kobach-used-flawed-research-to-defend-trumps-voter-fraud-panel/.

40. Jennifer Mascia, "Pro-Gun Researcher Uses Trump Voter Fraud Commission to Troll Democrats on Background Checks," *Trace*, September 12, 2017, https://www.thetrace.org/rounds/john-lott-trump-voter-fraud-background-checks-nics/.

41. Christopher Ingraham, "Trump's Voter Fraud Commission Is Hearing a Proposal to Make Every Voter Pass a Gun Background Check," *Washington Post*, September 12, 2017, https://www.washingtonpost.com/news/wonk/wp/2017/09/12/trumps-voter-fraud-commission-is-hearing-a-proposal-to-make-every-voter-pass-a-gun-background-check/.

42. See "Sheriff David Clarke to Attend National Capital Friends of NRA," Arsenal Attorneys, May 2, 2017, https://www.arsenalattorneys.com/firearms-blog/breaking-news-sheriff-david-clarke-to-attend-national-capital-friends-of-nra; Dave Gilson, "The NRA's Board Members Are—Shockingly—Mostly White Guys," *Mother Jones*, March 1, 2018, https://www.motherjones.com/politics/2018/03/nra-board-members-tom-selleck/. See also, "Who's Backing the Last Pro-gun 'Academic,' John Lott?" Coalition to Stop Gun Violence, https://www.csgv.org/whos-backing-last-pro-gun-academic/.

43. In 2014, during an interview with Guns.com, Nugent called President Barack Obama "a subhuman mongrel" and a "chimpanzee." Justin Sink, "Nugent: Obama a 'Subhuman Mongrel,'" *Hill*, January 22, 2014, http://thehill.com/video/administration/196156-nugent-obama-a-subhuman-mongrel; Amy Davidson Sorkin, "Ted Nugent's 'Subhuman Mongrel' Slur, in Translation," *New*

Yorker, February 22, 2014, https://www.newyorker.com/news/amy-davidson/ ted-nugents-subhuman-mongrel-slur-in-translation. In a 1990 interview with the *Detroit Free Press*, Nugent defended racial apartheid in South Africa. "Apartheid isn't that cut and dried. All men are not created equal," he said. He also excused his frequent use of the N— word. "I use the word N— a lot because I hang around with a lot of N—s." Duane Noriyuki, "Ted Nugent Grows Up?" *Detroit Free Press Magazine*, July 15, 1990, downloaded August 17, 2018, from https:// www.scribd.com/doc/214489436/ted-nugent-grows-up-the-detroit-free-press -magazine-july-15-1990.

44. In 2016, Nugent posted a message on Facebook about "who is really behind gun control." The post featured a "grid of photos of Jewish legislators and leaders who support gun control, labeling each photo with Israeli flags and descriptions . . . [including] 'Jew York City mayor Mikey Bloomberg,' and, under a photo of the late New Jersey senator Frank Lautenberg, 'Gave Russian Jew immigrants your tax money.'" Sarah Begley, "Ted Nugent Posts Anti-Semitic Facebook Message about Gun Control," *Time*, February 9, 2016, http://time.com/4213198/ted -nugent-anti-semitic-facebook-gun-control/. In the face of a storm of criticism, Nugent at first dug in and defiantly posted, "What sort of racist prejudiced POS could possibly not know that Jews for gun control are Nazis in disguise." Lindsey Bever, "Ted Nugent Digs in amid Anti-Semitic Accusations—And Calls for His NRA Ouster," *Washington Post*, February 10, 2016, https://www.washington post.com/news/post-nation/wp/2016/02/10/gun-rights-advocates-urge-nra -to-remove-ted-nugent-from-board-over-anti-semitic-outburst/. Finally, under pressure even from other pro-gun advocates, Nugent issued an apology claiming that—in spite of the Israeli flags pinned to each person's picture, "I made no connection whatsoever to any religious affiliation." Stephen Rex Brown, "Ted Nugent Apologizes for Anti-Semitic Facebook Post," *New York Daily News*, February 18, 2016, http://www.nydailynews.com/news/national/ted-nugent -apologizes-anti-semitic-facebook-post-article-1.2536411#.

45. In 2007, during an onstage rant, Nugent said, "Obama, he's a piece of shit. I told him to suck on my machine gun. Hey, Hillary, you might want to ride one of these [machine guns] into the sunset, you worthless b—." Elizabeth Goodman, "Ted Nugent Threatens to Kill Barack Obama, Hillary Clinton during Vicious Onstage Rant," *Rolling Stone*, August 24, 2007, https://www.rollingstone.com/music/music-news/ted-nugent-threatens -to-kill-barack-obama-and-hillary-clinton-during-vicious-onstage-rant-94687/. A video of the incident is at YouTube video at https://www.youtube.com/ watch?v=vy8RIiTyhMI. In April 2012, during what was described as "an impassioned plea for support for Republican presidential candidate Mitt Romney" at an NRA meeting, Nugent said, "We need to ride into the battlefield and chop

their heads off in November," adding, "If Barack Obama becomes the next president in November, again, I will either be dead or in jail by this time next year." Natalie Jennings, "Ted Nugent Comments Prompt Secret Service Investigation," *Washington Post*, April 19, 2012, https://www.washingtonpost.com/politics/ted-nugent-comments-prompt-secret-service-investigation/2012/04/18/gIQA5vvcRT_story.html?utm_term=.3b7b2abb8e56. Two U.S. Secret Service agents visited Nugent as a result of his remarks, but no further action was taken. The Reliable Source, "Ted Nugent: 'Good, Professional' Meeting with Secret Service Unfolds without Incident," *Washington Post*, April 19, 2012, https://www.washingtonpost.com/blogs/reliable-source/post/ted-nugents-meeting-with-secret-service-unfolds-without-incident/2012/04/19/gIQALXFnTT_blog.html?utm_term=.6bbfe83b2c38.

46. Alex Horton, "Ted Nugent Says Parkland Students 'Have No Soul,' Calls Them 'Mushy-Brained Children,'" *Washington Post*, March 31, 2018, https://www.washingtonpost.com/news/arts-and-entertainment/wp/2018/03/31/ted-nugent-says-parkland-students-have-no-soul-calls-them-mushy-brained-children/.

47. Kate Feldman, "Ted Nugent Doubles Down on attack of Parkland Survivor David Hogg: 'He Is Consumed with Hate,'" *New York Daily News*, April 3, 2018, http://www.nydailynews.com/entertainment/ted-nugent-doubles-attack-parkland-survivor-david-hogg-article-1.3911341#.

48. Noriyuki, "Ted Nugent Grows Up?"

49. David Mikkelson, "Ted Nugent Dodged the Draft?" Snopes.com, https://www.snopes.com/fact-check/the-artful-dodger/ (quoting 1977 *High Times* magazine interview with Nugent).

50. Noriyuki, "Ted Nugent Grows Up?"

51. Mikkelson, "Ted Nugent Dodged."

52. Mikkelson, "Ted Nugent Dodged."

53. Mikkelson, "Ted Nugent Dodged."

54. Glenn Thrush, "4 Hours at the White House with Ted Nugent, Sarah Palin and Kid Rock," *New York Times*, April 20, 2017, https://www.nytimes.com/2017/04/20/us/politics/sarah-palin-kid-rock-ted-nugent-white-house.html; Josh Nathan-Kazis, "Ted Nugent, Who Pinned Gun Control Efforts on Jews, Invited to White House," *Forward*, April 21, 2017, https://forward.com/fast-forward/369521/ted-nugent-who-called-obama-sub-human-invited-to-white-house-dinner/.

55. Meghan Keneally, "After School Shooting, Breaking Down the Conspiracy Theories Facing Parkland Students," ABC News, February 22, 2018, https://abcnews.go.com/US/school-shooting-breaking-conspiracy-theories-facing-parkland-students/story?id=53273847 (Capitals in original).

56. Cockburn, "The Wild, Wild World of Sheriff David Clarke," *Spectator USA*, March 2018, https://spectator.us/2018/03/the-wild-wild-world-of-sheriff-david-clarke/.

57. Cliff Schecter, "How David Clarke Bridges Donald Trump's Gun Nuts and Vladimir Putin's Kleptocrats," Daily Beast, December 5, 2016, https://www.thedailybeast.com/how-david-clarke-bridges-donald-trumps-gun-nuts-and-vladimir-putins-kleptocrats.

58. Cockburn, "The Wild, Wild World." Clarke filed for divorce from his wife of some twenty-two years in February 2018. Daniel Bice, "Former Sheriff David Clarke Files for Divorce in Milwaukee County," *Milwaukee Journal Sentinel*, February 23, 2018, https://www.jsonline.com/story/news/politics/2018/02/23/bice-former-sheriff-david-clarke-files-divorce-milwaukee-county/366426002/.

59. Pete Madden and Matthew Mosk, "Senate Democrats Probe NRA Donors' Contacts with Russians in Moscow," ABC News, July 26, 2018, https://abcnews.go.com/Politics/senate-democrats-probe-nra-donors-contacts-russians-moscow/story?id=56840406; Tim Mak, "Depth of Russian Politician's Cultivation of NRA Ties Revealed," *NPR Morning Edition*, March 1, 2018, https://www.npr.org/2018/03/01/590076949/depth-of-russian-politicians-cultivation-of-nra-ties-revealed; Tim Mak, "Top Trump Ally Met with Putin's Deputy in Moscow," Daily Beast, March 7, 2017, https://www.thedailybeast.com/top-trump-ally-met-with-putins-deputy-in-moscow.

60. Theo Keith, "Ex-Sheriff David Clarke's 2015 Trip Expenses Paid by Alleged Russian Agent's Group," Fox6Now, July 17, 2018, https://fox6now.com/2018/07/17/woman-charged-with-being-covert-russian-agent-had-ties-to-former-sheriff-david-clarke/.

61. Schecter, "How David Clarke Bridges."

62. Peter Stone and Greg Gordon, "FBI Investigating whether Russian Money Went to NRA to Help Trump," *McClatchy DC*, January 18, 2018, https://www.mcclatchydc.com/news/nation-world/national/article195231139.html.

63. Stone and Gordon, "FBI Investigating."

64. Greg Gordon and Peter Stone, "Russia Investigators Likely Got Access to NRA's Tax Filings, Secret Donors," *McClatchy DC*, July 2, 2018, https://www.mcclatchydc.com/news/politics-government/article214075459.html.

65. Cockburn, "The Wild, Wild World."

66. Andrew Restuccia, "Sheriff David Clarke Lands Job at Homeland Security," *Politico*, May 17, 2017, https://www.politico.com/story/2017/05/17/sheriff-david-clarke-homeland-security-job-238517.

67. Ron Nixon, "Milwaukee County Sheriff Says He Will Not Join Homeland Security Department," *New York Times*, June 18, 2017, https://www.ny

times.com/2017/06/18/us/politics/david-clarke-sheriff-homeland-security-job
.html.

68. Abby Phillip, "Milwaukee Sheriff David Clarke Rescinds Acceptance of Homeland Security Post," *Washington Post*, June 17, 2017, https://www.washington post.com/news/post-politics/wp/2017/06/17/milwaukee-sheriff-david-clarke -rescinds-acceptance-of-homeland-security-post/.

69. Matt Stevens, "David Clarke, Milwaukee County Sheriff and Trump Supporter, Resigns," *New York Times*, August 31, 2017, https://www.nytimes .com/2017/08/31/us/sheriff-clarke-resigns-milwaukee.html.

70. Cockburn, "The Wild, Wild World."

71. Phillip, "Milwaukee Sheriff David Clarke Rescinds."

72. U.S. Office of Personnel Management, National Background Investigations Bureau, "About Us," https://nbib.opm.gov/about-us/.

73. Lee Sullivan, "A Nonprofit Board's Fiduciary Responsibility," GuideStar Blog, October 17, 2014, https://trust.guidestar.org/blog/2014/10/17/a-nonprofit -boards-fiduciary-responsibility/.

74. Kevin D. Williamson, "An Epidemic of Dishonesty on the Right," *National Review*, February 22, 2018, https://www.nationalreview.com/2018/02/ parkland-shooting-hoax-latest-right-dishonesty-epidemic/.

75. Williamson, "An Epidemic of Dishonesty on the Right."

76. Alex Seitz-Wald, "Why Is the Media Rehabilitating John Lott?" *Salon*, December 21, 2012, https://www.salon.com/2012/12/21/why_is_the_media _rehabilitating_john_lott/.

77. Ali Rowhani-Rahbar et al., "Loaded Handgun Carrying among US Adults, 2015," *American Journal of Public Health* 107:12, December 2017, 1930–36, doi:10.2105/AJPH.2017.304072, 1932.

78. Emily Larsen, "Fact Check: Are Most Gun Crimes Committed with Handguns?" Daily Caller News Foundation, February 20, 2018, http://dailycaller newsfoundation.org/2018/02/20/fact-check-are-most-gun-crimes-committed -with-handguns/.

79. U.S. Department of Justice, Office of Justice Programs, Bureau of Justice Statistics. Michael Planty and Jennifer L. Truman, *Firearm Violence, 1993–2011*. Special Report. May 2013, NCJ 241730, 3.

80. For summaries of Canadian gun control efforts, see Peter Squires, *Gun Crime in Global Contexts* (New York: Routledge, 2014), 284–88; "History of Firearms Control," in Canada, Royal Canadian Mounted Police, *RCMP Canadian Firearms Program—Program Evaluation*, February 2010, 5. For an in-depth history and analysis, see generally R. Blake Brown, *Arming and Disarming: A History of Gun Control in Canada* (Toronto: University of Toronto Press, 2012).

81. David B. Kopel, *The Samurai, the Mountie, and the Cowboy: Should America Adopt the Gun Controls of Other Democracies?* (Buffalo: Prometheus Books, 1992), 164.

82. Brown, *Arming and Disarming*, 47–50 (on encouraging rifle use); Desmond Morton, *A Short History of Canada* (Toronto: McClellan & Stewart, 2017), 3, 88–89, 96–97, 100 (on fears of invasion and other incursions).

83. Morton, *A Short History*, 3.

84. Morton, *A Short History*, 88–89 (American Civil War), 96–97 (Fenians), 100 (Alaska, Red River).

85. See chapter 5, "Angry White Men: Resistance to Gun Control in Canada, 1946–1950," and chapter 6, "Flexing the Liberal State's Muscles: The Montreal Massacre and the 1995 *Firearms Act*, 1980–2006," in Brown, *Arming and Disarming*, 159–98.

86. See chapter 2, "'The Government Must Disarm All the Indians': Controlling Firearms from Confederation to the Late Nineteenth Century," in Brown, *Arming and Disarming*, 46–80.

87. See Pamela Haag, *The Gunning of America: Business and the Making of American Gun Culture* (New York: Basic Books, 2016), 94 ("Winchester was thinking of his rifle's post–Civil War future in foreign markets"); 99 (The gun industry "moved decisively into a commercially focused phase characterized by heavy investments in machine production . . . and fierce competition"); 110 (the American gun market was "abysmal" after the Civil War).

88. Brown, *Arming and Disarming*, 46.

89. Brown, *Arming and Disarming*, 71.

90. Brown, *Arming and Disarming*, 119.

91. See chapter 3, "'A Rifle in the Hands of Every Able-Bodied Man in the Dominion of Canada under Proper Auspices': Arming Britons and Disarming Immigrants from the Late Nineteenth Century to the Great War," Brown, *Arming and Disarming*, 81–131.

92. Squires, *Gun Crime*, 140.

93. Thad Morgan, "The NRA Supported Gun Control When the Black Panthers Had the Weapons," History.com, March 22, 2018, https://www.history.com/news/black-panthers-gun-control-nra-support-mulford-act; Winkler, *Gun Fight*, 230–44, 253–58.

94. Unless otherwise noted, the description of current Canadian firearms law in this section is based on Canada, Royal Canadian Mounted Police, *Commissioner of Firearms 2012 Report*, Ottawa, 2013.

95. United States, Library of Congress, Law Library of Congress, "Firearms-Control Legislation and Policy: Canada," PDF downloaded from https://www.loc.gov/law/help/firearms-control/canada.php.

96. Law Library of Congress, "Firearms-Control Legislation."

97. Kim Bolan, "RCMP See a Disturbing Shift in B.C. Where Majority of Guns Used Illegally Are Acquired through Legal Sources," *Vancouver Sun*, September 27, 2016, https://vancouversun.com/news/crime/criminals-now-getting -their-guns-in-canada-police.

98. Sigal Samuel, "Canada Is Raging against Gun Violence—But Not Like America," *Atlantic*, July 2018, https://www.theatlantic.com/international/ archive/2018/07/canada-gun-control-debate/566102/.

99. See, for example, Chelsea Parsons and Eugenio Weigend Vargas, "Beyond Our Borders: How Weak U.S. Gun Laws Contribute to Violent Crime Abroad," Center for American Progress, February 3, 2018, https://www.americanprogress .org/issues/guns-crime/reports/2018/02/02/445659/beyond-our-borders/.

100. Trevor Wilhelm, "The Pipeline: 'A Lot of People in Canada Want Guns,'" *Windsor Star*, December 17, 2013, https://windsorstar.com/news/local -news/gunrunners-a-grim-gateway.

101. Craig Pearson, "The Smuggler: 'Don't Stutter, Be Cool, Breathe,'" *Windsor Star*, December 17, 2013, https://windsorstar.com/news/local-news/ gunrunners-the-smuggler.

102. Sarah Kinosian and Eugenio Weigend, "We're Sending Guns, Crime to Mexico," *Los Angeles Times*, March 2, 2017, http://www.latimes.com/opinion/ op-ed/la-oe-kinosian-weigend-guns-mexico-20170302-story.html#. See also for examples of American gun trafficking to Mexico and other points south of the border, Jonathan Blitzer, "The Link between America's Lax Gun Laws and the Violence That Fuels Immigration," *New Yorker*, March 22, 2018, https:// www.newyorker.com/news/news-desk/the-link-between-americas-lax-gun -laws-and-the-violence-that-fuels-immigration; Christopher Ingraham, "Why Mexico's Drug Cartels Love America's Gun Laws," *Washington Post*, January 14, 2016, https://www.washingtonpost.com/news/wonk/wp/2016/01/14/ why-mexicos-drug-cartels-love-americas-gun-laws/?noredirect=on&utm _term=.1310d50cd078.

103. Topher McDougal et al., "The Way of the Gun: Estimating Firearms Traffic across the U.S.-Mexico Border," University of San Diego Trans-Border Institute, March 2013, 8, https://catcher.sandiego.edu/items/peacestudies/way _of_the_gun.pdf.

104. Kinosian and Weigend, "We're Sending Guns, Crime to Mexico"; McDougal et al., "The Way of the Gun," 2, 15.

105. Patrick Cain, "With Shootings on the Rise in Toronto and Edmonton, More Guns Are Being Seized at the Border," Global News, June 7, 2016, https://globalnews.ca/news/2743764/with-shootings-on-the-rise-in-toronto -and-edmonton-more-guns-are-being-seized-at-the-border/.

106. Garen Wintemute, "Inside Gun Shows: What Goes On When Everybody Thinks Nobody's Watching," Violence Prevention Research Program, Department of Emergency Medicine, UC Davis School of Medicine, Sacramento, California, September 2009, 1–20, https://health.ucdavis.edu/vprp/pdf/IGS/IGScoverprefweb.pdf.

107. Pearson, "The Smuggler."

108. Pearson, "The Smuggler."

109. William Marsden, "Canadians Crack Down on Guns, Alarmed by Flow from U.S.," *Washington Post*, February 14, 2016, https://www.washingtonpost.com/world/the_americas/us-gun-problem-is-creeping-into-canada/2016/02/13/a28cd1e4-c388-11e5-b933-31c93021392a_story.html?noredirect=on&utm_term=.17f7db396104.

110. U.S. Department of Justice, U.S. Attorney's Office, District of Vermont, Media release, "Quebec Man Pleads Guilty to Smuggling over 100 Handguns from Vermont to Quebec," January 29, 2018, https://www.justice.gov/usao-vt/pr/quebec-man-pleads-guilty-smuggling-over-100-handguns-vermont-quebec.

111. See, for example, Cain, "With Shootings on the Rise in Toronto."

112. Olivia Bowden, "Illegal Guns Sourced in Canada Are Surging, Compared to Those Smuggled from the U.S.," Canadian Press, July 24, 2018, https://nationalpost.com/news/illegal-guns-sourced-in-canada-surge-compared-to-those-smuggled-from-u-s.

113. Patrick Cain, "RCMP Ignores Data That Could Flag People Selling Guns to Criminals: Toronto Mayor," Global News, December 19, 2016, https://globalnews.ca/news/3135360/rcmp-ignores-data-that-could-flag-people-selling-guns-to-criminals-toronto-mayor/.

114. Cain, "RCMP Ignores Data."

115. Betsy Powell, "Toronto Police Memo Flags Surge in Domestic Handgun Trafficking," the star.com, November 19, 2016, https://www.thestar.com/news/crime/2016/11/19/toronto-police-memo-flags-surge-in-domestic-handgun-trafficking.html.

116. Powell, "Toronto Police Memo Flags Surge."

117. Elizabeth Thompson, "More Than a Million Restricted, Prohibited Guns in Canada," CBC News, May 25, 2017, https://www.cbc.ca/news/politics/guns-firearms-restricted-canada-1.4129994.

118. Unless otherwise noted, the following discussion of the Dark Net is based on U.S. Department of Justice, Federal Bureau of Investigation, "A Primer on DarkNet Marketplaces: What They Are and What Law Enforcement Is Doing to Combat Them," November 1, 2016, https://www.fbi.gov/news/stories/a-primer-on-darknet-marketplaces; Dr. Giacomo Persi Paoli, slide presentation,

"Arms Trafficking on the Dark-web 101: What Is It, How Does It Work and Why Is It Important," Open briefing of the Counter-Terrorism Committee on "Preventing Terrorists from Acquiring Weapons," RAND Europe, May 17, 2017; Matt Schroeder, "Beyond the Dark Web: Arms Trafficking in the Digital Age," *Medium*, https://medium.com/@SmallArmsSurvey/beyond-the-dark-web-arms-trafficking-in-the-digital-age-56ddd806587a; Major Jeremy Cole, USAF, "Dark Web 101," *Air & Space Power Journal* (2016), 1(2), 3–8, www.dtic.mil/dtic/tr/fulltext/u2/1005862.pdf.

119. Cole, "Dark Web 101," 4.

120. Cole, "Dark Web 101," 3–4.

121. "Federal Law Enforcement Agencies Continue Their Efforts to Penetrate Criminal Conspiracies on the DarkNet," federallawenforcement.org, January 17, 2017, https://www.federallawenforcement.org/2017/01/federal-law-enforcement-agencies-continue-their-efforts-to-penetrate-criminal-conspiracies-on-the-darknet/.

122. See J. Dailey, "The Intelligence Club: A Comparative Look at Five Eyes," *J Pol Sci Pub Aff* (2017), 5:2, doi:10.4172/2332-0761.1000261.

123. Jim Bronskill, "Guns Are Being Sold Illegally through the Darknet, Mounties Warn," Canadian Press, March 25, 2018, https://nationalpost.com/news/canada/illicit-gun-sales-made-to-canadians-through-dark-web-mounties-warn.

124. U.S. Department of Justice, U.S. Attorney's Office, Northern District of Georgia, Media releases, "Gun Traffickers Arrested for Allegedly Using the Darknet to Export Guns across the World," May 31, 2017, https://www.justice.gov/usao-ndga/pr/gun-traffickers-arrested-allegedly-using-dark-web-export-guns-across-world; "Darknet International Gun Traffickers Sentenced," April 17, 2018, https://www.justice.gov/usao-ndga/pr/darknet-international-gun-traffickers-sentenced.

125. Bronskill, "Guns Are Being Sold Illegally."

126. William J. Lewinski et al., "The Real Risks during Deadly Police Shootouts: Accuracy of the Naïve Shooter," *International Journal of Police Science & Management*, vol. 17(2) (2015), 117–217, 118, doi:10.1177/1461355715582975.

127. Jack Moore, "NYPD Officers Shot the Lowest Number of People Ever in 2017," *Newsweek*, December 24, 2017, http://www.newsweek.com/nypd-officers-shot-lowest-number-people-ever-2017-758205.

128. Lewinski et al., "The Real Risks," 118.

129. Al Baker, "A Hail of Bullets, a Heap of Uncertainty," *New York Times*, December 9, 2007, https://www.nytimes.com/2007/12/09/weekinreview/09baker.html.

130. Lewinski et al., "The Real Risks," 121.

131. "Eaton Centre Shooting Suspect Charged with Murder," CBC News, June 4, 2012, http://www.cbc.ca/news/canada/toronto/eaton-centre-shooting -suspect-charged-with-murder-1.1229300.

Chapter Three: When Lonnie Met Sandy

1. The personal events about Lonnie and Sandy Phillips related in this chapter are based on a series of interviews of them by the author, supplemented by other research noted as necessary.

2. See "Disney University 101—What It Is and Why You'll Love It," DisneyFanatic.com, https://www.disneyfanatic.com/disney-university-101-what-it -is-and-why-youll-love-it/.

3. Equal Justice Initiative, "Lynching in America: Confronting the Legacy of Racial Terror, Supplement: Lynchings by County, Third Edition," available at https://eji.org/reports/lynching-in-america.

4. *Miranda v. Arizona*, 384 U.S. 436 (1966), 444. ("[T]he prosecution may not use statements, whether exculpatory or inculpatory, stemming from . . . questioning initiated by law enforcement officers after a person has been taken into custody or otherwise deprived of his freedom of action in any significant way . . . [unless it demonstrates the use of procedural safeguards effective to secure the Fifth Amendment's privilege against self-incrimination]. . . . Prior to any questioning, the person must be warned that he has a right to remain silent, that any statement he does make may be used as evidence against him, and that he has a right to the presence of an attorney, either retained or appointed.")

5. Reproduction of Remington Arms Company, Inc. 1966 catalog in author's files.

6. Description of "Bannerman 1966 Surplus Military Goods Catalog (100th Anniv.)," Cornell Publications, https://www.cornellpubs.com/old-guns/item _desc.php?item_id=946.

7. Chris Eger, "Bannerman's Castle: The Ultimate Army-Navy Store," Guns .com, November 7, 2015, https://www.guns.com/2015/11/07/bannermans -legacy-ultimate-army-navy-store/.

8. Pamela Colloff, "96 Minutes," *Texas Monthly*, August 2006, https://www .texasmonthly.com/articles/96-minutes/.

9. Rebecca Johnston, "A Fitting Memorial: The Mental Health Legacy of the Whitman Murders," *Behind the Tower* (2016), http://behindthetower.org/a -fitting-memorial; Notes of Dr. Maurice Dean Heatley, March 29, 1966, PDF file downloaded from http://alt.cimedia.com/statesman/specialreports/whitman/ heatley.pdf.

10. *Mass Murderers* (Alexandria, VA: Time-Life Books, 1993), 56.

11. Gary M. Lavergne, *A Sniper in the Tower: The Charles Whitman Murders* (Denton: University of North Texas Press, 1997), 5, 116–18.

12. Lavergne, *A Sniper in the Tower*, 117.

13. Lavergne, *A Sniper in the Tower*, 71–72.

14. Lavergne, *A Sniper in the Tower*, 21.

15. Lavergne, *A Sniper in the Tower*, 51 (italics in original).

16. Lavergne, *A Sniper in the Tower*, 235.

17. *Mass Murderers*, 40.

18. *Mass Murderers*, 42.

19. *Mass Murderers*, 40.

20. Notes of Dr. Maurice Dean Heatley.

21. *Mass Murderers*, 42.

22. Lavergne, *A Sniper in the Tower*, 54–55.

23. Johnston, "A Fitting Memorial."

24. Colloff, "96 Minutes."

25. *Mass Murderers*, 47.

26. Johnston, "A Fitting Memorial."

27. *Mass Murderers*, 47.

28. Lavergne, *A Sniper in the Tower*, 88.

29. "Finding and Recommendations" of *Report to the Governor: Mental Health Aspects*, released at a press conference in Austin, Texas, September 8, 1966, 9.

30. Lavergne, *A Sniper in the Tower*, 73.

31. The description in this section of amphetamine, Dexedrine, their legal and illegal use, and their effects is based on the following sources: U.S. Department of Justice, Drug Enforcement Administration, *Drugs of Abuse: A DEA Resource Guide* (2017 edition); "Dexedrine Prescribing Information," DX:L58, GlaxoSmithKline (Research Triangle Park, NC: 2007); Uri Eliyahu et al., "Psychostimulants and Military Operations," *Military Medicine*, 172, 4:383, 2007; "Dexedrine Addiction, Abuse and Treatment," Addiction Center, February 14, 2018, https://www.addictioncenter.com/stimulants/dexedrine/; Elliot Borin, "The U.S. Military Needs Its Speed," wired.com, February 10, 2003, https://www.wired.com/2003/02/the-u-s-military-needs-its-speed/.

32. "Dexedrine Prescribing Information."

33. Drug Enforcement Administration, *Drugs of Abuse*.

34. *Mass Murderers*, 49; Lavergne, *A Sniper in the Tower*, 68.

35. *Mass Murderers*, 56; Notes of Dr. Maurice Dean Heatley.

36. Lavergne, *A Sniper in the Tower*, 92.

37. Lavergne, *A Sniper in the Tower*, 92–93.

38. Lavergne, *A Sniper in the Tower*, 93.

39. *Mass Murderers*, 31.

40. Colloff, "96 Minutes." But see, *Mass Murderers*, 5. ("Some authorities mark the dawn of the new age of mass murder as September 6, 1949, the day that Howard Unruh gunned down 13 people during a 12-minute walk through Camden, New Jersey.")

41. Colloff, "96 Minutes."

42. Roy Marcot, *The History of Remington Firearms* (New York: Chartwell Books, 2011), 89.

43. Lavergne, *A Sniper in the Tower*, 20.

44. See Mike R. Lau, *The Military and Police Sniper* (Manchester, CT: Precision Shooting, Inc., 1998), 180–81.

45. Colloff, "96 Minutes."

46. Isaac McQuistion, "Armed Civilians and the UT Tower Tragedy," *Behind the Tower*, http://behindthetower.org/armed-civilians-and-the-ut-tower-tragedy.

47. U.S. Department of Justice, Federal Bureau of Investigation, Molly Amman et al., *Making Prevention a Reality: Identifying, Assessing, and Managing the Threat of Targeted Attacks* (Washington, DC: U.S. Department of Justice, February 2017), 4.

48. See, for example, Leroy Thompson, *The M1 Carbine* (New York: Osprey Publishing, 2011), 42 (Second World War: "The M1 Carbine is very appealing because it is light and handy, but the .30 Carbine round lacked the stopping power and range to be a serious killing weapon."); S. L. A. Marshall, *Commentary on Infantry Operations and Weapons Usage in Korea: Winter of 1950–51* (West Chester, OH: Nafziger Collection, 2002), 61 (Korean War: "Where carbine fire had proved killing effect, approximately 95% of the time the target was dropped at less than 50 yards."); Gordon Rottman, *Green Beret in Vietnam, 1957–73* (Oxford: Osprey Publishing, 2002), 41 (Vietnam War: "these guns lacked hitting power and penetration, and they were eventually outclassed by the AK-47 assault rifle.").

49. Former 18 U.S.C. Section 922 (v)(3)(B)(1).

50. Former 18 U.S.C. 922, "Appendix."

51. Lavergne, *A Sniper in the Tower*, 268.

52. 103d Congress, 2d Session, H.R. 3932, introduced March 1, 1994, Section 204, "Federal Arsenal License." Interestingly, the proposed law included an appended list that specifically exempted several models of the Iver Johnson M1 carbine, as well as the Navy Arms TU-KKW Sniper Trainer, the Krico Model 600 Sniper Rifle, the McMillan M-86 and M-89 Sniper Rifles, and the Parker-Hale M-85 Sniper Rifle.

53. "About *Behind the Tower*," http://behindthetower.org/about/.

54. Isaac McQuistion, "Texas Gun Culture and the UT Tower Shooting," http://behindthetower.org/texas-gun-culture-and-the-ut-tower-shooting.

55. Joshua Fechter, "Texas Campus Carry Law Will Take Effect on 50th Anniversary of Charles Whitman Shooting at UT," *San Antonio Express-News*, October 8, 2015, https://www.mysanantonio.com/news/local/article/Texas -campus-carry-law-will-take-effect-on-50th-6558524.php.

56. Ali Sundermier, "The Most Terrifying Part about Getting Struck by Lightning Is What Happens to You Afterwards," *Business Insider*, April 20, 2016, https://www.businessinsider.com/what-to-expect-when-you-survive -lightning-2016-4.

57. *The Essential Brain Injury Guide*, 36.

58. *The Essential Brain Injury Guide*, 35.

59. Johnston, "A Fitting Memorial."

60. Kevin Davis, *The Brain Defense: Murder in Manhattan and the Dawn of Neuroscience in America's Courtrooms* (New York: Penguin Press, 2017), 167.

61. See Lindsay Dodgson, "Brain Injuries Can Cause Some People to Become Violent Criminals and Pedophiles—Here's What Scientists Know So Far about Why That Is," *Business Insider*, February 10, 2018, https://www.businessinsider .com/brain-damage-can-turn-people-into-criminals-2018-2; Micah Johnson, "How Responsible Are Killers with Brain Damage?" *Scientific American*, January 30, 2018, https://www.scientificamerican.com/article/how-responsible-are -killers-with-brain-damage/.

62. Jeffrey Rosen, "The Brain on the Stand," *New York Times*, March 11, 2007, https://www.nytimes.com/2007/03/11/magazine/11Neurolaw.t.html.

63. J. Reid Meloy and Jens Hoffman, eds., *International Handbook of Threat Assessment* (New York: Oxford University Press, 2014), 4.

64. Meloy and Hoffman, *International Handbook*, 4.

65. Federal Bureau of Investigation, *Making Prevention a Reality*, 51.

66. Lavergne, *A Sniper in the Tower*, 270.

67. See James B. Jacobs, *Can Gun Control Work?* (New York: Oxford University Press, 2002), 20–21.

68. See "Maryland School Gunman Confronted by Officer Shot Himself, Authorities Say," *New York Times*, March 26, 2018, https://nyti.ms/2pJREQP.

69. Other freestanding trauma centers are located in San Diego, Las Vegas, and Miami. Like the Baltimore center, they are affiliated with medical colleges. See, "Every Second Counts: A Day in the Trauma Center," UC San Diego News Center, June 5, 2014, http://ucsdnews.ucsd.edu/feature/every_second_counts_a _day_in_the_trauma_center; "Controlled Chaos at Las Vegas Hospital Trauma Center after Attack," *New York Times*, October 2, 2017, https://www.nytimes .com/2017/10/02/us/vegas-shooting-hospital.html; and "The Ryder Trauma

Center at University of Miami/Jackson Memorial Medical Center," http://
surgery.med.miami.edu/trauma.

70. Video, "Inside a Trauma Unit: A Ballet of Organized Chaos," *Wall Street
Journal*, December 7, 2012, https://www.wsj.com/video/inside-a-trauma-unit-a
-ballet-of-organized-chaos/017E2016-AFA8-43F2-BC67-6CE88C7ABCDD
.html.

71. Unless otherwise noted, all quotes from Dr. Scalea are from the author's
interview with him in his office on March 20, 2018.

72. Gina Kolata and C. J. Chivers, "Wounds from Military-Style Rifles? 'A
Ghastly Thing to See,'" *New York Times*, March 4, 2018, https://www.nytimes
.com/2018/03/04/health/parkland-shooting-victims-ar15.html.

73. *The Essential Brain Injury Guide Edition 5.0* (Brain Injury Association
of America, 2016), 4 (91 percent die); Loyola V. Gressot et al., "Predictors of
Outcome in Civilians with Gunshot Wounds to the Head upon Presentation,"
J. Neurosurg 121: 645–52 (2014), 645 (up to 66 percent die at scene).

74. David J. Lin et al., "'Time Is Brain' the Gifford [*sic*] Factor—or: Why Do
Some Civilian Gunshot Wounds to the Head Do Unexpectedly Well?" *Surgical
Neurology International* 3: 98 (2012), August 27, 2012, https://www.ncbi.nlm.nih
.gov/pmc/articles/PMC3463834/?report=pr, doi: 10.4103/2152-7806.100187.

75. Maia Szalavitz, "It Is Brain Surgery: Neurosurgeon Nirit Weiss on Treating Gunshot Victims Like Rep. Gabrielle Giffords," *Time*, January 10, 2011,
http://healthland.time.com/2011/01/10/it-is-brain-surgery-neurosurgeon-nirit
-weiss-on-treating-gunshot-victims-like-rep-gabrielle-giffords/.

76. *The Essential Brain Injury Guide*, 32.

77. For detailed overviews of the brain and the central nervous system, see
chapter 2, "Neuroanatomy and Neuroimaging," in *The Essential Brain Injury
Guide Edition 5.0* (Brain Injury Association of America, 2016); chapter 1, "Introduction to the Nervous System," in Todd W. Vanderah and Douglas J. Gould,
Nolte's The Human Brain, 7th ed. (Philadelphia: Elsevier, 2016).

78. Szalavitz, "It Is Brain Surgery."

79. Hernando Raphael Alvis-Mirandal et al., "Craniocerebral Gunshot Injuries;
A Review of the Current Literature," *Bull Emerg Trauma* 4(2): 65–74, 66 (2016).

80. *The Essential Brain Injury Guide*, 2.

81. Gressot et al., "Predictors of Outcome," 645.

82. For a good overview of the brain's structure and function in lay language,
see Brain Injury Association of America, "Functions of the Brain," https://www
.biausa.org/brain-injury/about-brain-injury/basics/function-of-the-brain.

83. Gressot et al., "Predictors of Outcome," 651 ("Bullet trajectory has been
shown to impact both mortality and morbidity from penetrating brain injuries,

with bihemispheric and posterior fossa injuries demonstrating worse outcomes"); "Researchers Develop System to Classify Gunshot Wounds to the Head and Other Similar Injuries," *Science Daily*, October 26, 2016, https://www.science daily.com/releases/2016/10/161026165833.htm ("The study also found that having only a single penetrating brain injury, rather than multiple penetrating brain injuries, was associated with 87 percent higher odds for survival"); Lin et al., "'Time Is Brain,'" 98 ("zona fatalis").

84. Mike Orcutt, "A Key Series of Events Helped Giffords Survive a Gunshot Wound to the Head," *Scientific American*, January 10, 2011, https://www .scientificamerican.com/article/gabrielle-giffords-gunshot-survival/.

85. Melissa Dahl, "If Gabby Giffords Still Struggles to Speak, How Can She Sing?" today.com, January 9, 2014, https://www.today.com/health/if-gabby -giffords-still-struggles-speak-how-can-she-sing-2D11888324.

86. National Aphasia Association, "Broca's (Expressive) Aphasia," https:// www.aphasia.org/aphasia-resources/brocas-aphasia/.

87. Dahl, "If Gabby Giffords Still Struggles."

88. Video accompanying story "Connor Stevenson 'Pretty Dizzy' after Being Shot at Eaton Centre," Canadian Press, November 13, 2014, http://www.cbc.ca/ news/canada/toronto/connor-stevenson-pretty-dizzy-after-being-shot-at-eaton -centre-1.2834051.

89. *The Survivor, Part Three*, CTV National News video posted at Lisa La Flamme, "The Inside Story: How a Trip to the Toronto Eaton Centre Turned into Horror," February 2, 2013, https://www.ctvnews.ca/w5/the-inside-story -how-a-trip-to-the-toronto-eaton-centre-turned-into-horror-1.1139769.

90. *The Survivor, Part One*, posted at La Flamme, "The Inside Story."

91. *The Survivor, Part One*, posted at La Flamme, "The Inside Story."

92. *The Survivor, Part Two*, posted at La Flamme, "The Inside Story."

93. *The Survivor, Part Two*, posted at La Flamme, "The Inside Story."

94. Lin et al., "'Time Is Brain.'"

95. *The Survivor, Part Three*, posted at La Flamme, "The Inside Story."

96. Lin et al., "'Time Is Brain.'"

97. Szalavitz, "It Is Brain Surgery."

98. Szalavitz, "It Is Brain Surgery."

99. Szalavitz, "It Is Brain Surgery."

100. *The Survivor, Part Three*, posted at La Flamme, "The Inside Story."

101. Jacques Gallant, "Supreme Court Won't Hear Crown Appeal over New Trial in 2012 Eaton Centre Shootings," *Toronto Star*, February 8, 2018, https:// www.thestar.com/news/crime/2018/02/08/supreme-court-wont-hear-crown -appeal-over-new-trial-in-2012-eaton-centre-shootings.html.

Chapter Four: Over the Double Rainbow

1. Telephone interview with Sandy and Lonnie Phillips, February 12, 2018.

2. James Silver, Andre Simons, and Sarah Craun, "A Study of the Pre-Attack Behaviors of Active Shooters in the United States between 2000–2013," U.S. Department of Justice, Federal Bureau of Investigation (2018), 6.

3. The description of the FN Five-seveN handgun and Major Nidal Hasan's use of it at Fort Hood is based largely on the discussion of the incident in Tom Diaz, *The Last Gun: How Changes in the Gun Industry Are Killing Americans and What It Will Take to Stop It* (New York: New Press, 2012), 6–9, where primary sources are noted.

4. The discussion of the role of Beretta and Glock in the American civilian handgun market is based on the discussion in Tom Diaz, *Making a Killing: The Business of Guns in America* (New York: New Press, 1999), 77–82, and primary sources noted therein.

5. For a more detailed history of the AR-15's development, see Duncan Long, "Chapter 1: Beginnings" in *The Complete AR-15/M16 Sourcebook: What Every Shooter Needs to Know* (Revised and Updated Edition) (Boulder, CO: Paladin Press, 2001), 3–21.

6. *Colt Defense v. Bushmaster Firearms*, No. 06-1696, U.S. Court of Appeals (1st Cir, 2007).

7. "Trademark and Copyright Information," https://www.colt.com/page/terms-of-use; "AR-15 Trademark Details," Justia Trademarks, https://trademarks.justia.com/722/53/ar-72253092.html.

8. Long, *The Complete AR-15/M16 Sourcebook*, 3.

9. Gary Paul Johnston and Thomas B. Nelson, "Foreword," *The World's Assault Rifles* (Lorton, VA: Ironside International Publishers, 2010).

10. A unit, or "round," of modern ammunition consists of the bullet, a metal case containing gunpowder, into the top of which the bullet is seated, and a primer in the base of the case. When struck by the gun's firing pin, the primer ignites the gunpowder and the bullet is expelled by expanding gas.

11. A magazine is a container (usually a rectangular box) into which ammunition rounds—commonly from ten to forty—are pre-loaded. Inserted into a well in a firearm, the magazine is the rifle's replaceable ammunition supply. A spring in the base of the magazine pushes the supply of ammunition into the firing chamber as the gun's mechanism expels empty cases and loads new rounds.

12. "In the Second 'Great War,' the selective-fire characteristic of the assault rifle would be joined by the straight-line stock, pistol grip, and high-capacity magazine, all of these comprising key elements on an assault rifle." Johnston and Nelson, "Introduction," *World's Assault Rifles*.

13. "Modern Sporting Rifle Facts," National Shooting Sports Foundation, https://www.nssf.org/msr/.

14. For a detailed description of the process of loading the M1, see chapter 3, "Operation and Functioning," in *U.S. Army M-1 Garand Technical Manual* (Seattle, WA: Pacific Publishing Studio, 2011), 18–22.

15. "Modern Sporting Rifle Facts," National Shooting Sports Foundation; "The name 'tactical carbine' appeared as a politically correct term for the much older moniker 'assault rifle,' which dates back to the days of World War II." Alan C. Paulson, *Weapons Evaluations for the Armed Professional and Advanced Collector* (Boulder, CO: Paladin Press, 2006), 109.

16. "AR-15–Style Rifles Are NOT 'Assault Weapons' or 'Assault Rifles.' An Assault Rifle Is Fully Automatic—A Machine Gun," National Shooting Sports Foundation, "Modern Sporting Rifle Facts."

17. National Shooting Sports Foundation, "Modern Sporting Rifle Facts." (Referring to the National Firearms Act of 1934.)

18. Duncan Long, *Assault Pistols, Rifles, and Submachine Guns* (Boulder, CO: Paladin Press, 1986), 3.

19. Earl J. Hess, *The Rifle Musket in Civil War Combat: Reality and Myth* (Lawrence: University Press of Kansas, 2008), 223.

20. United States Army Combat Developments Command, "Rifle Evaluation Study," December 20, 1962, 2, www.dtic.mil/cgi-bin/GetTRDoc?AD=ADA046961.

21. Thomas L. McNaugher, "Marksmanship, McNamara and the M16 Rifle: Organizations, Analysis and Weapons Acquisition," Rand Corporation, The Rand Paper Series, March 1979, www.rand.org/content/dam/rand/pubs/papers/2008/P6306.pdf.

22. Long, *The Complete AR-15/M16 Sourcebook.*

23. David Westwood, *Rifles: An Illustrated History of Their Impact* (Santa Barbara, CA: ABC-CLIO, 2005), 43.

24. Hess, *The Rifle Musket*, 16; "Side Arms, Standard Infantry," *The Oxford Companion to American Military History*, John Whiteclay Chambers II, ed. (New York: Oxford University Press, 1999), 659.

25. Westwood, *Rifles*, 20.

26. Hess, *The Rifle Musket*, 16.

27. Edward R. Crews, "The Mississippi Rifle," in *Gun Digest Book of Classic American Combat Rifles*, Terry Wieland, ed. (Iola, WI: Gun Digest Books, 2011), 27.

28. Westwood, *Rifles*, xi.

29. Ian V. Hogg, *Guns and How They Work* (New York: Everest House, 1979), 29.

30. McNaugher, "Marksmanship," 5.

31. Hess, *The Rifle Musket*, 30.

32. Hess, *The Rifle Musket*, 30.

33. Hess, *The Rifle Musket*, 31–32, 68, 218–19; McNaugher, "Marksmanship," 5–7.

34. McNaugher, "Marksmanship," 5.

35. J. F. C. Fuller, *The Conduct of War, 1789–1961* (New Brunswick, NJ: Da Capo Press, 1992), 184–85.

36. Westwood, *Rifles*, 115.

37. McNaugher, "Marksmanship," 8.

38. John Ellis, *The Social History of the Machine Gun* (Baltimore: Johns Hopkins University Press, 1986), 179.

39. Ellis, *The Social History of the Machine Gun*, 179.

40. Johnston and Nelson, *Assault Rifles*, 335.

41. On the development of the MP-18 submachine gun, see Hogg, *Guns and How They Work*, 115–19. On German storm troopers and their assault tactics generally, see Col. Frank D. Ely, "The German Assault Battalions and Shock Troops," *Infantry Journal* 14, 1917/18, available at https://catalog .hathitrust.org/Record/000544751; Bruce I. Gudmunsson, *Stormtroop Tactics: Innovation in the German Army, 1914–1918* (Westport, CT: Praeger, 1995); "German Assault Tactics and Allied Manpower Problems," in William R. Griffiths, *The Great War: Strategies and Tactics of the First World War* (The West Point Military History Series) (Garden City Park, NY: Square One Publishers, 2003), 134–37.

42. Johnston and Nelson, *Assault Rifles*, 11–14, 340.

43. Hogg, *Guns and How They Work*, 150.

44. For a detailed history of this development, see chapter 25, "Germany: The Sturmgewehr," in Johnston and Nelson, *Assault Rifles*, 333–80.

45. Paulson, *Weapons Evaluations*, 112.

46. Hogg, *Guns and How They Work*, 151.

47. Westwood, *Rifles*, 133.

48. McNaugher, "Marksmanship," 18.

49. Westwood, *Rifles*, 133. In fact, later tests made "very clear that the heavy recoil of the M14 rifle was almost impossible for an average soldier to control under actual combat conditions (as opposed to target style shooting)." Long, *The Complete AR-15/M16 Sourcebook*, 19.

50. McNaugher, "Marksmanship," 16.

51. Charles R. Shrader, *History of Operations Research in the United States Army*, vol. I (Washington, DC: U.S. Army, 2006), 102.

52. McNaugher, "Marksmanship," 23.

53. "Project AGILE & the M16 Rifle," http://www.darpa.mil/about-us/timeline/agile-and-M16.

54. Long, *The Complete AR-15/M16 Sourcebook*, 65.

55. Colt Defense LLC, Form 10-K/A, Amendment No. 2, filed with U.S. Securities and Exchange Commission, for fiscal year ended December 31, 2013, 5.

56. Jeff Brazil and Steve Berry, "Crackdown on Assault Weapons Has Missed Mark," *Los Angeles Times*, August 24, 1997, http://articles.latimes.com/1997/aug/24/news/mn-25528.

57. Phillip Peterson, *Gun Digest Buyers Guide to Assault Weapons* (Iola, WI: Gun Digest Books, 2008), 11.

58. Diaz, *Making a Killing*, 127, and examples cited therein.

59. U.S. War Department Tactical and Technical Trends (April 1945) quoted in Chris McNab, *German Automatic Rifles 1941–45* (New York: Osprey Publishing, 2013), 54.

60. Headquarters, U.S. Department of the Army, FM 3-22.9, *M16-/M4-Series Weapons*, August 2008, 7-12, 7-14. ("Automatic or burst fire is inherently less accurate than semiautomatic fire." 7-38.) See also the postings in response to "In What Situation Would a Modern Soldier Fire an Assault Rifle on Full Auto? Burst? Semi-Automatic?" at Quora, https://www.quora.com/In-what-situation-would-a-modern-soldier-fire-an-assault-rifle-on-full-auto-What-about-on-burst-What-about-on-semi-automatic.

61. Sean D. Naylor and Christopher Drew, "SEAL Team 6 and a Man Left for Dead: A Grainy Picture of Valor," *New York Times*, August 27, 2016, https://www.nytimes.com/2016/08/28/world/asia/seal-team-6-afghanistan-man-left-for-dead.html?_r=0.

62. Long, *Assault Pistols, Rifles*, 1.

63. In the late nineteenth century, Smith & Wesson produced a "revolving rifle," which was essentially a handgun (revolver) with a detachable stock. The gun's popularity was "limited." Dean K. Boorman, *The History of Smith & Wesson Firearms* (Guilford, CT: Lyons Press, 2002), 42.

64. "Smith & Wesson Enters Long-Gun Market," *Shooting Industry*, February 1, 2006.

65. "Q4 2006 Smith & Wesson Hldg. Corp. Earnings Conference Call," FD (Fair Disclosure) Wire, June 15, 2006.

66. "Smith & Wesson Boss Talks about Guns and Gun Laws," *Daily Oklahoman*, July 20, 2009, reproduced by HuntNetwork, http://huntnetwork.net/modules/news/index.php?start=1465&storytopic=4.

67. See M&P15-22 Sport, https://www.smith-wesson.com/firearms/mp-15-22-sport.

68. W. H. B. Smith and Joseph E. Smith, *Small Arms of the World: The Basic Manual of Military Small Arms* (Harrisburg, PA: Stackpole Books, 1962), 638.

69. Leroy Thompson, *The M1 Carbine* (Oxford: Osprey Publishing, 2011), 4–5.

70. Gordon Rottman, *Green Beret in Vietnam: 1957–73* (Oxford: Osprey Publishing, 2002), 41.

71. Thompson, *The M1 Carbine*, 68.

72. Thompson, *The M1 Carbine*, 69.

73. "Post WWII Commercially Manufactured M1 Carbines (U.S.A.)," http://www.m1carbinesinc.com/carbine_universal.html.

74. See, for example, David Maccar, "N.J. Court Says Man Can't Have Grandfather's M1 Carbine Back," Range365.com, September 22, 2015, https://www.range365.com/nj-court-says-man-cant-have-grandfathers-m1-carbine-back.

75. Adam Lankford, "Public Mass Shooters and Firearms: A Cross-National Study of 171 Countries," *Violence and Victims* 31 (2016): 187–99, http://dx.doi.org/10.1891/0886-6708.VV-D-15-00093, 188.

76. Neta C. Crawford, "United States Budgetary Costs of Post-9/11 Wars Through FY2018: A Summary of the $5.6 Trillion in Costs for the US Wars in Iraq, Syria, Afghanistan, and Pakistan, and Post-9/11 Veterans Care and Homeland Security," Watson Institute for International & Public Affairs (November 2017), 1–3. PDF downloaded from https://watson.brown.edu/costsofwar/papers/economic.

77. Tamara Baluja and Dakshana Bascaramurty, "Colorado Shooting Victim Narrowly Missed Eaton Centre Shooting," *Globe and Mail*, July 20, 2012, https://www.theglobeandmail.com/news/world/colorado-shooting-victim-narrowly-missed-eaton-centre-shooting/article4429853/.

78. German Lopez, "He Survived the Las Vegas Mass Shooting. Then He Died in the Thousand Oaks, California, Shooting," Vox.com, November 9, 2018, https://www.vox.com/2018/11/9/18079038/thousand-oaks-california-shooting-telemachus-orfanos; Jose A. Del Real, Jennifer Medina, and Tim Arango, "California Shooting Kills 12 at Country Music Bar, a Year after Las Vegas," *New York Times*, November 8, 2018, https://www.nytimes.com/2018/11/08/us/shooting-california-thousand-oaks.html.

79. Lopez, "He Survived the Las Vegas Mass Shooting."

80. "Mass Shootings," in *The Science of Gun Policy* (Santa Monica, CA: RAND Corporation, 2018), 267.

81. RAND, "Mass Shootings," 265.

82. Gun Violence Archive, "General Methodology," http://www.gunviolencearchive.org/methodology. (Capitals in original.)

83. RAND, "Mass Shootings," 265–67.

84. Lankford, "Public Mass Shooters," 190.

85. Iain Overton, *The Way of the Gun: A Bloody Journey into the World of Fire-arms* (New York: Harper, 2016), 68.

86. Adam Lankford, "Are America's Public Mass Shooters Unique? A Comparative Analysis of Offenders in the United States and Other Countries," *International Journal Of Comparative And Applied Criminal Justice*, 2016, 40 (2), 171–83, http://dx.doi.org/10.1080/01924036.2015.1105144, 173.

87. "Profile of an Active Shooter," in U.S. Department of Homeland Security, *Active Shooter—How To Respond* (Washington, DC, 2017), 2.

88. New York City Police Department, *Active Shooter: Recommendations and Analysis for Risk Mitigation* (2016 edition), 4.

89. Trace, https://www.thetrace.org/features/gun-violence-facts-and-solutions/mass-shootings-all-deaths-01/; Garen J. Wintemute, "The Epidemiology of Firearm Violence in the Twenty-First Century United States," *Annual Review Public Health* 36: 5–19, 8 (2015).

90. "The Showdown over the Concealed Carry Reciprocity Act," CBS *60 Minutes*, February 11, 2018, https://www.cbsnews.com/news/concealed-carry-reciprocity-act-showdown/.

91. James Alan Fox and Monica DeLateur, "Mass Shootings in America: Moving beyond Newtown," *Homicide Studies* 18 (2014), 125–45, 141, doi: 10.1177/1088767913510297.

92. Jessica Roy, "Bill O'Reilly Calls Mass Shootings 'the Price of Freedom,'" *Los Angeles Times*, October 2, 2017, http://www.latimes.com/nation/la-las-vegas-shooting-live-updates-bill-o-reilly-calls-mass-shootings-the-1506980448-htmlstory.html#.

93. Lankford, "Are America's Public Mass Shooters Unique?" 172.

94. Adam Winkler, *Gun Fight: The Battle over the Right to Bear Arms in the United States* (New York: W.W. Norton, 2013), xiv.

95. Lankford, "Public Mass Shooters," 187.

96. See Cathy Scott-Clark and Adrian Levy, *The Siege—68 Hours inside the Taj Hotel* (New York: Penguin Books, 2013).

97. Biography, "Adam Lankford, Criminology Professor, The University of Alabama," http://adamlankford.com/bio.htm.

98. Lankford, "Public Mass Shooters," 188.

99. Lankford, "Public Mass Shooters," 192.

100. Lankford, "Public Mass Shooters," 195.

101. Lankford, "Public Mass Shooters," 194.

102. Lankford, "Public Mass Shooters," 195.

103. Lankford, "Are America's Public Mass Shooters Unique?" 176.

104. Frederic Lemieux, "Effect of Gun Culture and Firearms Laws on Gun Violence and Mass Shootings in the United States: A Multi-Level Quantitative Analysis," *International Journal of Criminal Justice Sciences*, January–June 2014, vol. 9 (1), 74–93.

105. The countries were Australia, Austria, Belgium, Canada, Denmark, Finland, France, Germany, Greece, Holland, Hungary, Iceland, Ireland, Italy, Japan, Luxembourg, New Zealand, Norway, Poland, Portugal, Spain, Sweden, Switzerland, United Kingdom, and the United States.

106. Lemieux, "Effect of Gun Culture," 81–82.

107. Lemieux, "Effect of Gun Culture," 90.

108. Lemieux, "Effect of Gun Culture," 90.

109. Lemieux, "Effect of Gun Culture," 75.

110. Reuters, "Trump Says Pittsburgh Shooting Has Little to Do with Gun Laws," https://www.msn.com/en-us/news/politics/trump-says-pittsburgh -shooting-has-little-to-do-with-gun-laws/ar-BBOYHr2.

111. Dan MacGuill, "Does the United States Have a Lower Death Rate from Mass Shootings than European Countries? A Pro-Gun Rights Economist Uses Questionable Statistical Methods to Create a Misleading Impression," Snopes. com, March 9, 2018, https://www.snopes.com/fact-check/united-states-lower -death-shootings/.

112. "Family Living through 'Life Sentence' after Eaton Centre Shooting," CTV News, January 16, 2015, https://www.ctvnews.ca/w5/w5-family-living -through-life-sentence-after-eaton-centre-shooting-1.2192192.

113. Del Real, "California Shooting Kills 12."

Chapter Five: Tobacco Road

1. Jack Shepherd, "14 Stories that Prove Animals Have Souls," BuzzFeed, July 2, 2012, https://t.co/PTEyYzvS. ("Animals are capable of so much more compassion, love, bravery, and ingenuity than most people realize.")

2. Catherine Porter, "Shelagh Was Here—An Ordinary, Magical Life," *Star*, March 16, 2012, https://www.thestar.com/news/gta/2012/03/16/shelagh_was _here_an_ordinary_magical_life.html.

3. Nick Groke, "UFC 150 Back Where It All Started—In Denver," *Denver Post*, August 9, 2012, https://www.denverpost.com/2012/08/09/ufc-150-back -where-it-all-started-in-denver/.

4. Moms Demand Action, "Sandy Phillips Fights for Stronger, Smarter Gun Laws in the Aftermath of the Murder of Her Daughter in the Aurora Mass Shooting," July 17, 2013, https://momsdemandaction.org/out-of-the-darkness

-a-mother-who-lost-her-daughter-in-the-aurora-movie-theater-shooting
-advocates-for-stronger-smarter-gun-laws/.

5. Kelsey Fowler, "Tomato Battle Comes to Metro Denver for Outdoor Food Fight," *Denver Post*, July 4, 2012, https://www.denverpost.com/2012/07/04/tomato-battle-comes-to-metro-denver-for-outdoor-food-fight/.

6. Kelsey Fowler, "Tomato Battle."

7. "Complex Overview," Dick's Sporting Goods Park, https://www.dicks sportinggoodspark.com/stadium-field-complex/field-complex-info/complex -overview/.

8. "Gay Bowl XVIII," http://gaybowl.org/?tags=MA_VS_HMPG_439542 &utm_source=HMPG&utm_medium=VS&utm_campaign=MA_VS _HMPG_439542.

9. "Dick's Sporting Goods Scores Naming Rights for New Rapids Stadium Complex," https://www.coloradorapids.com/es/post/2010/06/28/dicks-sporting -goods-scores-naming-rights-new-rapids-stadium-complex. For a history of the company, see Dick's Sporting Goods, "About Us," https://www.dickssporting goods.com/s/about-us.

10. Laura M. Holson, "Dick's Sporting Goods Will Destroy the Assault-Style Weapons It Didn't Sell," *New York Times*, April 18, 2018, https://www.nytimes .com/2018/04/18/business/guns-dicks-sporting-goods.html.

11. See "People in Red: Thousands Hurl Tomatoes in Spanish Food Fight," Reuters, August 29, 2018, https://www.reuters.com/article/us-spain-culture -tomato-fight/people-in-red-thousands-hurl-tomatoes-in-spanish-food-fight -idUSKCN1LE1DO; Wikipedia, "La Tomatina," https://en.wikipedia.org/wiki/ La_Tomatina.

12. Angie Jackson, "Colorado Tomato War Revived after 20-Year Armistice," June 23, 2011, *Gazette* (Colorado Springs), https://gazette.com/news/colorado -tomato-war-revived-after—year-armistice/article_3890ec2c-ec0a-527a-bb9c -2cfbe965b5b1.html.

13. Angie Jackson, "Colorado Tomato War."

14. The biographical details of James Holmes's life in this section are derived from William H. Reid, *A Dark Night in Aurora: Inside James Holmes and the Colorado Mass Shootings* (New York: Skyhorse Publishing, 2018); "Profile: Aurora Cinema Shooting Killer James Holmes," BBC, July 17, 2015, https://www.bbc .com/news/world-us-canada-18937513; Carol D. Leonnig and Joel Achenbach, "James Holmes, Held in Colorado Shooting, Known as Shy but Pleasant," *Washington Post*, July 20, 2012, https://www.washingtonpost.com/national/ health-science/james-eagan-holmes-held-in-colorado-shooting/2012/07/20/ gJQA213UyW_story.html; and "James Holmes: Mass Murderer," A&E Television Networks, https://www.biography.com/people/james-holmes-20891561.

15. Jack Healy, "Aurora Killer's Parents Plead to Spare His Life," *New York Times*, July 28, 2015, https://nyti.ms/1DNo4Yz.

16. Leonnig and Achenbach, "James Holmes."

17. Leonnig and Achenbach, "James Holmes."

18. The dates and places of Holmes's purchases are from *Phillips v. Lucky Gunner*, Amended Complaint, filed in District Court, Arapahoe County, Colorado, on September 16, 2014.

19. "America's Ammunition Crisis: Few Laws Exist to Prevent Purchases by Dangerous People Online and in Stores," Giffords Law Center, July 30, 2012, https://lawcenter.giffords.org/americas-ammunition-crisis-few-laws-exist-to-prevent-purchases-by-dangerous-people-online-and-in-stores/; Andrew Jay McClurg and Brannon P. Denning, "Firearms Owners Protection Act," in *Guns and the Law: Cases, Problems, and Explanation* (Durham, NC: Carolina Academic Press, 2016), 48.

20. U.S. Department of Justice, Federal Bureau of Investigation, "National Instant Criminal Background Check System (NICS)," https://www.fbi.gov/services/cjis/nics.

21. See Kathleen Hall, "Do Filtered Cigarettes Lower the Risk of Lung Cancer?" *U.S. News & World Report*, July 25, 2017, https://health.usnews.com/health-care/patient-advice/articles/2017-07-25/do-filtered-cigarettes-lower-the-risk-of-lung-cancer; Pagan Kennedy, "Who Made That Cigarette Filter?" *New York Times Magazine*, July 6, 2012, https://www.nytimes.com/2012/07/08/magazine/who-made-that-cigarette-filter.html.

22. Quotes in this section are from a PDF copy of the diary in the author's files. It is available at several locations on the internet.

23. For a review of mental health professionals who had seen James Holmes as of July 2015, see Jordan Steffen, "A Guide to Mental Health Professionals Who Saw Theater Shooting Gunman," *Denver Post*, July 20, 2015, https://www.denverpost.com/2015/07/10/a-guide-to-mental-health-professionals-who-saw-theater-shooting-gunman/.

24. Reid, *A Dark Night*, 266.

25. Leonnig and Achenbach, "James Holmes."

26. Reid, *A Dark Night*, 102.

27. Reid, *A Dark Night*, 13.

28. Reid, *A Dark Night*, 20.

29. Reid, *A Dark Night*, 54.

30. Reid, *A Dark Night*, 57.

31. Reid, *A Dark Night*, 58.

32. Reid, *A Dark Night*, 66.

33. Reid, *A Dark Night*, 82 (italics in original). See also Noelle Phillips and John Ingold, "Aurora Theater Gunman Says He Hoped FBI Would Stop Him, Lock Him Up," *Denver Post*, May 29, 2015, https://www.denverpost .com/2015/05/29/aurora-theater-gunman-says-he-hoped-fbi-would-stop-him -lock-him-up/.

34. John R. Lott Jr., "Background Checks Are Not the Answer to Gun Violence," *New York Times*, February 12, 2018, https://www.nytimes.com/ 2018/02/12/opinion/politics/background-checks-gun-violence.html.

35. Michael R. Bloomberg, "Foreword," in Daniel W. Webster and Jon S. Vernick, eds., *Reducing Gun Violence in America—Informing Policy with Evidence and Analysis* (Baltimore: Johns Hopkins University Press, 2013), xii.

36. Webster and Vernick, *Reducing Gun Violence*, 22.

37. National Research Council of the National Academies (2005), *Firearms and Violence: A Critical Review*, Committee to Improve Research Information and Data on Firearms, 72.

38. Adam Winkler, *Gunfight: The Battle over the Right to Bear Arms in the United States* (New York: W.W. Norton, 2013), 295.

39. Excerpt from Glenn Harlan Reynolds, "A Critical Guide to the Second Amendment," 62 *Tennessee Law Review* 461 (1995), in Andrew J. McClurg, David B. Kopel, and Brannon P. Denning, eds., *Gun Control and Gun Rights: A Reader and Guide* (New York: New York University Press, 2002), 198.

40. Brooks Clark, "Irrepressible Contrarian," *Quest* (University of Tennessee), 2014, https://quest.utk.edu/2014/irrepressible-contrarian/.

41. Glenn Harlan Reynolds, "Looking for 'Solutions' to Mass Killings? Start with Punishing Failure," *USA Today*, April 9, 2018, https://www.usatoday .com/story/opinion/2018/04/09/mass-killings-failures-hold-law-enforcement -accountable-column/497285002/.

42. Glenn Harlan Reynolds, "Why the President Needs to Be White, Male and Republican: Glenn Reynolds," *USA Today*, May 26, 2016, https://www .usatoday.com/story/opinion/2016/05/26/donald-trump-imperial-presidency -obama-executive-action-order-power-column/84907556/.

43. Instapundit.com, November 23, 2010, https://pjmedia.com/instapundit/ 110310/.

44. Glenn Greenwald, "Extremist Bush Supporter Calls for Murder of Scientists," *Salon*, February 13, 2007, https://www.salon.com/2007/02/13/assassination _2/.

45. Kelsey Sutton, "USA Today Suspends Columnist Glenn Reynolds for One Month," *Politico*, September 22, 2016, https://www.politico.com/media/ story/2016/09/usa-today-columnist-glenn-reynolds-004780.

46. Joe Heim, Devlin Barrett, and Hannah Natanson, "Man Accused of Driving into Crowd at Charlottesville 'Unite the Right' Rally Charged with Federal Hate Crimes," *Washington Post*, June 27, 2018, https://www.washingtonpost.com/local/man-accused-of-driving-into-crowd-at-unite-the-right-rally-charged-with-federal-hate-crimes/2018/06/27/09cdce3a-7a20-11e8-80be-6d32e182a3bc_story.html.

47. *Heller*, 554 U.S. at 626–27 (2008).

48. *An Act to Regulate Commerce in Firearms*, Public Law 785, *U.S. Statutes at Large* 52 (1938), 1250–52.

49. *An Act to Regulate Commerce in Firearms*, Public Law 785, *U.S. Statutes at Large* 52 (1938), 1250.

50. James B. Jacobs, *Can Gun Control Work?* (New York: Oxford University Press, 2002), 22–23.

51. Jacobs, *Can Gun Control Work?*, 23.

52. McClurg and Denning, *Guns and the Law*, 45.

53. *An Act to Amend Title 18, United States Code, to Provide for Better Control of the Interstate Traffic in Firearms*, Public Law 90-618, *U.S. Statutes at Large* 82 (1968), 1213–36.

54. *An Act to Amend Title 18, United States Code, to Provide for Better Control of the Interstate Traffic in Firearms*, Public Law 90-618, *U.S. Statutes at Large* 82 (1968), 1220–21.

55. Jacobs, *Can Gun Control Work?*, 25.

56. Jacobs, *Can Gun Control Work?*, 30.

57. Jacobs, *Can Gun Control Work?*, 31.

58. David Hemenway, *Private Guns, Public Health* (Ann Arbor: University of Michigan Press, 2017), 170.

59. Wesley Lowery, "2.1 Million Gun Sales Stopped by Background Checks in 20 Years, Brady Report Finds," *Washington Post*, February 28, 2014, https://www.washingtonpost.com/news/post-politics/wp/2014/02/28/2-1-million-gun-sales-stopped-by-background-checks-in-20-years-brady-report-finds/.

60. Hemenway, *Private Guns*, 170–71; German Lopez, "After 2 Years of Increases, the US Murder Rate Officially Fell in 2017," Vox, September 24, 2018, https://www.vox.com/2018/9/24/17895572/murder-violent-crime-rate-fbi-2017. For a graphic view of the decline over the decades since the 1960s, see the chart in Lopez.

61. Hemenway, *Private Guns*, 171.

62. Philip J. Cook and Jens Ludwig, "The Limited Impact of the Brady Act," in Webster and Vernick, *Reducing Gun Violence*, 24–25.

63. Cook and Ludwig, "The Limited Impact," in Webster and Vernick, *Reducing Gun Violence*, 22–23.

64. RAND Corporation, *The Science of Gun Policy: A Critical Synthesis of Research Evidence on the Effects of Gun Policies in the United States* (Santa Monica, CA: RAND, 2018), 54.

65. RAND Corporation, *The Science of Gun Policy*, 55.

66. National Research Council, *Firearms and Violence*, 99.

67. National Research Council, *Firearms and Violence*, 100.

68. Hemenway, *Private Guns*, 167.

69. RAND Corporation, *The Science of Gun Policy*, xxiii.

70. For a detailed discussion of how "the gun industry and its relentless lobby have succeeded in preventing the federal government from collecting, organizing, analyzing, and—most of all—releasing detailed data about guns and gun death, injury and crime in America," see chapter 7, "Top Secret: America's Guns," in Tom Diaz, *The Last Gun: How Changes in the Gun Industry Are Killing Americans and What It Will Take to Stop It* (New York: New Press, 2012), 168–88.

71. RAND Corporation, *The Science of Gun Policy*, xix.

72. RAND Corporation, *The Science of Gun Policy*, xxiii.

73. Jacobs, *Can Gun Control Work?*, 109.

74. Martha Bellisle, Associated Press, "Gun Background Check System Riddled with Flaws," at *PBS News Hour*, March 10, 2018. https://www.pbs.org/newshour/nation/gun-background-check-system-riddled-with-flaws.

75. Gifford Law Center to Prevent Gun Violence, "Categories of Prohibited People," https://lawcenter.giffords.org/gun-laws/policy-areas/who-can-have-a-gun/categories-of-prohibited-people/.

76. Author's notes from video, "Theater Shooting Trial Day 31," YouTube, https://www.youtube.com/watch?v=xRmxY_JqxxI.

77. For a video of a sportsman shooting at the range, see Todd Toven, "Shooting Rifles at Colorado's Byers Canyon Shooting Range," September 10, 2014, https://www.youtube.com/watch?v=OxBrfZvPdJ4.

78. Colorado Parks and Wildlife, "Colorado's Byers Canyon Shooting Range Now Open," Outdoor News, March 22, 2012, https://www.outdoornews.com/2012/03/22/colorados-byers-canyon-shooting-range-now-open/.

79. For the story of Jablonski's injury and the company's fund-raising on his behalf, see "Sauce Hockey Helps Paralyzed Minnesota Hockey Player," CBS Sports, March 30, 2012, https://www.cbssports.com/nhl/news/sauce-hockey-helps-paralyzed-minnesota-hockey-player/. Jablonski is now a senior at the University of Southern California. He recently discovered that he can wiggle his toes, indicating that his spine was not completely severed. Sarah Horner, "Paralyzed Hockey Player Jack Jablonski Can Wiggle His Toes and He Has the Video to Prove It," *Pioneer Press*, July 10, 2018, https://www.twincities.com/2018/07/10/jack-jablonski-paralyzed-hockey-player-wiggle-toes-video/.

80. Author's notes from prosecutor's opening statement on Monday, April 27, 2015, YouTube, https://www.youtube.com/watch?v=eunOhCcVveM.

81. "Hunting and Target Shooting Participation, 2016 Edition," National Shooting Sports Foundation, in author's files.

82. "Shooting Sport Participation in the United States in 2014," National Shooting Sports Foundation, in author's files.

83. Ali Watkins, John Ismay, and Thomas Gibbons-Neff, "Once Banned, Now Loved and Loathed: How the AR-15 Became 'America's Rifle,'" *New York Times*, March 3, 2018, https://nyti.ms/2F8sMI9.

84. Watkins, "Once Banned, Now Loved."

85. Watkins, "Once Banned, Now Loved."

86. Charles Scudder, "Sticking to Their Gun: Aficionados Say the AR-15 Is Ideal for Civilian Sport Shooting, Self-Defense," *Dallas Morning News*, July 1, 2016, http://interactives.dallasnews.com/2016/gun-owners/.

87. Tara Isabella Burton, "The Cultlike Church behind a Ceremony with AR-15s and Bullet Crowns, Explained," Vox, March 1, 2018, https://www.vox.com/2018/3/1/17067894/church-bullet-crowns-ar15-world-peace-unification-sanctuary-moonies-moon.

88. "Declaration of James Curcuruto in Support of Plaintiffs' Motion for Preliminary Injunction," filed November 10, 2017, *Rupp v. Bercerra*, U.S. District Court for the Central District of California, Southern Division, Case No.: 8:17-cv-00746-JLS-JDE.

89. "Declaration of James Curcuruto," 4.

90. "Declaration of James Curcuruto," 5.

Chapter Six: Only in America

1. Robert Braile '77, "To Daniel Oates '77: An Essay on Idealism," *Bucknell Magazine*, https://www.bucknell.edu/about-bucknell/communications/bucknell-magazine/recent-issues/summer-2013/to-daniel-oates-77-an-essay-on-idealism.

2. Unless otherwise noted, quotes are from an interview with Chief of Police Daniel Oates at his office in Miami Beach, Florida, on February 26, 2018.

3. Russ Buettner and Charles V. Bagli, "How Donald Trump Bankrupted His Atlantic City Casinos, but Still Earned Millions," *New York Times*, June 11, 2016, https://www.nytimes.com/2016/06/12/nyregion/donald-trump-atlantic-city.html.

4. Jacquelyn Nixon, "New Police Chief Feels at Home in Ann Arbor," *Michigan Daily*, September 6, 2001, https://www.michigandaily.com/content/new-police-chief-feels-home-ann-arbor.

5. J. Pete Blair, Terry Nichols, David Burns, and John R. Curnutt, *Active Shooter: Events and Responses* (Boca Raton, FL: CRC Press, 2013), 2.

6. Blair, *Active Shooter*, 4.

7. Blair, *Active Shooter*, 4.

8. Blair, *Active Shooter*, 5.

9. Blair, *Active Shooter*, 6.

10. Radley Balko, *Rise of the Warrior Cop: The Militarization of America's Police Forces* (New York: Public Affairs, 2014), 334.

11. Blair, *Active Shooter*, 7.

12. Blair, *Active Shooter*, 9.

13. Blair, *Active Shooter*, 9.

14. Blair, *Active Shooter*, 8.

15. Details of the Columbine High School attack are from Blair, *Active Shooter*, 1–13, and David Cullen, *Columbine* (New York: Twelve, 1991), passim.

16. Cullen, *Columbine*, 57.

17. Cullen, *Columbine*, 56.

18. Cullen, *Columbine*, 56.

19. Cullen, *Columbine*, 56–57.

20. Blair, *Active Shooter*, 11.

21. Blair, *Active Shooter*, 12; Cullen, *Columbine*, 57, 61.

22. Blair, *Active Shooter*, 12; Cullen, *Columbine*, 353.

23. Blair, *Active Shooter*, 12.

24. Blair, *Active Shooter*, 12–13.

25. Blair, *Active Shooter*, 20.

26. Washington, DC, Police Executive Research Forum (PERF), *The Police Response to Active Shooter Incidents*, March 2014, 2.

27. Alex Norton, "'We're Making Entry:' Sergeant Killed in Thousand Oaks Pursued Gunman inside Club," *Washington Post*, November 8, 2018, https://www.washingtonpost.com/nation/2018/11/08/sheriffs-deputy-was-about-retire-instead-he-died-hero-thousand-oaks/.

28. PERF, *The Police Response*, 2.

29. The discussion of the Batman phenomenon in this section is based primarily on Les Daniels, *Batman: The Complete History* (San Francisco: Chronicle Books, 1999) and Jody Duncan Jesser and Janine Pourroy, *The Art and Making of the Dark Knight Trilogy* (New York: Abrams, 2012).

30. Steven D. Greydanus, "The 'Dark Knight' Trilogy: The Inconclusive Battle for Gotham's Soul," *National Catholic Register*, July 20, 2018, http://www.ncregister.com/daily-news/the-dark-knight-trilogy-the-inconclusive-battle-for-gothams-soul.

31. Manohla Dargis and A. O. Scott, "Super-Dreams of an Alternate World Order: 'The Amazing Spider-Man' and the Modern Comic Book Movie," *New York Times*, June 27, 2012, https://www.nytimes.com/2012/07/01/movies/the -amazing-spider-man-and-the-modern-comic-book-movie.html.

32. Brooks Barnes, "At CinemaCon, Theater Owners Are the Stars," *New York Times*, April 24, 2012, https://mediadecoder.blogs.nytimes.com/2012/04/24/at -cinemacon-theater-owners-are-the-stars/.

33. Erik Olsen, "Packing All the Heat a Movie Could Want," *New York Times*, May 17, 2012, https://www.nytimes.com/2012/05/20/movies/the -specialists-prop-weapons-supplier-to-men-in-black-3.html.

34. Manohla Dargis, "A Rejected Superhero Ends Up at Ground Zero," *New York Times*, July 18, 2012, https://www.nytimes.com/2012/07/20/movies/the -dark-knight-rises-with-christian-bale.html.

35. Dave Itzkoff, "Rotten Tomatoes Halts Comments on 'Dark Knight,'" ArtsBeat, *New York Times* blog, July 17, 2012, https://artsbeat.blogs.nytimes .com/2012/07/17/rotten-tomatoes-halts-reader-comments-amid-dark-knight -furor/.

36. For an in-depth account of Mitt Romney's history with Bain Capital, see Matt Taibbi, "Greed and Debt: The True Story of Mitt Romney and Bain Capital," *Rolling Stone*, August 29, 2012, https://www.rollingstone.com/ politics/politics-news/greed-and-debt-the-true-story-of-mitt-romney-and-bain -capital-183291/.

37. Nicholas Confessore, "Morgan Freeman Gives $1 Million to Obama Super PAC," The Caucus—The Politics and Government blog of the *New York Times,* July 19, 2012, https://thecaucus.blogs.nytimes.com/2012/07/19/morgan -freeman-gives-1-million-to-obama-super-pac/.

38. Unless otherwise noted, Sandy Phillips quotes in this section are from a telephone interview with the author on February 12, 2018.

39. Victoria Ptashnick, "Canadian Boyfriend of 'Batman' Shooting Victim Devastated," *Toronto Sun*, July 20, 2012, https://torontosun.com/2012/07/20/ boyfriend-of-batman-shooting-victim-devastated/wcm/0ffd64d2-4148-4d78 -92ca-0b8202ce19d8.

40. Pat Leonard, "Colorado 'Dark Knight' Massacre Victim Jessica Ghawi's Last Words Were with Former Daily News Hockey Writer Jesse Spector," *New York Daily News*, July 20, 2012, http://www.nydailynews.com/news/national/ colorado-dark-knight-massacre-victim-jessica-ghawi-words-daily-news-hockey -writer-jesse-spector-article-1.1118607.

41. Moms Demand Action, "Sandy Phillips Fights for Stronger, Smarter Gun Laws in the Aftermath of the Murder of Her Daughter in the Aurora Mass Shooting," July 17, 2013, https://momsdemandaction.org/out-of-the-darkness

-a-mother-who-lost-her-daughter-in-the-aurora-movie-theater-shooting
-advocates-for-stronger-smarter-gun-laws/.

42. Blair, *Active Shooter*, 82–83.

43. Blair, *Active Shooter*, 83.

44. Blair, *Active Shooter*, 66–70.

45. PERF, *The Police Response*, 6.

46. Jennifer Medina, Dave Philipps, and Serge F. Kovaleski, "Dueling Images: A Smiling Young Marine and a Killer Dressed in Black," *New York Times*, November 8, 2018, https://www.nytimes.com/2018/11/08/us/ian-david-long
-california-shooter.html.

47. Tess Owen, "Why California's 'Red Flag' Law Didn't Stop the Thousand Oaks Shooter," VICE News, November 9, 2018, https://news.vice.com/en_us/
article/wj38yz/why-californias-red-flag-law-didnt-stop-the-thousand-oaks-shooter.

48. "Governor Brown Vetoes Gun Violence Bill Introduced after Florida School Shooting," CBS13, September 27, 2018, https://sacramento.cbslocal
.com/2018/09/27/governor-brown-vetoes-gun-violence-bill/.

49. J. Reid Meloy and Jens Hoffman, eds., *International Handbook of Threat Assessment* (New York: Oxford University Press, 2014), 6.

50. Meloy, *International Handbook*, 10.

51. See Meloy, *International Handbook*, 10–12.

52. Meloy, *International Handbook*, 47.

53. PERF, *The Police Response*, 30.

54. PERF, *The Police Response*, 31.

55. "RECAP: 235 Bullet Trajectories Shown in Theater Shooting Trial, Day 16," Fox31 News, https://kdvr.com/2015/05/20/watch-live-day-16-of-aurora
-theater-shooting-trial/.

56. Carly Moore, "Friend Recalls Praying over Body of Jessica Ghawi in Theater Shooting," Fox31 Denver, May 20, 2015, https://kdvr.com/2015/05/20/i
-prayed-over-jessica-ghawis-body-during-theater-shooting-friend-testifies/.

57. Noelle Phillips and John Ingold, "Officers in Tears Testify of Ferrying Aurora Theater Shooting Victims in Holmes' Trial," *Denver Post*, April 30, 2015, https://www.denverpost.com/2015/04/30/officers-in-tears-testify-of-ferrying
-aurora-theater-shooting-victims-in-holmes-trial/.

58. Andrew Cohen, "Blood on the Tracks: The Aurora Theater Shooting Hearing," *Atlantic*, January 7, 2013, https://www.theatlantic.com/
national/archive/2013/01/blood-on-the-tracks-the-aurora-theater-shooting
-hearing/266899/.

59. Phillips and Ingold, "Officers in Tears."

60. Cohen, "Blood on the Tracks."

61. Moms Demand Action, "Sandy Phillips Fights."

Chapter Seven: The Right Not to Be Shot

1. Details of this incident are from Santa Barbara County Sheriff's Office, *Investigative Summary: Isla Vista Mass Murder, May 23, 2014* (February 18, 2015); and Todd Leopold, "Father of Rampage Victim: 'When Will This Insanity Stop?'" CNN, May 27, 2014, https://www.cnn.com/2014/05/24/us/santa-barbara-shooting-victims/index.html.

2. Leopold, "Father of Rampage Victim."

3. Jonathan Lowy and Kelly Sampson, "The Right Not to Be Shot: Public Safety, Private Guns, and the Constellation of Constitutional Liberties," 14 *Geo. J.L. & Pub. Pol'y* 187 (2016).

4. Lowy and Sampson, "The Right Not to Be Shot," 189–90.

5. Lowy and Sampson, "The Right Not to Be Shot," 190–91.

6. For a learned and thorough critique of the influence of student-run law journals on public debate, see Robert J. Spitzer, *Saving the Constitution from Lawyers: How Legal Training and Law Reviews Distort Constitutional Meaning* (New York: Cambridge University Press, 2008). For a discussion of the conservative law review article factory and its consequences for gun control specifically, see chapter 2, "Supreme Nonsense and Deadly Myths," in Tom Diaz, *The Last Gun: How Changes in the Gun Industry Are Killing Americans and What It Will Take to Stop It* (New York: New Press, 2013), 37–60.

7. This anecdote is based on the author's experience as a congressional committee staff member.

8. This anecdote was told to the author in a 2018 interview by the second activist leader, the person to whom the remark was made. The author recalls attending at least one of these summits and knows both of the parties.

9. See, Kristin A. Goss, *Disarmed: The Missing Movement for Gun Control in America* (Princeton, NJ: Princeton University Press, 2006), 66–67, 169.

10. Email from Sarah Brady to Paul Helmke, June 17, 2009, copy in author's files.

11. Dorothy Samuels, "The Deadly Myth of Gun Control in Electoral Politics," *New York Times*, May 8, 2009, https://www.nytimes.com/2009/05/09/opinion/09sat4.html.

12. Jason Horowitz, "Over a Barrel? Meet White House Gun Policy Adviser Steve Croley," *Washington Post*, April 11, 2011, https://www.washingtonpost.com/lifestyle/style/over-a-barrel-meet-white-house-gun-policy-adviser-steve-croley/2011/04/04/AFt9EKND_story.html.

13. "Meet White House Gun Policy Adviser Steve Croley," Tactical-Life.com, May 19, 2011, https://www.tactical-life.com/news/meet-white-house

-gun-policy-adviser-steve-croley/; description of magazine at https://outdoor
groupstore.com/p-1622-tactical-life-subscription.aspx.

14. Sarah Brady, "30 Years after the Reagan Shooting, Gun Violence
Still Reigns," *Washington Post*, March 29, 2011, https://www.washingtonpost
.com/opinions/30-years-after-the-reagan-shooting-gun-violence-still-reigns/
2011/03/28/AFEpxEyB_story.html.

15. Manuel Roig-Franzia, "As Presidential Campaign Ends, Hopes Dashed
for Issues Pushers," *Washington Post*, November 5, 2012, https://www.washington
post.com/lifestyle/style/as-presidential-campaign-ends-hopes-dashed-for
-issues-pushers/2012/11/05/8634df0a-26d3-11e2-8d6a-9b57d8a5215c_story
.html.

16. This phrase is sometimes hyphenated in Goss's text and sometimes not.
Quoted material is as written in *Disarmed*.

17. Goss, *Disarmed*, 193.

18. Goss, *Disarmed*, 22.

19. Goss, *Disarmed*, 30.

20. Goss, *Disarmed*, 22.

21. Goss, *Disarmed*, 22.

22. Goss, *Disarmed*, 23.

23. Goss, *Disarmed*, 23–24.

24. Goss, *Disarmed*, 24.

25. Goss, *Disarmed*, 24.

26. Goss, *Disarmed*, 28.

27. Goss, *Disarmed*, 47.

28. Goss, *Disarmed*, 47.

29. Goss, *Disarmed*, 48.

30. Goss, *Disarmed*, 30.

31. Goss, *Disarmed*, 145.

32. Goss, *Disarmed*, 147.

33. Goss, *Disarmed*, 29.

34. Goss, *Disarmed*, 147.

35. Goss, *Disarmed*, 172.

36. Goss, *Disarmed*, 170.

37. Goss, *Disarmed*, 193.

38. Goss, *Disarmed*, 175.

39. This description of the Empire State Building shooting is based on Robert D. McFadden, "Shots Send Empire State Crowd Fleeing," *New York Times*,
February 24, 1997, https://www.nytimes.com/1997/02/24/nyregion/shots-send
-empire-state-crowd-fleeing.html; Blaine Harden, "Shooter Bought Gun by

Using New Florida ID," *Washington Post*, February 25, 1997, https://www
.washingtonpost.com/archive/politics/1997/02/25/shooter-bought-gun-by-using
-new-florida-id/8bfb87f6-da54-4422-960c-3ad4bf5dc433/; Matthew Purdy,
"Empire State Gunman's Note: Kill 'Zionists,'" *New York Times*, February 26,
1997, https://www.nytimes.com/1997/02/26/nyregion/empire-state-gunman-s
-note-kill-zionists.html.

40. Harden, "Shooter Bought Gun."

41. Lawrence Downes, "After Oregon Shooting, Rudy Giuliani Bashes
Obama on Gun Control," *New York Times*, October 2, 2015, https://takingnote
.blogs.nytimes.com/2015/10/02/after-oregon-shooting-rudy-giuliani-bashes
-obama-on-gun-control/.

42. Melissa Healy, "Matthew Gross' Life Changed at the Empire State
Building," *Los Angeles Times*, January 24, 2011, http://articles.latimes.com/2011/
jan/24/health/la-he-matthew-gross-20110124.

43. Michelle Miller and Phil Hirschkorn, "Shooting Survivor May Show Giffords' Future," CBS News, January 29, 2011, https://www.cbsnews.com/news/
shooting-survivor-may-show-giffords-future/.

44. Healy, "Matthew Gross' Life."

45. Joyce Purnick, "Metro Matters; The Shots That Changed His Life,"
New York Times, June 1, 2000, https://www.nytimes.com/2000/06/01/nyregion/
metro-matters-the-shots-that-changed-his-life.html.

46. Nichole M. Christian, "A Year Later, Victim Forms a New Group
to Fight Guns," *New York Times*, February 24, 1998, https://www.nytimes
.com/1998/02/24/nyregion/a-year-later-victim-forms-a-new-group-to-fight
-guns.html.

47. Joyce Purnick, "Metro Matters."

48. Melanie Eversley, "Brady Gun-Control Organization Gets New
President," *USA Today*, February 6, 2012, http://content.usatoday.com/
communities/ondeadline/post/2012/02/brady-gun-control-organization-gets
-new-president/1#.W_AmXidRdE7.

49. Brady Campaign to Prevent Gun Violence, Form 990, "Return of Organization Exempt from Income Tax," 2012, dated November 2013.

50. Brady Campaign to Prevent Gun Violence, Form 990, "Return of Organization Exempt from Income Tax," 2016, dated November 2017.

51. The Brady Campaign and Center to Prevent Gun Violence, "Statement
from the Chairman of the Board, Kevin Quinn," September 6, 2017, http://
www.bradycampaign.org/press-room/statement-from-the-chai.

52. Michael Luca, Deepak Malhotra, and Christopher Poliquin, "The Impact
of Mass Shootings on Gun Policy," Harvard Business School, Working Paper
16-126 (October 2016).

53. Luca, "The Impact of Mass Shootings," 3.

54. Luca, "The Impact of Mass Shootings," 3.

55. Luca, "The Impact of Mass Shootings," 14.

56. Luca, "The Impact of Mass Shootings," 3–4 (italics in original).

57. Goss, *Disarmed*, 1.

58. Robert J. Spitzer, *The Politics of Gun Control: Sixth Edition* (Boulder, CO: Paradigm Publishers, 2015), 162.

59. Douglas Kellner, *Guys and Guns Amok: Domestic Terrorism and School Shootings from the Oklahoma City Bombing to the Virginia Tech Massacre* (Boulder, CO: Paradigm Publishers, 2008), 121.

60. Kellner, *Guys and Guns Amok*, 123.

61. Kellner, *Guys and Guns Amok*, 122.

62. Kellner, *Guys and Guns Amok*, 121–23.

63. Goss, *Disarmed*, 1–2.

64. Andrew Jay McClurg and Brannon P. Denning, *Guns and the Law: Cases, Problems, and Explanation* (Durham, NC: Carolina Academic Press, 2016), 351.

65. For a brief discussion of the basics of tort law as applied to guns, see Andrew J. McClurg, David B. Kopel, and Brannon P. Denning, eds., *Gun Control and Gun Rights: A Reader and Guide* (New York: New York University Press, 2002), 288–91.

66. McClurg and Denning, *Guns and the Law*, 349.

67. McClurg and Denning, *Guns and the Law*, 349.

68. McClurg and Denning, *Guns and the Law*, 349.

69. McClurg and Denning, *Guns and the Law*, 350.

70. Heidi Li Feldman, "Prudence, Benevolence, and Negligence: Virtue Ethics and Tort Law," 74 *Chi.-Kent L. Rev.* 1431–66 (2000), 1435.

71. Howard M. Erichson, chapter 5, "Private Lawyers, Public Lawsuits: Plaintiff's Attorneys in Municipal Gun Litigation," in Timothy D. Lytton, ed., *Suing the Gun Industry: A Battle at the Crossroads of Gun Control and Mass Torts* (Ann Arbor: University of Michigan Press, 2006), 129.

72. *Associated Press*, "Wendell Gauthier, 58, Dies; Lawyer in Big Damage Suits," *New York Times*, December 12, 2001, https://www.nytimes.com/2001/12/12/us/wendell-gauthier-58-dies-lawyer-in-big-damage-suits.html.

73. Erichson, "Private Lawyers," in Lytton, *Suing the Gun Industry*, 131.

74. Tom Diaz, chapter 3, "The American Gun Industry: Designing and Marketing Increasingly Lethal Weapons," in Lytton, *Suing the Gun Industry*, 89.

75. Timothy D. Lytton, chapter 6, "The NRA, the Brady Campaign & the Problem of Gun Litigation," in Lytton, *Suing the Gun Industry*, 166.

76. McClurg and Denning, *Guns and the Law*, 347.

77. McClurg and Denning, *Guns and the Law*, 370.

78. See Charity Navigator, "Ratings History, Brady Center to Prevent Gun Violence," https://www.charitynavigator.org/index.cfm?bay=search.history &orgid=5426, and "What Do Our Ratings Mean?" https://www.charitynavigator .org/index.cfm?bay=content.view&cpid=43. Charity Navigator rates organizations on a four-star system. Four stars is "exceptional" ("Exceeds industry standards and outperforms most charities in its Cause"). Three stars is "good" ("Exceeds or meets industry standards and performs as well as or better than most charities in its Cause"). Two stars is "needs improvement" ("Meets or nearly meets industry standards but underperforms most charities in its Cause"). One star is "poor" ("Fails to meet industry standards and performs well below most charities in its Cause"). As of its latest rating (October 10, 2018) and as of this writing, in four out of its five ratings since 2016 Charity Navigator gave Brady two stars ("needs improvement"). The fifth rating (on May 1, 2018) gave Brady one star ("poor").

BIBLIOGRAPHY

Abramowitz, Alan I. *The Great Alignment: Race, Party Transformation, and the Rise of Donald Trump*. New Haven: Yale University Press, 2018.

Achen, Christopher H., and Larry M. Bartels. *Democracy for Realists: Why Elections Do Not Produce Responsive Government*. Princeton, NJ: Princeton University Press, 2016.

Alschuler, Albert W. "Two Guns, Four Guns, Six Guns, More Guns: Does Arming the Public Reduce Crime?" 31 *Val. U. L. Rev.* 365 (1997).

Alvis-Mirandal, Hernando Raphael, Andres M. Rubiano, Amit Agrawal, Alejandro Rojas, Luis Rafael Moscote-Salazar, Guru Dutta Satyarthee, Willem Guillermo Calderon-Miranda, Nidia Escobar-Hernandez, and Nasly Zabaleta-Churio. "Craniocerebral Gunshot Injuries; A Review of the Current Literature," *Bull Emerg Trauma* 2016; 4(2): 65–74.

Anestis, Michael D. *Guns and Suicide—An American Epidemic*. New York: Oxford University Press, 2018.

Balko, Radley. *Rise of the Warrior Cop: The Militarization of America's Police Forces*. New York: Public Affairs, 2014.

Bishop, Bill. *The Big Sort: Why the Clustering of Like-Minded America Is Tearing Us Apart*. Boston: Mariner Books, 2009.

Blair, J. Pete, Terry Nichols, David Burns, and John R. Curnutt. *Active Shooter: Events and Responses*. Boca Raton, FL: CRC Press, 2013.

Boorman, Dean K. *The History of Smith & Wesson Firearms*. Guilford, CT: Lyons Press, 2002.

Brain Injury Association of America. *The Essential Brain Injury Guide Edition 5.0*. 2016.

Brown, R. Blake. *Arming and Disarming: A History of Gun Control in Canada*. Toronto: University of Toronto Press, 2012.

Canada. Ministry of Industry. Canadian Centre for Justice Statistics. "Firearms and Violent Crime in Canada." Adam Cotter, author. Catalogue no. 85-0020-X, 2014.

Connecticut, State of, Sandy Hook Advisory Commission. "Final Report." Presented to Governor Daniel P. Malloy, March 6, 2015.

Cook, Philip J., and John J. Donohue. "Saving Lives by Regulating Guns: Evidence for Policy." *Science* 358 (6368), December 8, 2017, 1259–61, doi: 10.1126/science.aar3067.

Cook, Philip J., and Kristin A. Goss. *The Gun Debate: What Everyone Needs to Know*. New York: Oxford University Press, 2014.

Crawford, Neta C. "United States Budgetary Costs of Post-9/11 Wars Through FY2018: A Summary of the $5.6 Trillion in Costs for the US Wars in Iraq, Syria, Afghanistan, and Pakistan, and Post-9/11 Veterans Care and Homeland Security." Watson Institute for International & Public Affairs. November 2017.

Cullen, David. *Columbine*. New York: Twelve, 1991.

Daniels, Les. *Batman: The Complete History*. San Francisco: Chronicle Books, 1999.

Davidson, Osha Gray. *Under Fire: The NRA and the Battle for Gun Control* (expanded ed.). Iowa City: University of Iowa Press, 1998.

Davis, Kevin. *The Brain Defense: Murder in Manhattan and the Dawn of Neuroscience in America's Courtrooms*. New York: Penguin Press, 2017.

Diaz, Tom. *The Last Gun: How Changes in the Gun Industry Are Killing Americans and What It Will Take to Stop It*. New York: New Press, 2012.

Diaz, Tom. *No Boundaries: Transnational Latino Gangs and American Law Enforcement*. Ann Arbor: University of Michigan Press, 2011.

Diaz, Tom, and Barbara Newman. *Lightning out of Lebanon: Hezbollah Terrorists on American Soil*. New York: Ballantine Books, 2006.

Doherty, Brian. *Gun Control on Trial: Inside the Supreme Court Battle Over the Second Amendment*. Washington, DC: Cato Institute, 2008.

Ellis, John. *The Social History of the Machine Gun*. Baltimore: Johns Hopkins University Press, 1986.

Feldman, Heidi Li. "Prudence, Benevolence, and Negligence: Virtue Ethics and Tort Law." 74 *Chi.-Kent L. Rev.* 1431–66, 2000.

Fiorina, Morris P. *Unstable Majorities: Polarization, Party Sorting & Political Stalemate*. Stanford, CA: Hoover Institution Press, 2017.

Fowlera, Katherine A., Linda L. Dahlberg, Tadesse Haileyesus, and Joseph L. Annest. "Firearm Injuries in the United States." *Prev. Med.* 2015 October; 79: 5–14, doi:10.1016/j.ypmed.2015.06.002.

Fox, James Alan, and Monica DeLateur. "Mass Shootings in America: Moving Beyond Newtown." *Homicide Studies* 18 (2014).

Fuller, J. F. C. *The Conduct of War, 1789–1961.* New Brunswick, NJ: Da Capo Press, 1992.

Goertzel, Ted. "Myths of Murder and Multiple Regression," http://www.crab.rutgers.edu/~goertzel/mythsofmurder.htm. (Originally published in *The Skeptical Inquirer*, volume 26, no. 1, January/February 2002, 19–23.)

Goss, Kristin A. *Disarmed: The Missing Movement for Gun Control in America.* Princeton, NJ: Princeton University Press, 2006.

Gressot, Loyola V., Roukoz B. Chamoun, Akash J. Patel, Alex B. Valadka, Dima Suki, Claudia S. Robertson, and Shankar P. Gopinath. "Predictors of Outcome in Civilians with Gunshot Wounds to the Head upon Presentation." *J. Neurosurg* 121: 645–52 (2014).

Griffiths, William R. *The Great War: Strategies and Tactics of the First World War* (The West Point Military History Series). Garden City Park, NY: Square One Publishers, 2003.

Grinshteyn, Erin, and David Hemenway. "Violent Death Rates: The US Compared with Other High-Income OECD Countries, 2010." *American Journal of Medicine* 129 (2016), 269, doi: 10.1016/j.amjmed.2015.10.025.

Gudmunsson, Bruce I. *Stormtroop Tactics: Innovation in the German Army, 1914–1918.* Westport, CT: Praeger, 1995.

Haag, Pamela. *The Gunning of America: Business and the Making of American Gun Culture.* New York: Basic Books, 2016.

Hemenway, David. *Private Guns, Public Health.* Ann Arbor: University of Michigan Press, 2017.

Hess, Earl J. *The Rifle Musket in Civil War Combat: Reality and Myth.* Lawrence: University Press of Kansas, 2008.

Hogg, David, and Lauren Hogg. *#Never Again.* New York: Random House, 2018.

Hogg, Ian V. *Guns and How They Work.* New York: Everest House, 1979.

Inglehart, Ronald. *The Silent Revolution: Changing Values and Political Styles among Western Publics.* Princeton, NJ: Princeton University Press, 1977.

Inglehart, Ronald, Jon Miller, and Logan Woods. "The Silent Revolution in Reverse: Trump and the Xenophobic Authoritarian Populist Parties." Paper presented at American Political Science Association Meetings in Boston, August 31, 2018.

Jacobs, James B. *Can Gun Control Work?* New York: Oxford University Press, 2002.

Jesser, Jody Duncan, and Janine Pourroy. *The Art and Making of the Dark Knight Trilogy.* New York: Abrams, 2012.

Johnston, Gary Paul, and Thomas B. Nelson. *The World's Assault Rifles*. Lorton, VA: Ironside International Publishers, 2010.

Karp, Aaron. "Estimating Global Civilian-Held Firearms Numbers." Briefing Paper, Small Arms Survey, Graduate Institute of International and Development Studies, Geneva (June 2018).

Kellner, Douglas. *Guys and Guns Amok: Domestic Terrorism and School Shootings from the Oklahoma City Bombing to the Virginia Tech Massacre*. Boulder, CO: Paradigm Publishers, 2008.

Klarevas, Louis. *Rampage Nation: Securing America from Mass Shootings*. Amherst, NY: Prometheus Books, 2016.

Kopel, David B. *The Samurai, the Mountie, and the Cowboy: Should America Adopt the Gun Controls of Other Democracies?* Buffalo: Prometheus Books, 1992.

Lankford, Adam. "Are America's Public Mass Shooters Unique? A Comparative Analysis of Offenders in the United States and Other Countries." *International Journal of Comparative and Applied Criminal Justice*, 2016.

Lankford, Adam. "Public Mass Shooters and Firearms: A Cross-National Study of 171 Countries." *Violence and Victims* 31 (2016).

Lau, Mike R. *The Military and Police Sniper*. Manchester, CT: Precision Shooting, 1998.

Lavergne, Gary M. *A Sniper in the Tower: The Charles Whitman Murders*. Denton: University of North Texas Press, 1997.

Leddy, Edward F. *Magnum Force Lobby: The National Rifle Association Fights Gun Control*. Lanham, MD: University Press of America, 1987.

Lemieux, Frederic. "Effect of Gun Culture and Firearms Laws on Gun Violence and Mass Shootings in the United States: A Multi-Level Quantitative Analysis." *International Journal of Criminal Justice Sciences*, January–June 2014, vol. 9 (1).

Lewiecki, E. Michael, and Sara A. Miller. "Suicide, Guns, and Public Policy." *J. Public Health*, 2013; 103:27–31, doi:10.2105/ AJPH.2012.300964.

Lin, David J., Fred C. Lam, Jeffrey J. Siracuse, Aiith Thomas, and Ekkehard M. Kasper. "'Time Is Brain' the Gifford Factor—or: Why Do Some Civilian Gunshot Wounds to the Head Do Unexpectedly Well?" *Surg Neurol Int*. 2012; 3:98, August 27, 2012.

Lipset, Seymour Martin. *Continental Divide: The Values and Institutions of the United States and Canada*. New York: Routledge, 1991.

Long, Duncan. *Assault Pistols, Rifles, and Submachine Guns*. Boulder, CO: Paladin Press, 1986.

Long, Duncan. *The Complete AR-15/M16 Sourcebook: What Every Shooter Needs to Know* (Revised and Updated Edition). Boulder, CO: Paladin Press, 2001.

Lott, John R. Jr. *More Guns, Less Crime—Understanding Crime and Gun-Control Laws*, third ed. Chicago: University of Chicago Press, 2010.

Lowy, Jonathan, and Kelly Sampson. "The Right Not to Be Shot: Public Safety, Private Guns, and the Constellation of Constitutional Liberties." 14 *Geo. J.L. & Pub. Pol'y* 187, 2016.

Luca, Michael, Deepak Malhotra, and Christopher Poliquin. "The Impact of Mass Shootings on Gun Policy." Harvard Business School, Working Paper 16-126, October 2016.

Lytton, Timothy D, ed. *Suing the Gun Industry: A Battle at the Crossroads of Gun Control and Mass Torts*. Ann Arbor: University of Michigan Press, 2006.

Marcot, Roy. *The History of Remington Firearms*. New York: Chartwell Books, 2011.

Marshall, S. L. A. *Commentary on Infantry Operations and Weapons Usage in Korea: Winter of 1950–51*. West Chester, OH: Nafziger Collection, 2002.

Mason, Lilliana. *Uncivil Agreement: How Politics Became Our Identity*. Chicago: University of Chicago Press, 2018.

Mass Murderers. Alexandria, VA: Time-Life Books, 1993.

McClurg, Andrew Jay, and Brannon P. Denning. *Guns and the Law: Cases, Problems, and Explanation*. Durham, NC: Carolina Academic Press, 2016.

McClurg, Andrew J., David B. Kopel, and Brannon P. Denning, eds. *Gun Control and Gun Rights: A Reader and Guide*. New York: New York University Press, 2002.

McNab, Chris. *German Automatic Rifles 1941–45*. New York: Osprey Publishing, 2013.

McNaugher, Thomas L. "Marksmanship, McNamara and the M16 Rifle: Organizations, Analysis and Weapons Acquisition." Rand Corporation, The Rand Paper Series. March 1979.

Meloy, J. Reid, and Jens Hoffman, eds. *International Handbook of Threat Assessment*. New York: Oxford University Press, 2014.

Melzer, Scott. *Gun Crusaders: The NRA's Culture War*. New York: New York University Press, 2009.

Morton, Desmond. *A Short History of Canada*. Toronto: McClellan & Stewart, 2017.

National Research Council of the National Academies. Committee to Improve Research Information and Data on Firearms. *Firearms and Violence: A Critical Review*. 2005.

New York City Police Department. *Active Shooter: Recommendations and Analysis for Risk Mitigation* (2016 edition).

Overton, Iain. *The Way of the Gun*. New York: HarperCollins, 2016.

Paulson, Alan C. *Weapons Evaluations for the Armed Professional and Advanced Collector*. Boulder, CO: Paladin Press, 2006.

Peterson, Phillip. *Gun Digest Buyers Guide to Assault Weapons*. Iola, WI: Gun Digest Books, 2008.

Police Executive Research Forum (PERF). *The Police Response to Active Shooter Incidents*. Washington, DC, March 2014.

Putnam, Robert D. *Bowling Alone: The Collapse and Revival of American Community*. New York: Simon & Schuster Paperbacks, 2000.

RAND Corporation. *The Science of Gun Policy: A Critical Synthesis of Research Evidence on the Effects of Gun Policies in the United States*. Santa Monica, CA: RAND, 2018.

Reid, William H. *A Dark Night in Aurora: Inside James Holmes and the Colorado Mass Shootings*. New York: Skyhorse Publishing, 2018.

Rottman, Gordon. *Green Beret in Vietnam, 1957–73*. Oxford: Osprey Publishing, 2002.

Shrader, Charles R. *History of Operations Research in the United States Army*, vol. I. Washington, DC: U.S. Army, 2006.

Siegel, Michael, Ziming Xuan, Craig S. Ross, Sandro Galea, Bindu Kalesan, Eric Fleegler, and Kristin A. Goss. "Easiness of Legal Access to Concealed Firearm Permits and Homicide Rates in the United States." *American Journal of Public Health* 107:12 (December 2017), 1923–29, doi:10.2105/AJPH.2017.304057.

Smith, W. H. B., and Joseph E. Smith. *Small Arms of the World: The Basic Manual of Military Small Arms*. Harrisburg, PA: Stackpole Books, 1962.

Spitzer, Robert J. *The Politics of Gun Control: Sixth Edition*. Boulder, CO: Paradigm Publishers, 2015.

Spitzer, Robert J. *Saving the Constitution from Lawyers: How Legal Training and Law Reviews Distort Constitutional Meaning*. New York: Cambridge University Press, 2008.

Squires, Peter. *Gun Crime in Global Contexts*. New York: Routledge, 2014.

Teles, Steven M. *The Rise of the Conservative Legal Movement: The Battle for Control of the Law*. Princeton, NJ: Princeton University Press, 2008.

Thompson, Leroy. *The M1 Carbine*. New York: Osprey Publishing, 2011.

U. S. Army Combat Developments Command. "Rifle Evaluation Study," December 20, 1962.

U.S. Department of the Army, Headquarters. FM 3-22.9, *M16-/M4-Series Weapons*, August 2008.

U.S. Department of Homeland Security. *Active Shooter—How To Respond*. Washington, DC, 2017.

U.S. Department of Justice, Federal Bureau of Investigation. Molly Amman. *Making Prevention a Reality: Identifying, Assessing, and Managing the Threat of Targeted Attacks*. Washington, DC, February 2017.

U.S. Department of Justice, Federal Bureau of Investigation. James Silver, Andre Simons, and Sarah Craun. "A Study of the Pre-Attack Behaviors of Active Shooters in the United States between 2000–2013." 2018.

U.S. Department of Justice, Office of Justice Programs, Bureau of Justice Statistics. Michael Planty and Jennifer L. Truman. *Firearm Violence, 1993–2011*. Special Report. May 2013, NCJ 241730.

Vanderah, Todd W., and Douglas J. Gould. *Nolte's The Human Brain*, seventh ed. Philadelphia: Elsevier, 2016.

Webster, Daniel W., and Jon S. Vernick, eds. *Reducing Gun Violence in America—Informing Policy with Evidence and Analysis*. Baltimore: Johns Hopkins University Press, 2013.

Westwood, David. *Rifles: An Illustrated History of Their Impact*. Santa Barbara, CA: ABC-CLIO, 2005.

Wieland, Terry, ed. *Gun Digest Book of Classic American Combat Rifles*. Iola, WI: Gun Digest Books, 2011.

Winkler, Adam. *Gun Fight: The Battle over the Right to Bear Arms in the United States*. New York: W.W. Norton, 2013.

Wintemute, Garen J. "The Epidemiology of Firearms Violence in the Twenty-first Century United States." *Annu. Rev. Public Health*, 2015, 35:5–19, doi: 10.1146/annurev-publichealth-031914-122535.

Wintemute, Garen. *Inside Gun Shows: What Goes on When Everybody Thinks Nobody's Watching*. Violence Prevention Research Program, Department of Emergency Medicine. UC Davis School of Medicine, Sacramento, California, September 2009.

INDEX

ABOUT THE AUTHOR

Tom Diaz is a graduate of the University of Florida and of the Georgetown University Law Center. He clerked for Chancellor William Duffy of the Delaware Court of Chancery after graduation from law school. Although he practiced law in Washington, D.C., from time to time, he has generally preferred to follow his muse into research and writing projects, eventually focusing on books about guns, gangs, and terrorism.

Diaz was a reporter covering national security affairs at the *Washington Times* newspaper from 1982 to 1985, after which he was promoted to assistant managing editor responsible for overseeing the paper's overall news operations. During this period he also traveled to and reported from Central America during the conflicts of the mid-1980s, as well as India, Pakistan, the former Soviet Union in transition, and the Middle East (where he covered the first Gulf War, "Operation Desert Storm"). After leaving the *Washington Times*, he studied and wrote about terrorism and international organized crime at a small think tank, the National Strategy Information Center in Washington, from 1991 to 1993.

He was Democratic counsel to the U.S. House of Representatives Subcommittee on Crime and Criminal Justice from 1993 to 1997, where his subject-matter specialties included terrorism and firearms regulation. He later became senior policy analyst at a Washington-based gun violence reduction organization, where he wrote monographs about the American gun industry, its products, and their impact on public health and safety.

Diaz grew up in the family of a career army officer and learned to shoot in the Boy Scouts. He enlisted in the U.S. Air Force in 1958. After his active duty he served in the air force reserve and in the District of Columbia Air National Guard, where he was a firearms instructor. He was honorably discharged in 1964 but joined the Maryland Army National Guard in the 1970s, where he became an antitank platoon sergeant. He also served as a reserve police officer in the District of Columbia Metropolitan Police Department. As a result of his military service and his continuing personal interest in recreational firearms, Diaz is familiar with most types of military and civilian firearms. He handled his first AR-15 (later M16) assault rifle in 1965 in Bangkok, Thailand, while serving as the civilian administrative officer for an Advanced Research Projects Agency joint military research and development field unit. Diaz supports responsible gun ownership. But largely as a result of his work on the issue as a congressional staff member, he came to believe that the gun industry and its allies have grossly and dangerously distorted the American domestic gun market.

Lonnie and Sandy Phillips are the parents of Jessica Ghawi, who was murdered in the massacre at the midnight showing of *The Dark Knight Rises* in the summer of 2012 at an Aurora, Colorado, movie theater. In order to attend the trial of Jessi's killer, they rented out their home, bought a camper trailer, and lived on their friend's property for four months. After the trial, Lonnie and Sandy decided they would live off their retirement money so they could travel the country speaking on gun violence prevention and forming coalitions with other survivor groups. In the six years since their daughter's death, they have been on the ground in the immediate aftermath of ten mass shootings and founded the nonprofit "Survivors Empowered," which provides resources, guidance, and a soft place to land for survivors of gun violence.